Religious Confession and Evidential Privilege in the 21st Century

Edited by Mark Hill QC and A. Keith Thompson

SHEPHERD STREET PRESS

Published in 2021 by Connor Court Publishing Pty Ltd under the imprint Shepherd Street Press.

Shepherd Street Press is an imprint of Connor Court Publishing and The School of Law, The University of Notre Dame Australia, Broadway.

Shepherd Street Press Editorial Executive:

Michael Quinlan
A. Keith Thompson
Iain T. Benson

Connor Court Publishing Pty Ltd
PO Box 7257
Redland Bay QLD 4165
sales@connorcourt.com
www.connorcourtpublishing.com.au
Phone 0497-900-685

Printed in Australia

ISBN: 9781922449900

Front Cover Painting: Ships in a Storm, William Joy (1803-1867), Wikipedia Commons.

Peer Review Policy

This book has been prepared in compliance with the Peer Review Policy of the Shepherd Street Press which provides for double blind peer review by at least two expert reviewers.

The editors also wish to acknowledge the assistance they have received from Jesse Gibson, a final years Honours student. Among other tasks, Jesse has assisted in ensuring compliance with the fourth edition of the Australian Guide to Legal Citation.

Previous Shepherd Street Press Titles

Editorial Executive:

Michael Quinlan, A. Keith Thompson and Iain T. Benson

Religious Freedom in Australia – a new Terra Nullius?
Edited by Iain T. Benson, Michael Quinlan and A. Keith Thompson

Current Issues in Law and Religion
Edited by A. Keith Thompson

Inclusion, Exclusion and Relgious Freedom in Contemporary Australia
Edited by Michael Quinlan and A. Keith Thompson

Current Issues in the Law of Evidence
Edited by A. Keith Thompson

Available from
www.connorcourtpublishing.com.au

Table of Contents

Part III – Issues of priest / penitent privilege in the USA

Foreword

Lord Williams of Oystermouth
Archbishop of Canterbury 2002-2012

The words for 'faith' and 'trust' coincide in most languages; so it is natural to think that no community of faith can exist without a foundation of trust. We rightly feel that when religious authorities are responsible for betrayals of trust – through financial dishonesty, manipulative and dishonest behaviour or, most serious of all, the mental and physical abuse of those for whom they are meant to care, some very basic bond has been shattered. And historically one central aspect of that trust is the assurance that what has been said in confidence will normally be respected as such. Duties of confidence similarly arise in the medical profession and in therapeutic counselling, but religious communities, especially the largest of the historic Christian churches, have developed a systematic practice and discipline of confession. For the Roman Catholic and Eastern Orthodox Churches, and for significant strands of practice and teaching in the Anglican Communion, there is a recognition that, in certain carefully defined circumstances, confiding in a priest who stands for the whole community of believers has a sacramental character; it is governed by canon law, and what passes between the priest and the penitent is sacrosanct, as the penitent is understood as speaking not to the priest as an individual but to God, with the priest as witness.

The 'seal' of confession is not – as some critics would argue – a form of malign secrecy but an assurance that all kinds of destructive and damaging behaviour can be spoken out, named and acknowledged for what they are. The purpose of the confessional discipline is the restoration of the penitent to the life of the community – with all the healing and reparation that might imply. When a priest hearing a confession imposes a penance, the priest is not looking backwards at an offence that needs to be covered over but forwards to a perhaps painful process of truthfulness and repairing of relation with God and with the human community. It is precisely the assurance of confidentiality that is supposed to allow the penitent to be honest, to bring into the open what may seem too shameful, too humiliating or shocking, to speak of. Where grave offence and lasting injury are confessed, serious steps must be imposed and demanded.

Are there ever, then, circumstances in which the assurance of confidentiality should be waived? This is currently a matter of much debate, in the wake of our much enhanced recognition of the enormously serious character of abuse, especially the abuse of children and vulnerable persons. The contributions to this timely volume discuss the law and theology of the inviolability of the seal of the confessional as a matter of canon law, but they also consider the actual practice and custom of a variety of denominations on issues of confidence, confession and repentance, and assess the extent to which the state law of various countries impacts upon the free exercise of religion, whether through mandatory reporting of abuse of children and vulnerable adults or in other respects.

Both international instruments and domestic law in general recognise the institutional autonomy of religions to govern their own affairs; until recently there has been in modern times a high level of consensus that state interference in sacramental practice is an infringement of fundamental religious liberties. Any challenge to a doctrine that has been lived out in the historic practice of the churches, will understandably be seen as cutting to the heart of commitments to freedom of thought, conscience and religion, which are matters of both individual and collective rights. Granted that the issue of confessional 'privilege ' is far from straightforward, it needs to be recognized that the precedent of mounting a legal attack on some aspect of long-enshrined religious practice is a troubling one. In much of the current discussion, it seems to be assumed that the seal of the confessional is routinely a contributing factor in the institutional concealment or minimizing of the outrage of abuse. Is this an assumption that can properly be made? On what precise grounds does it stand? And are these grounds strong enough to outweigh the opportunity provided by assured confidentiality for individuals to recognize and begin to deal with all kind of other matters of painful sensitivity and complexity?

There are no easy answers. However, by collating a range of views across denominations and continents, the contributors to this book have provided a clear account of the issues that arise where sincere and rigorously disciplined confessional practice intersects with questions of evidential privilege in state courts. This volume will undoubtedly help to stimulate discussion, and to inform a deeper understanding on all sides of this tangled and urgent issue.

Rowan Williams

July 2021

Introduction

In 1991, the Supreme Court of Canada decided as a matter of common law that confidential religious communications could be privileged from admission as evidence in court cases in that country.[1] However, despite article 2(a) of the *Charter of Rights and Freedoms*, there was no constitutional requirement that courts except confidential religious communications from admission as evidence in every case. The minority (2) said that all confidential religious communications should be privileged to avoid chilling the free exercise of religion. The majority (7) considered the judiciary could be safely trusted with oversight of such privilege as a matter of discretion. All nine judges considered the evidence was properly admitted in the case before them because there was no expectation of confidentiality when the communication took place.

That decision came nine years after Canada constitutionalised human rights in its *Charter of Rights and Freedoms* in 1982 and 15 years after ratification of the *International Covenant on Civil and Political Rights* (*ICCPR*) in 1976. Canada's constitutional *Charter of Rights and Freedoms* followed her earlier statutory *Bill of Rights* in 1960. The Court's majority judgment in *Gruenke* referred to its own decision in *R v Big M Drug Mart Ltd* in 1985 with approval. In that case the majority had said:

> A truly free society is one which can accommodate a wide variety of beliefs, diversities of taste and pursuits, customs and codes of conduct. A free society is one which aims at equality with respect to the enjoyment of fundamental freedoms.[2]

---

1   *R v Gruenke* (1991) 3 SCR 263.
2   *R v Big M Drug Mart Ltd* (1985) 1 SCR 295, 336.

Though the *Big M Drug Market* majority had also said this ecumenical recognition of diverse beliefs did not rely on s 15 of the *Charter*, the *Gruenke* majority said that ss 2(a) and 27 of the *Charter* required a non-denominational approach to religious belief and practice.[3]

Those Canadian constitutional values were informed by the *Universal Declaration of Human Rights* and *ICCPR* following World War II, and saw a different resolution of the question whether confidential religious communications should be excepted from judicial scrutiny as a matter of curial evidence process from that which had emerged in the United States of America (US). The US history saw all of its state legislatures pass religious confession privilege statutes between 1828 and the 1960s. Those state statutes directed courts not to admit religious confessional material as evidence in court proceedings. Most of those state statutes were passed because the legislatures considered that judges had admitted relevant religious confession evidence in court cases that should have been excluded for public policy reasons.

Both of these approaches to the exclusion of confidential religious communications as evidence in court cases accept the wisdom of Knight-Bruce VC in England in 1846 when he said:

> The discovery and vindication and establishment of truth are main purposes certainly of the existence of Courts of Justice; still for the obtaining of these objects, which however valuable and important, cannot be usefully pursued without moderation, cannot be either usefully or creditably pursued unfairly or gained by unfair means, not every channel is or ought to be open to them. The practical inefficacy of torture is not, I suppose, the most weighty objection to that mode of examination... Truth, like all other good things, may be loved unwisely – may be pursued too keenly – may cost too much.[4]

Canadian and US jurisprudence was also informed by Professor Wigmore's canons of interpretation which he designed in the

---

3 *Gruenke* (n 1), 291.
4 *Pearse v Pearse* (1846) 63 ER 950, 957-958.

twentieth century to help courts work out whether a new confidential communications privilege should be recognised. He suggested that such privilege should be recognised if:

1   The communications ... originate in a *confidence* that they will not be disclosed.

2   The element of *confidentiality is essential* to the full maintenance of a satisfactory maintenance of the relation between the parties.

3   The *relation* is one which in the opinion of the community ought to be sedulously fostered.

4   The *injury* that would inure to the relation by the disclosure of the communications is *greater than the benefit* thereby gained for the correct disposal of litigation.[5]

In England however, there was never legislative direction that any religious confidences should be excluded as evidence in courts of law, largely, one assumes, because the seal of the confessional was maintained by the canon law of the Church of England, which was and remains the law of the land, due to establishment. As can be seen in the Hill/Grout chapter within this book, Anglican canon law protects disclosures made during the sacrament of penance, but wider question of confidential communications for the Church of England and other denominations remains unclear. Establishment also complicates the status of confidential communications within churches that were or are established in Scandinavia as the Aarflot chapter explains. But the Ferrante chapter shows that it is not just religious establishment that can affect the legal status of confidential religious communications. Where there is even a residue of customary identity between one church and the state, it is unlikely that confidential communications within that church will be easily adduced as evidence in court. And, by a principle analogous to gravitational pull, that legacy of respect to religious confidentiality

---

5   Emphasis original, J H Wigmore, *Evidence in Trials at Common Law*, Revised by John T. McNaughton (Boston: Little Brown, 1961), Vol. 8, 527.

can and does benefit other churches in a more ecumenical age.

However, the elephant in the religious communications privilege room, is the revelation in the US and Canada, and more recently in Australia and Ireland, that some clergy in large Christian churches have been using their positions of responsibility to groom and sexually abuse the youth and children entrusted to their care. In those four countries where Wigmore's principles have previously exerted some interpretive influence, there is no doubt that his third is no longer met. Few in those countries want law or policy to 'sedulously foster' relationships with potentially abusive clergy, and the result is that the statutes which had been passed to formalise religious confession privilege are being amended so that they can no longer shelter abusive behaviour, even theoretically.

Some have criticised the wisdom of those amendments because they will not protect a single child[6] and because the perpetrators of sexual abuse who do confess, do not provide information specific enough to activate a duty to report to enforcement authorities.[7] There is also the Irish insight that mandatory reporting is not always in the best interests of a child.[8] But despite these criticisms, there is little doubt that the public interest

---

6   Frank Brennan, "Breaking the Seal of the Confessional a Red Herring that will not Save One Child", *Weekend Australian* (3–4 December 2016).

7   See for Marie Keenan, *Child Sexual Abuse and the Catholic Church: Gender, Power and Organizational Culture* (Oxford, Oxford University Press, 2012), 163-4 where she observed that the small group of priests whom she interviewed during their prison sentences had not confessed sufficient information to reveal that their partner in immorality was a child.

8   Note that while legislation passed after the Ryan Commission made its findings, made it an offence for anyone who 'has information which … might be of material assistance in securing the apprehension, prosecution or conviction' of an offence (including a child sex offence) against another person and does not report it to the Garda Síochána (literally, the Guardians of the Peace, which is the name of the Irish Police force), there were generous exemptions. Parents, guardians, doctors, nurses and many other persons working with children, are exempt if, for bona fide reasons, they do not believe it would be in the best interests of that child to report the matter. And abused children were mature enough to express the view that they do not want to have an offence reported to the Garda, then that view is to be respected and constitutes a defence for the person accused of non-disclosure (Criminal Justice (Withholding of Information on Offences against Children and Vulnerable Persons) Bill 2012 (Ireland).

in preserving confidential religious relationships will not prevent the admission of such evidence in the future where the matter is left to judicial discretion. But is that a healthy outcome? What of Ros Burnet's warning about the gross injustices that this and other moral panics are perpetrating upon western societies hell-bent on abrogating evidential rules that were designed to prevent injustice?[9] And what of Brian Grim's warning that religious freedom generally is a canary in the coal mine where human rights in general and even democracy itself are concerned?[10] Has the West's growing disinterest in freedom of conscience and religion somehow precipitated the plight of Uighur Muslims in China, Rohinga Muslims in Myanmar, Bahais in Iran, Jehovah's Witnesses in Russia and Christians in general in Iraq?

Confidential religious communications are a multi-textured example of religious practice. The fact that they engage both the *forum internum* and the *forum externum* in art. 18 of the *ICCPR* can be seen in a traditional Roman Catholic confession. In that faith, an expressive act is required to fulfill and satisfy the doctrinal practice of the penitent. And while that expression may not reveal harm to anyone other than the penitent attending the confession, can the state really claim that the disclosure of that communication by the priest is 'necessary to protect public safety, order, health, or morals of the fundamental rights and freedoms of others' within the meaning of the limitation in art. 18(3)? Are J. Noel Lyon and Jeremy Bentham right that the foreclosure of confidential religious confession is tantamount to state coercion of conscience and even torture?[11] The fact that every penitent confesses her sins differently also complicates analysis under the *forum internum/externum* dichotomy. For while rigid adherence to a confessional formula may satisfy religious

---

9   Ros Burnet ed., *Wrongful Allegations of Sexual and Child Abuse* (Oxford: Oxford University Press, 2016).

10 See for example Brian Grim, "Canary in the Coal Mine (Part 1), December 8, 2014, *Centre for Public Christianity*.

11 J. Noel Lyon "Privileged Communications – Penitent and Priest" [1964-65] 7 *Crim LQ* 327; Jeremy Bentham, *Rationale of Judicial Evidence* (New York and London, Garland Publishing Inc.,1978 (Reprint of the 1827 ed published by Hunt and Clarke, London)), Vol 4, 589-591.

imperatives, it will not yield much in the way of admissible evidence and may also be excluded under other applicable evidence rules.

But there is also the question of whether the formulation of any privilege that does exist in common law or statute, has the equalitarian and non-denominational character which the *Gruenke* majority in the Supreme Court of Canada advocated.[12] What of Christian religions that do not have a formal confessional practice, and non-Christian religions which require their members to adhere to forms of conduct which include the imposition of discipline when members depart from the expected standards of personal behaviour? Does the greater society of the nation have an interest in encouraging individual citizen reform as Bentham said justified an evidential privilege in the case of Catholic confessional practice?[13]

This book will not and cannot answer all these questions, but it does advance the conversation. In a sense, its three part division is geographical – Australia, Europe and then the US. But the divisions are also thematic. The Australian section engages with the reforms to religious confession privilege laws that have followed the Royal Commission's recommendations in that country. The first two chapters engage with both the justifiability and the practicality of the reform legislation that has been passed, as well as its advisability. Those chapters also observe that confidential religious communications practice in Australia is not constitutionally protected as part of religious freedom writ large, because Australia has neither an entrenched constitutional bill of rights nor a comprehensive statutory regime protecting religious freedom under a domestic implementation of the *ICCPR*. Monica Doumit's chapter responds to the question whether the worldwide Roman Catholic Church should have amended its canon law in response to, and in the manner recommended by the Australian Royal Commission.

The chapters which form Part II manifest the diversity of European

---

12 *Gruenke* (n 1), 291.
13 Bentham (n 11).

treatment of confidential religious communications. While Mario Ferrante's chapter confirms that Italy no longer has a state church, the legacy of historical establishment and concordatarian arrangements with the Vatican after the invasion of Rome in 1870, ensure that the Roman Catholic Church still enjoys a place of privilege though modern equalitarian values protect other faith practices by analogy. Professor Ferrante also identifies Europe's commitment to privacy as a secular value which operates to protect religious confidences in Italy. The Hill/Grout chapter addresses the status of the established Church's canonical seal of the confessional in secular law, which many commentators fail to distinguish from more general principles of confidentiality. Will criminal laws and procedural rules of evidence override church laws or are they equal? How will judges exercise their discretion when asserted questions of admissibility cut across church laws about the seal of the confessional in particular, and confidentiality more generally? Will courts find themselves having to debate, define and legitimise church doctrine, something from which they have traditionally refrained from doing?[14]

Andreas Henriksen Aarflot's chapter is likely to introduce readers to some of the strongest laws protecting confidential religious communications they have ever seen. For not only have religious confidences been exempted from discovery in secular court proceedings in Norway and Sweden; until recently there have been secular laws in both countries which made any disclosure of religious confidences, a criminal offence. Recent amendments probably abrogate the priest's duty of confidentiality in Norway but the position in Sweden is less clear although there is a duty to avoid future harm to others with a particular emphasis on protecting children. Stephen Farrell explains that even though there are uncertainties about the metes and bounds of religious confession privilege in Ireland, the *Children First Act 2015* reduces the scope of the traditional privilege though no significant legal conflicts

---

14   See, by way of example, *Khaira v Shergill* [2014] UKSC 33.

have arisen between the two imperatives in the past, and not even since the new Act was passed. Because of the new Act, Farrell also doubts that the Wigmore principles of interpretation, which were quoted with approval by Gavan Duffy J in *Cook v Carroll* in 1945,[15] will protect confidential religious communications from courtroom disclosure in future since Irish society is no longer committed to 'sedulously fostering' relations between priests and parishioners.

Part III provides three quite different perspectives on confidential religious communications law in the US. In the first, Greg Zubacz reflects with sadness on the terrible abuses which have been perpetrated upon children by priests who were previously seen as beyond reproach. He notes how prevalent such abuse became, the volume of the settlements that have been paid and a downturn in reporting after 1985 but then an uptick again in 2018 although suggesting that apparent rise may be a statistical aberration. He also suggests that religious confession privilege statutes will continue to be scrutinized and that they will be diluted if not abrogated in child abuse cases in coming years. The late George Morelli discusses pastoral confessional practice in the Orthodox tradition and reflects on confession as the means of reconciliation between human beings and God. He insists that confessional secrecy must and will be maintained to enable those who commit sin to be healed and restored to the God who made them.

Eric Lieberman's chapter adds a thoroughly ecumenical dimension to the US discussion. He first explains auditing practice in Scientology and then how it is or should be protected by the First Amendment and more specific state religious confession statutes. Though confidential communications in Scientology are heard by more than one 'confessor', by analogy to the protection that has been afforded to confessions heard by multiple ministers in some other Christian church cases, he makes a compelling argument that auditing practice in Scientology does come within US constitutional and state statutory protection.

---

15   *Cook v Carroll* [1945] IR 515.

Overall, as editors we hope that this volume will provide readers with new perspectives on confidential religious communications. We believe that confidentiality and trust are important in all counselling relationships including those with a foundation in pastoral care. But we recognise that in the past, many church officers have mistakenly preferred the protection of the reputational interests of their institutions over the physical, emotional and psychological needs of those they were trusted to serve. We hope that this volume also contributes to a greater understanding of the need for human character improvement which often does require the help of others, since many of us cannot extract ourselves from our potholes using self-help tools. There is an enduring public interest in confidentiality, and the Irish insight suggests that even the paramount interests of the welfare of children will sometimes prevail over the utility of mandatory reporting.

We are indebted to Lord Williams of Oystermouth for contributing a Foreword to this volume. As a theologian and poet, Rowan Williams has the rare gift of communicating in accessible language truths which are profound and challenging. The clarity of his observations provides the perfect curtain raiser for the rich analysis in the chapters that follow.

Professor Mark Hill QC
United Kingdom

Dr A. Keith Thompson
Professor of Law
School of Law and Business
The University of Notre Dame Australia

June 30, 2021

Contributors

Andreas Henriksen Aarflot is a Senior Adviser on Church Law to the National Council and General Synod of the Church of Norway and a Lecturer in Church Law at the MF Norwegian School of Theology, Religion and Society in Oslo, Norway. He is also a member of the Governing Board of the Conference of European Churches, and the Vice-Chair of the Norwegian Society of Church Law.

Monica Doumit is the Director of Public Affairs and Engagement for the Catholic Archdiocese of Sydney and an adjunct senior lecturer in law at the University of Notre Dame Australia. She has worked as a corporate lawyer in Sydney and London, and holds degrees in law and medical science, and a masters in bioethics.

Stephen Farrell is an Irish Anglican priest and the Registrar for the Church of Ireland Province and Diocese of Dublin. He is a member of the European Consortium for Church State Research, the Colloquium of Anglican and Roman Catholic Canon Lawyers and a Fellow at the Centre for Law and Religion at the University of Cardiff.

Mario Ferrante is an Adjunct Professor at the University of Notre Dame, Law School, Sydney and Professor of Canon Law and Ecclesiastical Law at the Department of 'Jurisprudence' (University of Palermo, Italy). He is also a Rotal lawyer specialised in matrimonial and criminal Canon Law with more than 20 years of professional experience.

Christopher Grout is Registrar of the Qatar International Court and Dispute Resolution Centre. He practises at the Bar in London and is a Deputy District Judge of England and Wales and a Member of the Chartered Institute of Arbitrators.

Mark Hill QC is a lecturer at the Open University and an Associate Professor at Cardiff University; the University of Pretoria; Notre Dame University Law School, Sydney; and the Dickson Poon School of Law at King's College, London.

He is a Fellow of the Center for the Study of Law and Religion at Emory University, and Distinguished Fellow of the University of Notre Dame London Law Program.

Eric Lieberman is a constitutional lawyer in New York, specializing in First Amendment issues. He graduated magna cum laude from Harvard Law School and then received a prestigious post-graduate fellowship with the Arthur Garfield Hays Civil Liberties Program at New York University Law School. Since 1972 he has practiced at the New York firm Rabinowitz, Boudin, Krinsky & Lieberman. He has argued cases in the Supreme Court, most federal courts of appeals, and numerous state appellate courts.

Giorgio (George) Morelli was an assistant pastor of St. George's Antiochian Orthodox Church, San Diego California, who previously taught courses in psychology at Kean University in Union, New Jersey, and university and seminary courses on pastoral theology. He died in March 2021, as this volume went to print.

Robert Natanek is a recent graduate from the University of Queensland, with combined degrees in Arts and Law. He is an enthusiastic public speaker and writer, and intends to channel his skills towards a career at the bar. His main research interests include child protection, law reform and the complex legal issues regulating the interface between religious freedom and civil society.

Patrick Parkinson is a professor at the TC Beirne School of Law, University of Queensland. In addition to his work on law and religion issues he is a specialist in family law, child protection and the law of equity and trusts. He co-founded and chairs the organisation Freedom for Faith. He is an evangelical Christian.

A. Keith Thompson is a professor at the Sydney School of Law of The University of Notre Dame Australia. He previously worked as International Legal Counsel for The Church of Jesus Christ of Latter-day Saints through the Pacific and African continent and as a partner in a commercial law firm in Auckland, New Zealand.

The Reverend Dr **Gregory Joseph Zubacz** is a professor of business law and associate provost of Fresno Pacific University. He is a bi-ritual Ukrainian Catholic priest of the Eparchy of Chicago serving a mission parish in California, and is a member of the Child Protection Review Board of the eparchy.

Part I

Responses to the Royal Commission into Institutional Responses to Child Sexual Abuse

1

A. Keith Thompson

How does long term wisdom resist the pressure of a moral panic? The case of religious confession privilege

Abstract

The *Royal Commission into Institutional Responses to Child Sexual Abuse* recommended that Australian state governments abrogate religious confession privilege (RCP) where the communication involved the disclosure of child sexual abuse. That recommendation was said to be justified because the religious freedom underlying the practice of religious confession was not absolute under the *International Covenant on Civil and Political Rights* and must yield to the need to protect the rights and freedoms of others – in this case children. But the *Commission's* evidence and findings did not prove abrogation was necessary within the meaning of that *Covenant*. Indeed, objectively considered the *Commission's* evidence suggested that the problem of child sexual abuse in institutions had been resolved in Australia before 2000. In this chapter, the logic which underpins RCP is considered in light of its Australian history. The conclusion is that RCP should be protected in any society that values freedom of conscience and belief.

Keywords:

Seal of the confessional – Religious Confession Privilege – Royal Commission into Institutional Responses to Child Sexual Abuse – mandatory reporting – forum internum – freedom of conscience and religion

Introduction

Peter Jackson's heroic image of Tolkien's Gandalf resisting all that the Balrog of Morgoth can throw at him in *The Fellowship of the Ring*, is iconic because it presents as an aspect of human character and history that endlessly repeats itself. Gandalf's words of defiant yet hopeless moral courage, "You Shall Not Pass!", ring in our souls and we wish that all human souls might successfully withstand the blast with him. But while Gandalf slays his demon, he only survives through his resurrection as Gandalf the White. While Gandalf made his stand against a flood of evil, most of the time humans only have to stand against tides of misinformation, public hysteria and moral panic.

Why do I thus introduce an article about RCP in Australia? Because the moral outrage in the New South Wales Parliament which finally produced a statutory RCP in 1989 (which became the template for s 127 in the *Uniform Evidence Act* of 1995), is being diluted following the flawed recommendations of the *Royal Commission into Institutional Responses to Child Sexual Abuse*[1] (the Royal Commission) in Australia in relation to RCP. I suggest that because RCP is founded in sound human rights principle, history will identify some of the findings of the Royal Commission as misguided. But that will take time. As other authors of chapters in this book have noted, the renewed persecution of the Catholic Church because of its failure to protect children from abusive priests before the 1990s, has not yet run its course.

---

1   The Royal Commission into Institutional Responses to Child Sexual Abuse was announced by Prime Minister the Honourable Julia Gillard on 12 November 2012 and handed down its final report on 15 December 2017.

In this chapter I discuss the evolution and then the dilution of RCP in three parts. In the first, I review the Australian history of the privilege down to its statutory iteration in the *Uniform Evidence Act* of 1995. That review includes the first statutory iteration of the privilege in Victoria in 1864. It also includes the steadfast resistance of Queensland, South Australia and Western Australia to the idea of a uniform *Evidence Act* including any statutory expression of RCP. In Part Two I discuss efforts to dilute that statutory privilege once it was established including Nick Xenophon's unsuccessful efforts to abrogate it in South Australia. The major focus of part two however, is on the Royal Commission's flawed assertion that the abrogation of RCP is necessary (within the meaning of Article 18(3) of the *International Covenant on Civil and Political Rights* (the *ICCPR*)) in child sexual abuse cases to protect children from harm. I also discuss the question of whether RCP is entitled to complete protection from abrogation as an inviolable part of the *forum internum* under the *ICCPR*. In Part Three I discuss the logic which continues to underpin RCP in the face of moral panics about the protection of children and renewed persecution of the Catholic Church and its clergy in Australia since 1990. I begin that part by discussing the unlikely affirmation of RCP by Jeremy Bentham who was an opponent of every other form of privilege and an ardent critic of religious belief and practice. I conclude that RCP is required in any society that respects freedom of conscience.

Part One - The Australian history of RCP

RCP at common law

Australia inherited its common law from England.[2] Absent a RCP statute in England before 1865 when the *Colonial Laws Validity Act* granted all the British colonies a degree of law-making autonomy, the question whether RCP was recognised in the common law in 1865 was moot because there

---

2   See for example, Patrick Parkinson, *Tradition and Change in Australian Law*, 5th ed., (Australia: The Law Book Company), 3-5.

were no Australian cases about the privilege to answer the question. In England, most of the evidence law texts say there was no common law privilege citing precedents that do not stand up to scrutiny.[3] And even though the evidence law text writers who researched more carefully noted that there must have been such a privilege even after the Reformation since Edward Coke acknowledged it when he prosecuted Jesuit Father Henry Garnet to execution in 1606, as later in Australia they observe a lack of directly relevant cases to conclusively determine the point ever after.[4]

For the purposes of this chapter, the point is to identify the relevant law in Australia and how it has been affected by the statutes that have been passed and how it is affected by the *Constitution's* denial of Commonwealth power to pass laws that prohibit the free exercise of religion.

Even if it incorrect to assert that RCP was abolished by:

- the English Reformation,
- the Restoration of the monarchy after Cromwell's Commonwealth in 1660,
- anti-Catholic prejudice and persecution in the wake of the Reformation
- the passage of legislation affirming its existence
- authoritative judicial dicta expressed against it[5]

or that the recognition of RCP was inconsistent with religious neutrality in English colonies granted independence without a state church,[6] there has never been a decision in Australia that authoritatively settles the question. The closest we have come was Dixon J's obiter assertion in *McGuinness v Attorney-General (Vic)* in 1940 that there were very "few relations where paramount considerations of general policy appeared to

---

3   A. Keith Thompson, *Religious Confession Privilege at Common Law* (Leiden: Martinus Nijhoff, 2011), 13-28.
4   Ibid.
5   Ibid 155-180.
6   Ibid 181-216.

require that there should be a special privilege".[7] In that case he denied that such a privilege extended to the protection of journalists' sources, but his certainty in that case may have been affected by the early World War II context. But he did include "priest and penitent" among the cases where what he had earlier called "paramount considerations of general policy appeared to require that there should be a special privilege". But it is unclear whether he was acknowledging that such privileges were acknowledged in the common law, or whether, as in his home state of Victoria,[8] he was acknowledging that they could be created by statute but did not exist at common law.

While one might expect that subsequent obiter mentions of RCP in intermediate courts of appeal and in the High Court might be more helpful, they are not. For though Spigelman CJ and Beazley JA (as she then was) both quoted this same Dixon passage in R v Young in 1999,[9] they both came to different conclusions about the sexual assault communications privilege at issue in that case.

When religious confessions were earlier mentioned in obiter statements by three of the seven judges who decided Baker v Campbell in 1983,[10] they all inferred that the reason such communications were not privileged was because they were not part of the administration of justice.[11] But two of those judges (Gibbs CJ and Mason J) were dissenters and did not think that even legal professional privilege prevailed over the police search warrants which were at issue in that case, and those views about

---

7   *McGuinness v Attorney-General (Vic)* (1940) 63 CLR 73, 102-103.
8   There were three Australian jurisdictions that recognised religious confession privilege by statute when Dixon J handed down this judgment in 1940. They were Victoria, Tasmania and the Northern Territory (s 55 of the *Evidence Act 1890* (Vic), s 96 of the *Evidence Act 1910* (Tas) and s 12 of the *Evidence Act 1939* (NT)).
9   *R v Young* (1999) 46 NSWLR 681.
10   *Baker v Campbell* (1983) 153 CLR 52.
11   Ibid 66 (per Gibbs CJ); 75 (per Mason J) and 128 (per Dawson J).

legal professional privilege were further discountenanced in later cases.[12] And in his dissent, Justice Mason also doubted that legal professional privilege rested on any better justification than could be advanced for RCP among other privileges.[13]

Indeed for Justice Beazley in *R v Young*, as for Lord Hailsham in the House of Lords in *D v NSPCC*[14] and for Professor Wigmore in the very first edition of his magisterial *Law of Evidence*,[15] the categories of public interest and the privileges that flow are not closed and "must alter from time to time whether by restriction or extension as social conditions and social legislation develop."[16]

Following the NSWCCA's majority decision in *R v Young* which the New South Wales Parliament seem to have regarded as unsatisfactory, there was prompt legislative intervention[17] as two of those appeal judges had

---

12 Note for example, that in *Esso Australian Resources Limited v The Commissioner of Taxation* (1999) 201 CLR 49 the High Court found that legal professional privilege should be recognised even if obtaining legal advice was only the dominant rather than the sole purpose for which the communication had taken place. This decision overruled the decision in *Grant v Downs* (1976) 135 CLR 674 which had implemented the sole purpose test over earlier findings that obtaining legal advice need only be one of the purposes for which the communication took place. The majority in *Esso* found that the majority decision of the High Court in *Grant v Downs* was out of step with the rest of the British common law world ([56] per Gleeson CJ, Gaudron and Gummow JJ and [168] per Callinan J).

13 *Baker v Campbell* (1983) 153 CLR 52, 75.

14 *D v NSPCC* [1971] AC 171.

15 JH Wigmore, *A Treatise on the Anglo-American System of Evidence in Trials at Common Law Including the Statutes and Judicial Decisions of All Jurisdictions of the United States* (Boston, Little Brown and Company, 1904).

16 *D v NSPCC* [1971] AC 171, 230 as quoted by Beazley JA in *R v Young* (1999) 46 NSWLR 681, 711 [63]. In 1904, Wigmore proposed four canons that he recommended courts consider when deciding whether new categories of evidentiary privilege should exist. His canons are unchanged in the 3rd edition in 1940, Volume 5 [2396] (*A Treatise on the Anglo-American System of Evidence in Trials at Common Law Including the Statutes and Judicial Decisions of All Jurisdictions in the United States and Canada*) or the 1961 revision.

17 The *Evidence Amendment (Confidential Communications) Act* (NSW) was passed in 1997 to amend the *Evidence Act 1995* (NSW) "to protect the counselling communications of sexual abuse complainants." After the decision in *R v Young* (1999) 46 NSWLR 681 those provisions were expanded to make it clear that they applied to documents requested before trial on sub poena and removed from the *Evidence Act 1995* (NSW) and placed in the *Criminal Procedure Act 1986* (NSW). They have been enlarged again subsequently. See also "Sexual Assault Communications Privilege", *Sexual Assault Trials Handbook*, 29 August 2020.

anticipated might happen.[18]

In this judicial context, it cannot thus be said that the existence of RCP at common law in Australia is "settled" as a "rule of substantive law" within the meaning of Gleeson CJ, Gaudron, Gummow and Hayne JJ in *Daniels Corporation v ACCC* in 2002.[19] And though the question of when a privilege is "well settled in law" was later the subject of significant debate between the justices Crennan, Kiefel and Bell writing together and Justice Heydon in *Australian Crime Commission v Stoddart* in 2011,[20] if the existence of the spousal privilege at issue in that case was not well settled for the majority, then the prospects of RCP at common law in the highest courts of Australia look pretty slim.

So what about RCP statutes in Australia? When did they originate and how have they been developed?

RCP in Australia in statute

The first statute to confirm RCP in an Australian jurisdiction was the *Statute of Evidence 1864* (Vic). Section 47 provided:

> No clergyman of any church or religious denomination shall without the consent of the person making the confession divulge in any suit action or proceeding whether civil or criminal any confession made to him in his professional character according to the usage of the church or religious denomination to which he belongs.

This provision was immediately followed by a physician/patient privilege and both were repeated word for word as s 55 of the *Evidence Act 1890* (Vic) except that they were no longer joined by the conjunction "and".

---

18 *R v Young* (1999) 46 NSWLR 681, 696 [70] and 702 [105] (per Spigelman CJ) and 749 [352] (per James JA). Abadee and Barr JJ said it was for parliament to create a new privilege rather than the courts if they intended to abrogate the right of an accused person to call evidence that had not previously been privileged (722 [220]).

19 *Daniels Corporation v ACCC* (2002) 192 ALR 561, 564-565 [9-10].

20 *Australian Crime Commission v Stoddart* (2011) 282 ALR 620.

Tasmania followed with s 96(1) of the *Evidence Act 1910* (Tas) which read more simply:

> No clergyman of any church or religious denomination shall divulge in any proceeding any confession made to him in his professional character, except with the consent of the person who made such confession.

In 1939, the Northern Territory legislators expressed their privilege as follows:

> A clergyman of any church or religious denomination shall not, without the consent of the person who made the confession, divulge in any proceeding any confession made to him in his professional character.

All of these provisions descend genealogically from the original RCP statute which was passed by the New York legislature in 1828. That statute appears to have been passed in response to the decision in an Anglican case (*People v Smith*[21]) which had reversed the decision in *People v Phillips* which had recognised a common law privilege in the case of a Catholic confession.[22] The 1828 ground breaking New York statute read:

> No minister of the gospel or priest of any denomination whatsoever, shall be allowed to disclose any confession made to him in his professional character, in the course of discipline enjoined by the rules or practice of such denomination.[23]

Most RCP statutes have been passed to affirm a privilege that judges denied existed at common law,[24] and Suzanne McNicol has confirmed that was the case with the first New South Wales RCP statutes in 1989.[25] Section 3 of the *Evidence (Religious Confessions) Amendment Act 1989* (NSW)

---

21 *People v Smith* N.Y. City Hall Rec, 77 (1817).

22 *People v Phillips* N.Y. Ct. of Gen. Sess. (1813).

23 N.Y. Rev. Stat. 72, pt. 3m ch. VII, tit. III, art. 8 (1828).

24 Vincent Allred has confirmed that history for the first New Jersey religious confession privilege statute ("The Confession in Court" (1953) 13 *The Jurist* 2, 9) and Seward Reese confirmed a similar story in Delaware in "Confidential Communications to the Clergy" (1963) 24 *Ohio St LJ* 55.

25 Suzanne McNicol, *Law of Privilege*, (Australia, Law Book Co, 1992), 330.

created the first RCP statute in New South Wales by inserting a much more detailed provision into the *Evidence Act 1898* (NSW). It provided:

> 10. (1) A person who is or was a member of the clergy of any church or religious denomination is entitled to refuse to divulge that a religious confession was made, or the contents of a religious confession made, to the person when a member of the clergy.
>
> (2) Subsection (1) does not apply of the communication involved in the religious confession was made for a criminal purpose.
>
> (3) This section applies even in circumstances where an Act provides:
>
> (a) that the rules of evidence do not apply or that a person or body is not bound by the rules of evidence: or
>
> (b) that a person is excused from answering any question or producing any documents or other thing on the ground of privilege or any other ground.
>
> (4) Without limiting the generality of subsection (3), this section applies:
>
> (a) to any hearing or proceedings to which the Royal Commissions Act 1923, the Special Commissions of Inquiry Act 1983 or the Independent Commission Against Corruption Act 1988 applies; or
>
> (b) in relation to a witness summoned to attend and give evidence before either House of Parliament (or a Parliamentary Committee) as referred to in the Parliamentary Evidence Act 1901.

McNicol explained that the first RCP statute in New South Wales was a response to a finding of contempt against a Catholic priest in Lithgow (Father Mark McGuigan) who had declined to answer prosecution questions about a confession received from Pamela Young who was charged with a murder on New Year's Eve in 1988.[26] The New South Wales version of the statutory privilege responded to the Australian

---

26 Ibid. See also "Submission in connection with Case Study 50: Final hearing into Catholic Church authorities in Australia. The Catholic Church: Then and Now", 22 December 2016, *Royal Commission into Institutional Responses to Child Sexual*, 66.

Law Reform Commission's (ALRC) Interim Evidence Law Report in 1985 which had found that a statutory form of RCP in Australia only afforded "protection...to those denominations with an institutionalised system of confession...[and] not...to those denominations or religions in which spiritual advisers give assistance on a personal and private basis" which was said to be "discriminatory." The ALRC had also found that in jurisdictions without a statutory privilege, "[t]he potential for the courts to compel disclosure by a spiritual adviser...constitutes at least in theory a barrier to free and unfettered practice of religion."[27] The ALRC therefore recommended the legislature create a wider and ecumenical "judicial discretion to protect confidential communication between a clergyman and a member of his church."[28] In its 1987 38th Report recommending what has become known as a *Uniform Evidence Act*, the ALRC reaffirmed its recommendation of "a discretionary approach", but with the President dissenting and recommending the creation of "a separate privilege for confidential communications passing between a member of the clergy and a person making a confession to or seeking religious or spiritual advice or comfort from that member."[29]

The President's dissenting view prevailed and the *Uniform Evidence Act* in 1995 included the following provision which was immediately adopted in the Commonwealth, the ACT and New South Wales, and then in Tasmania in 2001, Victoria in 2008, and the NT in 2012. It provides:

> (1) A person who is or was a member of the clergy of any church or religious denomination is entitled to refuse to divulge that a religious confession was made, or the contents of a religious confession made, to the person when a member of the clergy.

---

27 Australian Law Reform Commission 26 Evidence (Interim) Report 1985, [460]-[461].
28 Ibid [909].
29 Australian Law Reform Commission 38 Evidence Report 1987, [204]-[213]. The Honourable Xavier O'Connor AO QC succeeded the Honourable Michael Kirby AC CMG as President of the ALRC after the Honourable Murray Wilcox AO QC had served as Acting President from September 1984 to 1985. Justice O'Connor served as President from 6 May 1985 to 11 December 1987.

(2) Subsection (1) does not apply if the communication involved in the religious confession was made for a criminal purpose.

(3) This section applies even if an Act provides:

(a) that the rules of evidence do not apply or that a person or body is not bound by the rules of evidence: or

(b) that a person is not excuse from answering any question or producing any document or other thing on the ground of privilege or any other ground

(4) In this section:

"*religious confession*" means a confession made by a person to a member of the clergy in the member's professional capacity according to the ritual of the church or religious denomination concerned.

It will be observed that the ALRC's recommendation that the privilege needed to be broadened and made ecumenical if it was to respect the "free and unfettered practice of religion" was observed to the letter. That recommendation in the ALRC's Interim Report in 1985 appears to have picked up the spirit of Justice Robin Cooke's (as he then was[30]) language in the New Zealand Court of Appeal in R v Howse in 1983 when he observed that the rationale behind any statutory RCP "must be that a person should not suffer temporal prejudice because of what is uttered under the dictates or influence of spiritual belief".[31] And that language in its turn alluded to discussion in two English cases immediately before Australia's first RCP statute was passed in Victoria in 1864. In the first of the two English cases, Baron Alderson had admonished prosecuting counsel in R v Griffin in England in 1853 not to seek to adduce evidence

---

30 Sir Robin Cooke served as President of the New Zealand Court of Appeal from 1986 until he was granted a British life peerage as Baron Cooke of Thorndon becoming a member of the Appellate Committee of the House of Lords where he sat as a Lord of Appeal until his retirement in 2001, Geoff McLay, "Sir Robin Cook" (2006) 37 VUWLR 335, (<http://www.nzlii.org/nz/journals/VUWLawRw/2006/15.pdf>)

31 R v Howse [1983] NZLR 246, 251.

of a religious confession because there was an analogy between the necessity for privilege in the case of an attorney to enable legal advice to be given and the case of a clergyman enabling spiritual assistance to be given. Though Baron Alderson said he was not laying this down "as an absolute rule", he did not "think such evidence ought...to be given".[32] Baron Alderson's advice to prosecuting counsel in the *Griffin* case stood in contrast to the interchange between Justice Hill and Father Kelly in *R v Hay* seven years later when Justice Hill likewise said he would not ask the priest to disclose anything said to him in the confessional, but gaoled him for contempt because he would not answer the simple factual question where he got the stolen watch he had handed into the police.[33]

The statutory privilege in New Zealand which was first created in 1885 perhaps in similar response to Sir George Jessel MR's celebrated obiter denial of the existence of such a privilege in the English Court of Appeal in *Wheeler v LeMarchant* in 1881,[34] has been similarly broadened. The latest 2006 iteration of the New Zealand privilege reads:

> (1) A person has a privilege in respect of any communication between that person and a minister of religion if the communication was –
>
> (a) made in confidence to or by the minister in the minister's capacity as a minister of religion, and

---

32 *R v Griffin* (1853) 6 Cox Cr Cas 219.

33 *R v Hay* (1860) 175 ER 933. Note that the ensuing debate in the English press about religious confession privilege continued for some time and flared again due to the case of Constance Kent (*R v Constance Kent* (1865) unreported but referred to in Attlay's Famous Trials of the Nineteenth Century, 1899, 113). Constance Kent had confessed to the murder of her half-brother when she was 16 in 1860 and precipitated a storm of high level judicial argument (mostly in the House of Lords) as to whether religious confession privilege had ceased to exist in England and Wales. After she was released from prison in 1885, she assumed a different name (Ruth Emilie Kaye) and moved to Australia where she died aged 100 in Strathfield, New South Wales in 1944.

34 *Wheeler v LeMarchant* (1881) 17 Ch D 675. Sir George Jessel said:
In the first place, the principle protecting confidential communications is of a very limited character. ... There are many communications, which, though absolutely necessary because without them the ordinary business of life cannot be carried on, still are not privileged. ... Communications made to a priest in the confessional on matters perhaps considered by the penitent to be more important than his life or his fortune, are not protected (ibid 681).

(b) made for the purpose of the person obtaining or receiving from the minister religious or spiritual advice, benefit or comfort.

(2) A person is a **minister of religion** for the purposes of this section if the person has a status within a church or other religious or spiritual community that requires or calls for that person –

(a) to receive confidential communications of the kind described in subsection (1); and

(b) to respond with religious or spiritual advice, benefit or comfort (emphasis original).[35]

Justice Claire L'Heureux-Dubé of the Supreme Court of Canada drew many of these threads together in her concurring minority judgement in *R v Gruenke* in 1991.[36] She was concerned that her Court's recognition of a case-by-case discretionary privilege would chill the free exercise of religion in Canada.[37] Recognition of the privilege in only a discretionary form focused only "on the palpable need for evidence in the individual case and...neglect[ed] more intangible and long-term interests".[38] As Knight Bruce VC had said in 1846, truth may be loved unwisely – may be pursued too keenly – and may cost too much.[39] Society's interest in promoting religious communications and privacy, and the fact that compelling disclosure could bring the justice system into disrepute, were other values that needed to be taken into account and that would be left out too easily when a trial judge was exercising a discretion focused on the need for evidence in the here and now.[40]

Justice Heydon has expressed similar concern about the exercise of discretion in criminal cases. In 1974 as Dean of the Law School at the

---

35 *Evidence Act 2006* (NZ) s 58.
36 *R v Gruenke* [1991] 3 SCR 263.
37 Ibid 311.
38 Ibid.
39 *Pearse v Pearse* (1846) 63 ER 950, 957.
40 *R v Gruenke* [1991] 3 SCR 263, 297-304.

University of Sydney he observed that

> the use of discretion...should be regarded as at most an ancillary aid...[because i]t leads to uncertainty in practice and differences from judge to judge: the accused's counsel will therefore never know how far the defence can safely go. Reliance on discretion to solve problems of evidence tends to confuse the actual rules of law and to cause loss of contact with fundamental principle; and it tends towards the reversal of established rules without express recognition of or adequate reason for that change.[41]

Thirty-seven years later as a Justice of the High Court of Australia, in a case about the admissibility and relevance of expert evidence, he reiterated his concern that reliance on discretion undermines the rule of law by reducing certainty and predictability. He said:

> [A] discretionary power of exclusion...eschews the primary technique of a rule of strict inadmissibility and instead falls back on a weaker device...For defendants in particular, it is necessary to know with reasonable certainty before the trial begins whether the expert evidence tendered by the moving party is admissible. If it is, it may be necessary to incur the expense of meeting it. If it is not, that expense can be avoided. To make the criterion of admissibility turn not on the satisfaction of a rule but on the invocation of a discretion is to abandon the search of reasonable predictability.[42]

The advent of statutory RCP in Australia is a manifestation of our Westminster choice that accountable elected parliamentarians rather than judicial technicians should have the final say on the nature and meaning of all our law except the *Constitution*. Though Queensland, South Australia and Western Australia have resisted calls to implement the *Uniform Evidence Act* including its statutory recognition of RCP, they are still morally bound to recognise the free exercise of religious conscience expressed in the *ICCPR* and Queensland and Western Australia have

---

41 "Can the Accused attack the Prosecution?", (1974) 7 *Sydney Law Review* 2, 166, 176.
42 *Dasreef Pty Ltd v Hawchar* (2011) 243 CLR 588, 635 [119].

enacted general law protections against religious discrimination.[43] And all three states are also practically bound to respect the political opinion of the religious believers who remain a majoritarian part of their electorates.[44]

Part Two – RCP under pressure – How does RCP relate to freedom of conscience and religion in international law?

Recommendations 33 to 35 of the Royal Commission's Final Report interact with religious confession and RCP directly. Recommendation 35 in particular suggested that all Australian state and territory governments amend their RCP statutes to the extent necessary to make the recommended new criminal failure to report offences effective. In effect, recommendation 35 says RCP should be abrogated to the extent necessary to ensure that it does not exempt or exonerate any failure to report. The abrogation of RCP is recommended where a person receiving a confession knew, or should have suspected that a child sexual abuse offence had been committed because of what was learned in the confession. The Royal Commission justified this recommendation in the following terms:

> We were told in submissions that any intrusion by the civil law on the practice of religious confession would undermine the principle of freedom of religion. In a civil society, it is fundamentally important that the right of a person to freely practise their religion in accordance with their beliefs is upheld.
>
> However, that right is not absolute. This is recognised in article 18 of the *International Covenant on Civil and Political Rights* on the freedom of religion, which provides that the freedom to manifest

---

43 "Factsheet: Guide to the protections for freedom of religion (2019)", 9 July 2019, *Australian Human Rights Commission.* See also s 20 *Human Rights Act 2019* (Qld) and Part IV of the *Equal Opportunity Act 1984* (WA).

44 In the 2016 Australian census, more than 60% of the Australian population still expressed a religious affiliation though "no religion is rising fast" ("2016 Census: Religion", 27 June 2017, *Australian Bureau of Statistics.*

one's religion or beliefs may be the subject of such limitation as are prescribed by law and are necessary to protect public safety, order, health or morals or the fundamental rights and freedoms of others.

The right to practise one's religious beliefs must accommodate civil society's obligation to provide for the safety of all and in particular, children's safety from sexual abuse. Institutions directed to and caring for and providing for children, including religious institutions, must provide an environment where children are safe from sexual abuse. Reporting information relevant to child sexual abuse to the police is critical to ensuring the safety of children.

We have concluded that the importance of protecting children from child sexual abuse means that there should be no exemption from the failure to report offence for clergy in relation to information disclosed in or in connection with a religious confession.[45]

In the balance of this Part, I review that justification in two ways. I first explain what the words of qualification in Article 18(3) of the *ICCPR* quoted by the Royal Commission mean, and then I discuss whether they justify the abrogation of RCP as the Royal Commission says they do. Because that analysis involves recognising the difference between that part of religious freedom in the *ICCPR* which is said to be inviolable (the *forum internum*) and that part which can be limited (the *forum externum*), I then also discuss whether the words used by the framers of the *ICCPR* place religious confession within the *forum internum* or the *forum externum*. That is, whether the practice of religious confession or any part of it is inviolable under Article 18(1) of the *ICCPR* or whether the only thing those framers intended to recognise as inviolable was what we think about inside our minds which no one else can access without our voluntary disclosure or some form of coercion. I conclude Part Two with a brief survey, as of the date of this writing, on how the Australian states and territories have responded to Royal Commission's recommendation that they abrogate RCP to the extent necessary to implement the failure to report offence and make it effective. That discussion includes reference

---

45 "Criminal Justice report: Failure to report offence", *n.d., Royal Commission into Institutional Responses to Child Sexual Abuse*, 2.

to Nick Xenophon's unsuccessful private member's bill introduced to the South Australian Parliament in September 2003 – ironical because the defeat of that bill in a state that has no statutory RCP arguably endorsed RCP's existence at common law.

Article 18 of the ICCPR

Because I refer to this article in detail, I set it out in full. It reads:

> 1. Everyone shall have the right to freedom of thought, conscience and religion. This right shall include freedom to have or to adopt a religion or belief of his choice, and freedom, either individually or in community with others and in public or private, to manifest his religion or belief in worship, observance, practice and teaching.
>
> 2. No one shall be subject to coercion which would impair his freedom to have or to adopt a religion or belief of his choice.
>
> 3. Freedom to manifest one's religion or beliefs may be subject only to such limitations as are prescribed by law and are necessary to protect public safety, order, health, or morals or the fundamental rights and freedoms of others.
>
> 4. The States Parties to the present Covenant undertake to have respect for the liberty of parents and, when applicable, legal guardians to ensure the religious and moral education of their children in conformity with their own convictions.

Subsection 1 essential repeats the original aspirational idea that was expressed in Article 18 of the UDHR in 1948:

> Everyone has the right to freedom of thought, conscience and religion; this right includes freedom to change his religion or belief, and freedom, either alone or in community with others and in public or private, to manifest his religion or belief in teaching, practice, worship and observance.

The nations that signed the follow-on *ICCPR* covenant promised to implement the terms of the covenant in their national law. Though Australia was one of seven charter members of the United Nations in 1948 and signed the *UDHR* almost immediately, it did not ratify the *ICCPR* until 14 years after it was promulgated and has never implemented it in domestic law. Initially Australia explained that some delay in domestic implementation was expected because the then federal executive was not sure it had the constitutional power to pass a national implementation law and would therefore have to persuade the states and territories to do so.[46] But within two years of ratification, the High Court's decision in the *Koowarta* case confirmed by a 4-3 majority that such an international covenant could be passed under the *Constitution's* external affairs power.[47] That interpretation of s 51(xxxi) of the *Constitution* was confirmed with a further 4-3 majority the following year in the *Tasmanian Dam Case*.[48] But despite that judicial confirmation of the federal government's power to pass laws making good on its international commitments, no succeeding federal government has been unable to gather the support necessary to implement the *ICCPR* and keep the commitment made to the international community in 1980. But while that means the provisions of the *ICCPR* including Article 18 do not yet bind in domestic law, they are now so well accepted that most experts in international law consider that they are binding as international customary law.[49] However, the fact that Article 18 is now a binding international custom does not mean a lot since there is no supra-national enforcement body that has the coercive power to sanction breaches.

In its explanation for why the abrogation of RCP was justified, the Royal Commission accepted that religious confession was a practice protected

---

46 The full text of Australia's reservation to the implementation of the *ICCPR* in Australian domestic law is set out in Appendix I to this chapter.

47 *Koowarta v Bjelke-Petersen* (1982) 153 CLR 168.

48 *Commonwealth v Tasmania (Tasmanian Dam Case)* (1983) 158 CLR 1.

49 In her text, *International Law: Contemporary Principles and Practice* (LexisNexis Butterworths, 2006), Gillian Triggs has written that "many of the provisions of the ICCPR" have achieved "customary law status" including the "rights of minorities to enjoy their own culture, profess their own religion [and] to use their own language" (ibid 14.5 and 14.8).

by Article 18 of the *ICCPR*, but it relied on the limitation language in Article 18(3). It said that like all other manifestations of religious belief, the confidentiality of religious confession including the seal in Catholicism could be formally limited by a law change if that change was necessary to protect the fundamental rights and freedoms of children. The problem is the necessity requirement under Article 18(3). Is it really necessary to pass a law to abrogate RCP to protect children as the Royal Commission stated?

The necessary standard in Article 18(3) of the ICCPR

The first question is what does necessary mean in the *ICCPR*'s context? Does it mean that a legislature or government committed to implementing the freedom of religion contemplated by the right expressed in the *ICCPR* can limit that freedom any time it is reasonable, or reasonably necessary to do so? Anytime it thinks society might be benefitted in any way for however short a period? Or did the framers of the *ICCPR* intend to specify a higher more objective threshold?

The answer is that a higher more objective standard was intended because the framers of the *ICCPR* said that such changes should only be made by the passage of formal laws, presumably so that the limitation might be clearly known, and so that it would not be the result of mere administrative action or the dictate of a passing executive whim. But the problem is that, as of this writing the three state and territory legislatures that have passed laws they say were intended to implement the right set out in Article 18 of the *ICCPR*, have either misunderstood this objective requirement or they have purposely diluted it to ensure the passage of their version of a religious liberty law with less political opposition.[50] Perhaps in that context, the Royal Commission can be forgiven for thinking that Article 18(3) meant that a religious practice could be abrogated any time a government or legislature wanted to limit it or thought it reasonable to do so. But that is not what the international standard says. Again, the *ICCPR* requirement is that to meet the international standard, no religious practice can be abrogated other than by the legislative passage of a formal law in circumstances where it was necessary to take that step. The meaning of the word necessary cannot be accurately conveyed by replacing it with the word reasonable. An accurate expression of the idea intended by the *ICCPR* framers is that a religious practice cannot be limited unless the legislative goal cannot be achieved in any other way. To use language familiar from American jurisprudence, the government must have a compelling reason to impose this limitation and the law chosen must pass a strict scrutiny test meaning that objective observers must agree as a matter of inexorable logic that there is either no other way or no better way to achieve this pressing government need without imposing on this particular religious practice. This is a form of proportionality analysis, but the word necessity and the synonymous American strict scrutiny phrase teach that it is high level proportionality analysis.

So what does such high level proportionality analysis say about the Royal Commission's assertion that it is necessary to abrogate RCP to protect children where a religious confession raises issues of child sexual abuse?

---

50 The *Human Rights Act 2004* (ACT) includes a note at the beginning of Part 3 which states that "[t]he primary source of these rights is the International Covenant on Civil and Political Rights" and the provisions from the *ICCPR* which are relied on are set out in schedule 1. In relation to Victoria's *Charter of Human Rights and Responsibilities Act 2006*, see the *Charter of Human Rights Bench Book* (Melbourne: Judicial College of Victoria, 2016-2018) where those authors state "[t]he 20 rights contained in the Charter were primarily drawn from the ICCPR" but were "adjusted...to improve the drafting" (ibid [12]) to "maintain parliamentary sovereignty" (ibid [6]) and because some of the rights in the ICCPR were "not suited to legislation by an Australian state" (ibid [13]). In its "Guide for Public Entities", the Queensland Human Rights Commission states that the *Human Rights Act 2019* (Qld) "protects 23 human rights" and says "that human rights are not absolute and may be subject under the law to reasonable limits that can be justified". None of these three acts uses the necessity language to which Australia agreed in the *ICCPR* in 1980.

Is it necessary to abrogate RCP in Australia when the confession raises issues of child sexual abuse?

This proposal is problematic when it is considered carefully. For it does not withstand careful thought. The first and oldest hurdle that the proposal to abrogate RCP must overcome is Jeremy Bentham's early nineteenth century insight that the moment the constabulary were known to have harvested their very first confessional secret, the well of such secrets would dry up. That is not to say that religious believers would stop confessing their sins and otherwise seeking help from spiritual advisors. But Bentham believed that those who might have confessed to the abuse of children would not discuss those sins with their priests and spiritual advisors once it was known that those confessions were not protected. Bentham was emphatic on the point. Though he opposed every other form of privilege including both legal professional privilege and parliamentary privilege, despite his atheism, he considered that nineteenth century proposals to extinguish RCP were nothing less than an institutionalised effort to persecute the Catholic Church. He does not seem to have even considered the confessional practices of the other churches of his age because he did not consider they were being targeted by the limitations proposed by his contemporaries.

The second hurdle to a finding that the abrogation of RCP is necessary to protect children from sexual abuse is the idea that those who sexually abuse children routinely confess their sins. While John Cornwell famously wrote in *The Dark Box* that a former Catholic priest named Michael Joseph McArdle had confessed more than 1500 times to 25 different priests over a 30 year period,[51] in fact that was McArdle's own self-serving and uncontested assertion before the Queensland Court of Appeal when he was trying to get his six year gaol term reduced. McArdle's story was rejected by the Court and his gaol term unchanged.[52] Cornwell's implication that many of those who sexually abuse children

---

51 John Cornwell, *The Dark Box, A Secret History of Confession* (New York: Basic Books, 2014) 189.
52 *R v McArdle* [2004] QCA 7.

routinely confess those sins to a priest stands in stark contrast to Gerald Risdale's infamous testimony before the Royal Commission on 27 May 2015 that 'he never told anyone about his sexual abuse of boys, even during confession, because the "overriding fear would have been losing the priesthood"'.[53] Risdale's approach is also more consistent with what Irish sociologist Dr Marie Keenan uncovered when she interviewed nine priests who were serving time for child sexual abuse offences. While two of them confirmed that they had gone to confession and mentioned their child sexual abuse sins, when Dr Keenan pressed them, they revealed that they had not told the priest receiving the confession enough information to reveal that the other party to their illicit sexual encounter was a child and therefore had not said enough to create knowledge or suspicion of child sexual abuse requirements to activate any of the mandatory reporting laws recommended by the Royal Commission.[54]

A third hurdle to proving that the abrogation of RCP is necessary to protect children from child sexual abuse comes from the Royal Commission's own data. That data suggested that child sexual abuse claims in religious institutions had fallen dramatically since 1990.[55] Not only do those numbers coincide with efforts by the churches to weed child sexual abusers out of their ranks during the 1990s, but they also coincide with the Queensland government's successful implementation of its Blue Card child care worker or volunteer scheme.[56] While New South Wales was slow to follow Queensland's lead and relied on a soft declaration system for child care volunteers until 2012,[57] cloned versions of the Queensland scheme seem to have driven the child sexual abusers

---

53 Andrew Koubaridis and AAP, "Vile paedophile Gerald Risdale will give evidence at Royal Commission today", May 27, 2015, *News.com.au*.

54 Marie Keenan, *Child Sexual Abuse and the Catholic Church: Gender, Power and Organizational Culture* (Oxford University Press, 2012), 162-164.

55 See for example Figure 3 in the Royal Commission's June 2017 "Analysis of Claims of Child Sexual Abuse made with respect to Catholic Church Institutions in Australia", 21 and supporting text.

56 *Working with Children (Risk Management and Screening Act 2000* (Qld). For details of how the scheme operates, see "The Blue Card system explained" 31 August 2020, *The Queensland Government*.

57 *The Child Protection (Working with Children) Act 2012* (NSW) came into effect on 15 June 2013.

who remained within the ranks of those who volunteered and worked with children in churches after 1990 from those ranks after 2000.

All of these hurdles suggest that the stories of confessions from perpetrators and victims that the Royal Commission heard, came from cases that predated 2000 and even 1990 so that the Commission's work and recommendations might have been more usefully focused on how those who had suffered from child sexual abuse as children could receive healing and compensation in the face of state and territory laws passed in the early 1990s to prevent recovery through the courts.[58] While the Royal Commission did recommend that those states and territories who still had such limitation laws on their books should repeal them immediately, there was no inquiry as to why those laws had been passed in the first place. That inquiry would have revealed state and territory concern about their own joint liability in most of those claims because they had either referred the victims to the institutions concerned or had

---

58 Before the Royal Commission commenced its hearings, all Australian jurisdictions had passed laws preventing child sexual abuse victims bringing claims against the perpetrators of their abuse, the institutions which engaged those perpetrators or the state and territory governments that referred and were charged with supervising those institutions. For example, s 50C (1) (b) of the NSW Limitation Act 1969 provided a "12 year long-stop limitation period", though that period could be extended by a Court exercising its discretion under Division 4 of Part 3. Section 27E of the Victorian Limitation of Actions Act 1958 provided that a person under a disability could bring an action before the earliest to occur of six years after a disability ended or twelve years from when the action accrued. Section 11 of the Queensland Limitation of Actions Act 1974 provided a three year limitation period in respect of personal injuries. Section 29 provided that period was extended by six years from the date when a disability ceased. Section 36 of the South Australian Limitation of Actions Act 1936 provided a three year limitation period for personal injury claims, or three years after the claimant became aware of the relevant injury. Section 14 of the West Australian Limitation Act 2005 provided a three year sunset on personal injury actions. Part 3 of the same Act made various provisions for extension depending on the nature of the disability (different minority ages and mental disability). In Tasmania, sections 5 and 5A of the Limitation Act 1974 made a distinction between causes of action accrued before and after the date of the commencement of the Act, with extensions possible under Part III for similar reasons that applied in NSW and Victoria. In the ACT, s 11 of the Limitation Act 1985 provided a six year limitation on all causes of action, but s 35 granted the court discretion to enlarge that time after reviewing specified criteria. Section 12 of the Limitation Act 2008 in the Northern Territory prescribed a three year limitation period on actions in tort. But s 36 provides for an extension of three years after the disability ended.

failed in their duty to supervise and ensure the safety of children within those institutions. Anecdotal evidence suggests that state and territory governments have been quietly settling all of those newly available cases out of court lest they attract some of the opprobrium that has attached to the churches because of the Royal Commission's focus on their shortcomings.[59]

But what changes to RCP have the states and territories made in response to the Royal Commission's recommendations that they make the reporting of knowledge or suspicion of child sexual abuse mandatory for everyone including those who learn it through religious confession?

State and territory responses to the mandatory reporting and abolish RCP recommendations of the Royal Commission

With the benefit of hindsight, Nick Xenophon's 2003 private member's bill to abrogate RCP in child abuse cases seems prescient even though it was unsuccessful. He certainly foresaw the coming media storm, but for the reasons already discussed it is doubtful that his abrogation of RCP goal in child sexual abuse cases was ever necessary. While the South Australian political party which he founded continued to press for further amendments to abolish RCP in child sexual abuse cases in addition to mandatory reporting,[60] there was arguably no need to seek the abrogation of RCP in that state because it was not protected in statute.

The ACT has amended its version of the *Uniform Evidence Act* and

---

59 See for example "Submission to the New South Wales Department of Justice, Discussion Paper, Limitation periods in civil claims for child sexual abuse", *n.d., knowmore* and Shine Lawyers, "Child Sex Abuse: Statute of Limitations", 1 October 2020, *Shine Lawyers.* See also "Model Litigant Policy for Civil Litigation and Guiding Principles for Civil Claims for Child Abuse, Premier's Memorandum M2016-03", *n.d., NSW Government, Communities and Justice.*

60 C. Bonaros, "SA-Best introduces bill to close loophole on mandatory reporting by priests of child abuse", 11 September 2018. The *Children and Young Person Safety Act 2017* (SA) took effect in two stages in February and October 2018.

subsection 2 now reads:

> Subsection (1) does not apply if
>
> (a) the communication involved in the religious confession was made for a criminal purpose: or
>
> (b) the religious confession includes information relating to –
>
> (i)   a child or young person that is experiencing, or has experienced, sexual abuse or non-accidental physical injury: or
>
> (ii)   a substantial risk that a child or young person may experience sexual abuse or non-accidental physical injury.

This amendment avoids inconsistency with the reporting obligation now included in the *Ombudsman Act 1989* which requires that the heads of designated entities including religious bodies must report to the Ombudsman, a variety of conduct including that now excepted from the protection of RCP in s 127 of the *Evidence Act 2011* (ACT).[61] While the exception of "non-accidental physical injury" goes beyond the recommendations of the Royal Commission, it appears that once the ACT legislature considered that injury to children was a reasonable exception to RCP, there was no reason to limit the abrogation of RCP in child abuse cases only to cases of abuse where sexual abuse arose. No other Australian jurisdictions have made legislative changes that go this far.

Section 127 (2) of the *Evidence Act 2008* (Vic) has been similarly amended. It now reads:

> (3) Subsection (1) does not apply –
>
> (a) if the communication involved in the religious confession was made for a criminal purpose; or
>
> (b) in a proceeding for an offence against section 184 of the Children, Youth and Families Act 2005; or
>
> (c) in a proceeding for an offence against section 327(2) of the Crimes Act 1958.

---

61   See Division 2.2A ss 17D to 17P of the *Ombudsman Act 1989* (ACT).

Section 184 of the *Children, Youth and Families Act* 2005 (Vic) makes it clear that persons in religious ministry are mandatory reporters and s 184(2A) restates that s 127 of the *Evidence Act 2008* (Vic) does not exempt such persons from mandatory reporting obligations under the *Children, Youth and Families Act 2005* (Vic). Section 327(2) and (7) of the *Crimes Act 1958* (Vic) similarly make it clear that anyone who fails to disclose knowledge or reasonable suspicion of a sexual offence against a child as soon as practicable after gaining that knowledge commits an offence and is not exempted from such disclosure by RCP.

New South Wales, Tasmania and the Northern Territory have not made similar amendments to s 127 of their versions of the *Uniform Evidence Act*[62] even though they have passed mandatory reporting laws which apply to persons likely to hear confidential religious confessions.[63] Tasmania has however stated in s 14(7) of their *Children, Young Persons and Their Families Act 1997* that RCP in s 127 of the *Evidence Act 2001* (Tas) does not exempt a member of the clergy from the duty to disclose which is confusing since s 127(3)(b) of the *Evidence Act 2001* (Tas) still says in effect that a member of the clergy is entitled to refuse to disclose confessional information even if another Act says that a member of the clergy is "not excused from answering any question...on the ground of privilege or any other ground." Perhaps the provision in the *Children, Young Persons and Their Families Act 1997* is specific enough as subsequent legislation that a court interpreting the apparent inconsistency would consider that the later amendment overruled the former.

Though the mandatory reporting laws in New South Wales and the Northern Territory do not add this Tasmanian element of confusion,

---

62 The *Evidence Act 1995* (NSW), the *Evidence Act 2001* (Tas) and the *Evidence (National Uniform Legislation) Act 2011* (NT).

63 Section 27(1)(c) of the *Children and Young Persons (Care and Protection) Act 1998* (NSW); s 14(1)(ja) of the *Children, Young Persons and Their Families Act 1997* (Tas) and s 26(1) of the *Care and Protection of Children Act 2007* (NT).

they do not answer the question whether a member of the clergy can avoid answering questions about a failure to report or disclose knowledge or suspicion of child sexual abuse because s 127 of these *Evidence* laws have not been amended in the same way as in Victoria and the ACT.

Laying aside these changes and potential inconsistencies in state and territory legislation because of varied responses to the 'abrogate RCP recommendation' of the Royal Commission, there is still the question of whether any of this legislation should have been passed at all given the arguably inviolable nature of the *forum internum* under the *ICCPR*.

What are the bounds of the *forum internum* under the ICCPR?

Carolyn Evans and Paul Taylor have suggested that defining what is protected without limitation by the *ICCPR* is problematic.[64] It will be remembered that Article 18(2) and (3) of the *ICCPR* provide that

> 2. No one shall be subject to coercion which would impair his freedom to have or to adopt a religion or belief of his choice.

> 3. Freedom to manifest one's religion or beliefs may be subject only to such limitations as are prescribed by law and are necessary to protect public safety, order, health, or morals or the fundamental rights and freedoms of others.

But does a law that would compel a member of the clergy to disclose a religious confession, impair his or her freedom to have or adopt that belief? Or are decisions required in conscience to follow that belief? That is, must a decision by a member of the clergy to refuse to disclose the contents of a religious confession or the fact that a religious confession took place, be protected under the inviolable *forum internum*

---

64 Carolyn Evans, *Freedom of Religion under the European Convention on Human Rights* (Oxford University Press, 2001) 67–102, 204–209; Paul M Taylor, *Freedom of Religion: UN and European Human Rights Law and Practice* (Cambridge University Press, 2005) 115–202.

set out in the *ICCPR*?

And similarly, when does the penitent's decision to confess become a limitable manifestation of religion under Article 18(3)? When she walks into the church, when she crosses the threshold of the confessional box or when she opens her mouth to speak the words of a confession believing that she is confessing those words to a member of the clergy as a proxy for God?

A related but not identical question that arose centuries ago in relation to those who provided translation services for lawyers was whether those translators were protected by the legal professional privilege of their principals? That question was answered in the affirmative.[65] But back to RCP and the *forum internum*. Does it matter that the member of the clergy considers that she does not hear what she hears in the confessional communication herself but only as a proxy for God?

This discussion and other hypothetical questions that can follow, disclose an irony in human rights law. For though we say that conscience is inviolable, in criminal law we make conviction of the most serious crime dependent on proof of intent. But because we cannot physiologically see inside someone's mind, even though we say we are proving intent, what we are really doing is adducing or proving more facts from which the judge or jury deduces the intention of the accused. But when King Henry VIII required Thomas More to take an Oath under the *Act of Succession 1534*, we now accept that King Henry was seeking to coerce Thomas's conscience in violation of the *forum internum*. In recognition of that inviolability of conscience, s 116 of the *Australian Constitution* now provides that a religious oath cannot be made a condition of appointment to any office of public trust under the Commonwealth.

But Thomas More never uttered the oath so his thoughts famously

---

65   *Du Barré v Livette* (1791) 1 Peake 108; 170 ER 86.

stayed within his mind. Is that the difference? Does that mean that the *forum internum* is not violated when there is an expression because an expression or utterance of any kind is a manifestation of religion which can therefore be limited? But if that is the answer, then perhaps it is easier to understand why some of those who do not feel comfortable with what King Henry VIII required of Thomas More, do not feel comfortable with what the Royal Commission recommended to the Australian Commonwealth, state and territory governments where RCP is concerned. That is because to the extent that those recommendations suggest that Australian state and territory governments abrogate RCP by requiring members of the clergy to disclose what has been told them in absolute confidence, they are being asked to pass laws that are genealogically similar to the law which King Henry VIII relied on against Thomas More between 1534 and 1536.

Now some final thoughts on whether RCP can still be intellectually justified in Australia in the 21st century.

Part Three – Can RCP be intellectually justified in modern secular Australia?

I have already referred to Jeremy Bentham's early nineteenth century view that the proposed abrogation of RCP was nothing less than a thinly veiled attempt to persecute adherents of the Catholic Church. His argument against the abrogation of RCP despite his wish to abrogate every other legal privilege in English society, is best captured by this extract from his 1827 *Rationale of Judicial Evidence*. He wrote:

> [A] coercion...is altogether inconsistent and incompatible [with any idea of toleration]....The advantage gained by the coercion – gained in the shape of assistance to justice – would be casual, and even rare; the mischief produced by it, constant and extensive...this institution is an essential feature of the catholic religion, and...the catholic religion is not to be suppressed by force...Repentance, and consequent abstinence from future misdeeds...are the well-known

consequences of the institution.[66]

When Wigmore also considered whether RCP was a class of privilege that was justified in modern Anglo-American society, he tested that proposal using his own canons of construction.[67] He then argued that the confidentiality of confession expected under church disciplinary rules was justified in the interests of character reform, and essential if character reform was to be its result; that the state intolerance implicit in seeking disclosure of religious confidences was inconsistent with any meaningful free exercise of religion and he followed Bentham in stating that the abrogation of RCP would damage society more by its interference with this religious institution than it would benefit the administration of justice by the disclosure of 'the party's own confession'.[68] But he also believed that coercion was an unsatisfactory foundation for any system of criminal law, an idea echoed in J. Noel Lyon's view that the best reason for religious confession privilege is that it denies police access to any evidence obtained under any form of duress.[69] While Australian evidence practice does not follow North American practice in excluding any evidence from trial where there is any suggestion that it was illegally obtained,[70] the admission of confessional evidence has never simply been

---

66 Jeremy Bentham, *Rationale of Judicial Evidence* (New York and London: Garland Publishing, Inc, 1978 (Reprint of the 1827 ed published by Hunt and Clarke, London), Vol. IV, 589-590.

67 Wigmore, JH, *Evidence in Trials at Common Law* (Boston: Revised by John T Mc-Naughton, Little Brown, 1961) Vol. 8, 527. Those canons of construction are:
The communications must originate in a *confidence* that they will not be disclosed. This element of *confidentiality* must *be essential* to the full and satisfactory maintenance of the relation between the parties.
The *relation* must be one which in the opinion of the community ought to be sedulously *fostered*.
The *injury* that would inure to the relation by the disclosure of the communications must be *greater than the benefit* thereby gained for the correct disposal of litigation.

68 Ibid Vol. 8, 878.

69 "Privileged Communications – Penitent and Priest" (1964-1965) 7 *Crim. L.Q.* 327.

70 Australian practice allows judges to decide whether illegally obtained evidence should be adduced in Australian courtrooms as matter of discretion. In Uniform Evidence Act jurisdictions, the factors to be considered by judges in the exercise of that discretion is set out if s 138(3) of the relevant Evidence Acts. In other Australian jurisdictions, similar discretionary considerations apply following principles developed in *R v Ireland* (1970) 126 CLR 321; *Bunning v Cross* (1978) 141 CLR 54 and *Ridgeway v The Queen* (1995) 184 CLR 19.

a matter of weighing its probative value. Indeed, Henry E. Smith has observed that because of the excesses of the prerogative courts during the Tudor and Stuart periods of English history, by the late eighteenth century, English courts had accepted that "a confession forced from the mind by the flattery of hope, or by the torture of fear, c[a]me...in so questionable a shape when it is to be considered as the evidence of guilt that no credit ought to be given to it".[71]

Professor Suzanne McNicol in Victoria found three further arguments in favour of a modern RCP compelling when she wrote her *Law of Privilege* in 1992:

> First, there is the civil libertarian argument which relies upon a citizen's fundamental right to the unfettered practice of religion without interference from the law. Secondly, there is the clear unyielding ethical duty imposed upon ministers not to divulge what is said to them in confidence....Thirdly, there is the undeniable fact that ministers will universally disobey a law compelling confidential confessional communications, preferring incarceration over violation of their spiritual duty.[72]

When all these arguments and many others have been considered, there are really only five policy justifications for RCP. L'Heureux-Dubé J name[d] three [in her concurring minority judgement in *R v Gruenke* in the Supreme Court of Canada]:

a) society's interest in religious communications;
b) freedom of religion;

---

71 Henry E Smith., "The Modern Privilege: Its Nineteenth-Century Origins," in *The Privilege Against Self-Incrimination, Its Origins and Development*, Helmholz R.H., Gray C.M., Langbein J.H., Moglen E., Smith H.E., and Alschuler A.W., eds., (Chicago and London: The University of Chicago Press, 1997) 154 citing *Warickshall's Case* (1783) 1 Leach 263-264; 168 ER 234, 235. However, note that Smith thinks that the decision of the court in *R v Gilham* (1828) 1 Moody Cr Cas 186; 168 ER 1235 is difficult to understand in the context of *Warickshall's Case* since though the prisoner's confessions in *Gilham* were not made to a member of the clergy, they were 'compelled' by religious influence and the court did not explicitly say that the "cautions" given the prisoner outweighed that influence (ibid 155).
72 Nichols, S, *Law of Privilege* (Butterworths, Australia, 1992), 328.

c) privacy interests.[73]

Wright and Graham were more specific than both L'Heureux-Dubé J and McNicol when they broke "practical considerations"[74] down into two succinct ideas which they name:

a) the futility rationale,[75] and
b)the legitimacy rationale,[76]

and finally, there is

(a)   the eighteenth century idea that no one should be 'compelled' to give evidence at all.[77]

As has been written elsewhere

Professors Jeremy Waldron and Michael Perry have both suggested that human rights generally (including freedom of conscience and belief encompassing freedom of religion) cannot be satisfactorily justified in purely secular terms.[78] In essence, they concede that the religious ideas of the fatherhood of God and the brotherhood of man are the only moderately convincing reasons so far expressed which explain why anyone would protect the rights of another human being. Even John Rawls' supposedly secular 'original position' from which every thinking soul would choose equalitarian rights as the moral framework for life, has a theological dimension though none is claimed.[79] And of course, this chapter...is not the place to tease out that discussion. But the underlying question that all are trying to answer is – why it is that many human beings think that human rights and particularly the right to freedom of religion [including

---

73 R v Gruenke [1991] 3 SCR 263, 297.
74 CA Wright and KW Graham, Federal Practice and Procedure: Evidence, 3rd ed, (St Paul Minnesota: West Publishing Co, 1992), 303-304; Nichols, S, Law of Privilege, 328.
75 Wright and Graham, Federal Practice and Procedure, 84.
76 Ibid 86.
77 Smith, "The Modern Privilege", 153-156.
78 Jeremy Waldron, God, Locke and Equality; Christian Foundations in Locke's Political Thought, (Cambridge University Press, 2002), 235-243; Michael J. Perry, The Idea of Human Rights: Four Inquiries, (Oxford University Press, 1998).
79 Waldron does not suggest that Rawls' work has a theological dimension. But the idea that one might contemplate life and social interaction in a future life on earth from an 'original position' resonates which many theologies includ-ing those which posit that the currently human soul passes through many phases of existence all of which have an influence on the phase to follow.

RCP] as a part of universal freedom of conscience and belief, are justified or necessary in an ideal society? And the answer seems to be that if we do not accept that the fatherhood of God and the brotherhood of man are satisfactory reasons to explain this western liberal democratic obsession, then all that remains is the pragmatic reason that the accommodation of this freedom is essential if we are to avoid civil strife in the long term. Professor John Garvey suggests in the US context that freedom of religion can be justified simply because we think religion is a good[80] and that is why the US constitutional framers placed it in their bill of rights. But when one reviews his following logic, it is always buttressed by the idea that "freedom of religion prevents political strife".[81] Indeed he specifically renounces the alternate semi-theological idea that the reason religion is a good is because it protects human agency and autonomy and specifically the right to make choices[82] which Ahdar and Leigh have also noted has its problems.[83]

Once again however, we come full circle. Any meaningful policy justification [for RCP] depends upon society's interest in fostering freedom of religion. If the majority in Australian society believe that religion is good for society, they will endorse [RCP in statutory evidence law].[84]

---

80 See for example, John Garvey, *What are Freedoms for?* (Harvard University Press, 1996).
81 John Garvey, "Why should religious freedom have distinctive constitutional protection?", *The First Amendment, The Free Exercise of Religion Clause*, Berg, T.C., ed., (Amherst, New York: Prometheus Books, 2008), 121.
82 Ibid 122.
83 Rex Ahdar and Ian Leigh, *Religious Freedom in the Liberal State* (Oxford University Press, 2005) 57-64. In particular Ahdar and Leigh explain that personal autonomy alone does not explain why a Jewish rabbi in the US military has a better reason to wear his *yarmulke* than a cowboy hat (citing a John Garvey example) (ibid 61) and they are concerned that personal autonomy does not explain the sense of duty which lies behind many religious beliefs.
84 A. Keith Thompson, *Religious Confession Privilege at Common Law* (Leiden: Martinus Nijhoff, 2011) 352-353.

Conclusion

I began this chapter with an account of the history and current status of RCP in Australian evidence law. There were no reported cases where the confidentiality of religious confession was questioned before Victoria passed its first statute on the subject in 1864. That statute appears to have responded to the uncertainty in England following the decision in R v Hay in 1861. New Zealand's 1885 statute may have similarly responded to Sir George Jessel's obiter comments against the privilege in Wheeler v LeMarchant in 1881, but that cannot be proven. The writer has not been able to find any contemporary case in the 1860s or the 1880s that raised the question whether there should be a RCP statute in Australia and New Zealand. But New South Wales' 1989 statute certainly followed that pattern. It was a direct response to the prosecution's argument that Father Mark McGuigan should be imprisoned for contempt when he would not disclose what Pamela Young said to him in confession following a homicide in Lithgow on New Year's Eve in 1988. That statute responded to the dissenting view of President Xavier O'Connor of the ALRC in 1987 and his dissenting ideas were crystallised further when the Uniform Evidence Act was implemented in the Commonwealth, New South Wales and the ACT in 1995. That provision not only recognised a broad ecumenical RCP in Australian law; it prevented judicial question of the member of the clergy's decision as to whether a confession had even taken place and overrode provisions in other legislation that other evidential privileges did not apply. But I then detailed the jurisdictions in Australia where that respect for RCP has been diluted in response to the Royal Commission's 35th recommendation.

In the introduction I also suggested that the Royal Commission's recommendation that RCP should be abrogated in child sexual abuse cases was an under-theorised reaction to a moral panic. In this chapter I have explained why that recommendation was not justified by the limitation provision in Article 18(3) of the ICCPR upon which the Royal Commission directly relied. The evidential reasons why the recommendation was not justified were fourfold.

First, Jeremy Bentham's early nineteenth century view that religious confessions would dry up the moment they lost their confidentiality in relevant cases has not lost its cogency with the elapse of time. Second, Bentham's insight resonates with an inference that is readily drawn from Dr Marie Keenan's contemporary Irish research and Gerald Risdale's infamous testimony before the Royal Commission. Despite John Cornwell's flawed contrary suggestions using Michael Joseph McArdle's unsuccessful but self-serving efforts to have his sentence reduced in the Queensland Court of Appeal, very few of those who perpetrate child sexual abuse reveal their sins in religious confession and not in enough detail to activate mandatory reporting by those who hear them.

Third, the Royal Commission's own data affirmed that child sexual abuse in Australian institutions was in steep decline by 1990. Further, such abuse in institutions was pretty much extinguished after 2000 in states that followed Queensland's lead in introducing mandatory police checks for anyone employed or volunteering to work with the children – the so-called Blue Card scheme.

In that context, it is pretty hard to argue that it was necessary to abrogate RCP to eliminate the institutional child sexual abuse cases that remain. Given that data, there is also a strong argument that the Royal Commission should have focused more of its attention on how the victims of historic child sexual abuse might obtain the redress that had been foreclosed to them by state and territory legislation which prevented their law suits from the early 1990s. Though the Royal Commission did recommend that such legislation should indeed be repealed, there was no analysis of why the states and territories had passed it in the first place. The obvious answer is that the legislative foreclosure of civil suits for historic child sexual abuse in institutions would protect state and territory governments since they had referred many of the victims and should have protected them following referral. That lack of focus from the Royal Commission's is surprising since such inquiry was well within its terms of reference.

I concluded this discussion of the Royal Commission's misinterpretation of Article 18(3) of the *ICCPR*, by suggesting that the abrogation of RCP recommendation may also amount to a recommendation that the Australian states and territories breach the *ICCPR's* inviolable *forum internum*. That was because since the execution of Thomas More for conscience sake, it has been accepted that conscience should never be coerced. And that idea has been reiterated in the *Australian Constitution's* prohibition on any religious test as a condition for an office of public trust under the Commonwealth.

However, after all this analysis, I concluded that RCP will only be respected in Australia in the future if the religious freedom upon which it is founded is still celebrated as an enduring and important Australian virtue. There is thus a sense in which RCP is a litmus test for the status of religious freedom in Australian consciousness at the moment. Sadly, its importance has been diminished in the ACT and Victoria, but the jury is still out in the other states as of this writing.

Appendix I

The full text of Australia's reservation to the implementation of the ICCPR in Australian domestic law

Articles 2 and 50

Australia advises that, the people having united as one people in a Federal Commonwealth under the Crown, it has a federal constitutional system. It accepts that the provisions of the Covenant extend to all parts of Australia as a federal State without any limitations or exceptions. It enters a general reservation that Article 2, paragraphs 2 and 3 and Article 50 shall be given effect consistently with and subject to the provisions in Article 2, paragraph 2.

Under Article 2, paragraph 2, steps to adopt measures necessary to give effect to the rights recognised in the Covenant are to be taken in accordance with each State Party's constitutional processes which, in the case of Australia, are the processes of a federation in which legislative, executive and judicial powers to give effect to the rights recognised in the Covenant are distributed among the federal (Commonwealth) authorities and the authorities of the constituent States.

In particular, in relation to the Australian States the implementation of those provisions of the Covenant over whose subject matter the federal authorities exercise legislative, executive and judicial jurisdiction will be a matter for those authorities; and the implementation of those provisions of the Covenant over whose subject matter the authorities of the constituent States exercise legislative, executive and judicial jurisdiction will be a matter for those authorities; and where a provision has both federal and State aspects, its implementation will accordingly be a matter for the respective constitutionally appropriate authorities (for the purpose of implementation, the Northern Territory will be regarded as a constituent State).

To this end, the Australian Government has been in consultation with the responsible State and Territory Ministers with the object of developing co-operative arrangements to co-ordinate and facilitate the implementation of the Covenant.

2

Robert Natanek and Patrick Parkinson

Thou shalt not seal: Will requiring priests to report abuse disclosed in the confessional make children safer?

Abstract

The Royal Commission into Institutional Responses to Child Sexual Abuse (2013–7) was a crucial development in the history of child protection reform in Australia. Despite a generally positive reception, one recommendation of the Commission has been the topic of considerable controversy. This is the recommendation that Australian states and territories legislate to override the confidentiality of religious confessions, despite the confessional privilege contained in several federal and state Evidence Acts.

In this article, we assess the efficacy of recent changes to mandatory reporting that have emerged in the wake of the Commission's report. To the extent that these changes require priests to report abuse disclosed in the confessional, we argue that the Commission was led by the principle that all possible measures need to be taken to identify and prosecute child sex abusers. The Commission did not adequately consider whether requiring priests to break the confessional seal would actually improve the child protection system.

We conclude, with reference to the available evidence, that the enacted changes will serve no practical benefit in terms of child protection and may leave children less protected than before. There are also more intangible costs that may result from the legislative changes, including undermining respect for the law and increasing alienation between people of faith and the secular majority.

Keywords:

Child sexual abuse – Seal of the Confessional – Religious Confession Privilege – Mandatory Reporting Legislation – Child Protection

Introduction

For decades, the Catholic Church has been the object of severe public criticism as a consequence of the involvement of many in the perpetration and concealment of child sexual abuse. The Catholic Church's track record in this area is a story of moral failure.[1] With the assistance of witness testimonies from survivors and the findings of various investigative reports, these lamentable failures have come to light and the impetus for legal intervention has arisen. One notable investigation—conducted on an Australia-wide scale—was the *Royal Commission into Institutional Responses to Child Sexual Abuse* (2013-17) (hereafter 'Royal Commission' or 'Commission').

The Royal Commission 'laid bare the sobering reality of institutional child sexual abuse and its profoundly negative impact on individuals,

---

1   Patrick Parkinson, 'Child Sexual Abuse and the Churches: A Story of Moral Failure?' (2014) 26(1) *Current Issues in Criminal Justice* 119.

families and communities'.[2] It particularly drew attention to the magnitude of this problem within Catholic institutions. Among other proposed reforms, the Royal Commission recommended that state and territory parliaments legislate to require priests to report abuse disclosed in the context of a religious confession, notwithstanding the confessional privilege contained in several federal and state evidence laws.[3] Recommendation 7.4 of the Final Report said that mandatory child protection reporting laws 'should not exempt persons in religious ministry from being required to report knowledge or suspicions formed, in whole or in part, on the basis of information disclosed in or in connection with a religious confession.'

Confession – the sacrament of penance – plays an important role in Catholic life. Canon 959 of the Code of Canon Law,[4] explains its importance:

> In the sacrament of penance the faithful who confess their sins to a legitimate minister, are sorry for them, and intend to reform themselves obtain from God through the absolution imparted by the same minister forgiveness for the sins they have committed after baptism and, at the same time, are reconciled with the Church which they have wounded by sinning.

Central to the sacrament is its absolute confidentiality. Canon 983 says that '[t]he sacramental seal is inviolable; therefore it is absolutely forbidden for a confessor to betray in any way a penitent in words or in any manner and for any reason'.

Not surprisingly, the Royal Commission's recommendation has paved the way for a heated debate between religious advocates on one side, and child protection advocates on the other. From the latter angle, critics argue that the confessional seal promotes the interests of the

---

2   Kathleen McPhillips, 'Religion after the Royal Commission: Challenges to Religion-State Relations' (2020) 11(1) *Religions* 1, 1.

3   Kirsty Magarey, 'Priests, Penitents, Confidentiality and Child Sexual Abuse', *FlagPost* (Blog Post, 24 November 2012).

4   *The Code of Canon Law: In English Translation* (Collins, 1983).

Catholic Church at the expense of justice for victims of child sexual abuse.[5] However, leaders of the Church reject this argument,[6] with advocates contending that any attempt to undermine the secrecy of the confessional is fundamentally contrary to principles of religious liberty that are considered well settled.[7]

When the Royal Commission was established in 2013, it was hoped that a new dawn would await survivors of child sexual abuse. Although the Commission has made strides to aid child protection in a range of institutional environments, its recommendation to override the confidentiality of religious confessions has given rise to religious, legal, and political controversy. There continues to be a push by governments in other countries also to override the confidentiality of religious confessions, on the assumption that this confidentiality perpetuates child endangerment.[8] This assumption aside, a newly emerging body of literature suggests that the move to abolish religious confession privilege is to effectively punish the Catholic Church, 'with no golden pot of evidence at the end of the rainbow'.[9]

The central issue this article explores is whether the Royal Commission's advice to remove the confessional seal, and the ensuing response by state and territory Parliaments in Australia, can be justified in the interests of child protection. In taking a more conservative stance on this issue, we wish to clarify that our intention is not to downplay the seriousness of

---

5 See, eg, Mary Mitchell, 'Must Clergy Tell? Child Abuse Reporting Requirements Versus the Clergy Privilege and Free Exercise of Religion' (1987) 71(3)
   Minnesota Law Review 723, 728; Joe Harman, 'The Power of Confession: Mandatory Reporting, Confession and the Evidence Act' (2013) 38(4) *Alternative
   Law Journal* 239.

6 Australian Catholic Bishops Conference and Catholic Religious Australia,
   'Response to the Royal Commission into Institutional Responses to Child
   Sexual Abuse' (August 2018) 40.

7 See, eg, Michael Quinlan, 'Strengthening Child Sexual Abuse Laws in NSW'
   (Discussion Paper, Department of Justice, 2017) 2.

8 Keith Thompson, 'The Persistence of Religious Confession Privilege', in Rex
   Ahdar (ed), *Research Handbook on Law and Religion* (Edward Elgar Publishing,
   2018) 442, 442.

9 Keith Thompson, 'Should Religious Confession Privilege Be Abolished in
   Child Abuse Cases? Do Child Abusers Confess Their Sins?' (2017) 8 *The Western Australian Jurist* 95, 109.

the Commission's findings or to suggest that the best response is to take no action at all. However, there is a need to examine policy responses dispassionately and by reference to the available evidence. We argue, in the light of this evidence, that abolishing the seal of confession will serve no practical benefit for child abuse victims. The Commission failed to adequately make out the empirical case for overriding the seal of the confessional.

In essence, the Royal Commission founded its recommendation to remove the exemption for religious confession on a principle - that the police and child protection authorities need to know if a child is being sexually abused, and that this child protection imperative should not be compromised or qualified by reference to any other value.[10] The Commission also relied on evidence and accounts given to it that both victims and perpetrators utilised the confessional to disclose child sexual abuse.[11]

The context of this recommendation is of course, a concern about the way in which institutions of all kinds – and not just Catholic or even religious ones – covered up cases of child sexual abuse, typically because of the impact of scandal on the reputation of the organisation. A regular theme of the Royal Commission case studies was a failure of organisations to report known, and even admitted, sexual abuse of children.[12] A theme therefore of a number of recommendations was the need to strengthen mandatory reporting laws.

The question was whether the confessional seal should still be protected as an exception to expanded reporting laws. In making its

---

10 See generally *Royal Commission into Institutional Responses to Child Sexual Abuse* (Criminal Justice Report, 2017) pts III–VI, 216–24 [16.7.2] ('*Criminal Justice Report*')

11 Ibid. See also *Royal Commission into Institutional Responses to Child Sexual Abuse* (Final Report, 2017) vol 16, bk 2, 849 ('*Final Report*').

12 See, eg, *Royal Commission into Institutional Responses to Child Sexual Abuse* (Report of Case Study No 29, October 2016). Since 1950 the JW's had recorded allegations, reports or complaints of child sexual abuse against 1,006 members of the organisation. The great majority were cases of intrafamilial abuse which had been investigated through the JW's disciplinary processes. There were admissions made by 579 members.

recommendation not to exclude confessions, the Royal Commission gave due consideration to the '[doctrinal] significance of religious confession', as well as the legal argument that 'any intrusion by the civil law on the practice of religious confession would undermine the principle of freedom of religion' in art 18 of the *International Covenant on Civil and Political Rights*.[13] Both arguments were rejected by the Commission on the ground that freedom of religion under art 18 is not absolute, but rather may be subject to such limitations as are 'necessary to protect public safety and, in this case, the rights and freedoms of children'.[14]

In this article, we will examine the recent legislative changes in relation to reporting of child sexual abuse in the Australian states and territories and explore their efficacy in terms of child protection.

I Royal Commission into Institutional Responses to Child Sexual Abuse

According to the Final Report of the Commission, there were more complaints and allegations of child sexual abuse in religious organisations than in any other type of institution.[15] This is not in itself surprising, since it was religious organisations that ran so many of the orphanages, children's homes and boarding schools in which a large number of children were abused. Secular organisations which ran similar services (for example, state-run children's homes) had similarly poor records of child sexual abuse.[16]

However, the Commission expressed particular concern regarding the inadequacy of responses by entities of the Catholic Church, which were characterised by a 'general secretive approach' and

---

13 *Criminal Justice Report* (n 10).
14 Thompson, 'The Persistence of Religious Confession Privilege' (n 8) 459.
15 *Final Report* (n 11) vol 16, bk 2, 76.
16 See, eg, *Royal Commission into Institutional Responses to Child Sexual Abuse* (Report of Case Study No 7, October 2014).

distanced relationship with the secular world of law enforcement.[17] Although abuse is by no means confined to the Catholic Church, the findings of the Commission reflect a commitment to prioritising accountability and transparency within the Catholic Church, in response to evidence that it has suffered a disproportionate problem in relation to child sexual abuse.[18]

Key Findings

The Royal Commission estimated that there are around 60,000 survivors of institutional child sexual abuse in Australia.[19] As at 31 May 2017, the Commission had heard from 6,875 survivors in private sessions, of whom 4,029 (58.6%) referred to abuse in a religious institution.[20] Among the 4,029 survivors who reported abuse at the hands of a religious organisation, 2,489 (61.8%) survivors specified abuse by a Catholic institution.[21] These 2,489 survivors account for almost two-thirds of all people who came forward in private sessions, reinforcing the alarming rate at which Catholic organisations were implicated in the sexual abuse of children. Anglican institutions recorded the second highest rate of child sexual abuse (14.7% of private session survivors who reported abuse in religious organisations),[22] followed by Salvation Army institutions (at 7.3%)[23] and the Jehovah's Witnesses (at 1.7%).[24] Although these figures may in part be explained by the large Catholic representation in this

---

17 Marie Keenan, *Child Sexual Abuse and the Catholic Church: Gender, Power, and Organizational Culture* (Oxford University Press, 2012) 37–9, cited in Anthony Gray, 'Is the Seal of the Confessional Protected by Constitutional or Common Law?' (2018) 44(1) *Monash University Law Review* 112, 114.

18 Patrick Parkinson, 'Mandatory Reporting of Child Sexual Abuse by Religious Leaders', in Ben Matthews and Donald C Bross (eds), *Mandatory Reporting Laws and the Identification of Severe Child Abuse and Neglect* (Springer, 2015) 295. See generally *Final Report* (n 11) vol 16, bk 2, 76–6 [13.3.1].

19 *Royal Commission into Institutional Responses to Child Sexual Abuse* (Redress and Civil Litigation Report, 2015) 8.

20 *Final Report* (n 11) vol 16, bk 2, 75.

21 Ibid.

22 *Final Report* (n 11) vol 16, bk 1, 16.

23 Ibid bk 3, 10.

24 Ibid 71.

country during the periods when the recorded abuse occurred,[25] they are broadly consistent with overseas and domestic research confirming a proportionately higher rate of abuse in the Catholic Church compared with other faith communities.[26]

Most of the abuse uncovered by the Royal Commission occurred prior to 1990, but the Commission warned that it would be a mistake to regard child sexual abuse as purely historical. Indeed, the Commission heard directly from some 200 survivors about child sexual abuse that was said to have occurred since 1990.[27] Disclosures of sexual abuse are notoriously prone to delay,[28] with the effect that figures reported by the Commission may fail to accurately reflect the extent of child sexual abuse in a contemporary sense.[29]

Contributing Factors

The Royal Commission specifically identified a range of factors that have contributed to elevated rates of child sexual abuse in Catholic institutions and undermined institutional responses to such abuse. While the problem was partially underscored by psychosexual factors related to individual perpetrators, a range of institutional factors were also implicated, including governance, theological and cultural factors.

---

25 See also Patrick Parkinson, 'Child Sexual Abuse in the Catholic Church: the Australian Experience' (Berkley Center for Religion, Peace & World Affairs, Georgetown University, 25 September 2019).

26 See, eg, Desmond Cahill, Submission to Family and Community Development Committee, Parliament of Victoria, *Inquiry into the Handling of Child Abuse by Religious and Other Organisations* (August 2012); John Jay College of Criminal Justice, *The Nature and Scope of Sexual Abuse of Minors by Catholic Priests and Deacons in the United States, 1950–2002* (Report, February 2004).

27 *Final Report* (n 11) vol 16, bk 1, 12.

28 Patrick Parkinson, Kim Oates and Amanda Jayakody, 'Breaking the Long Silence: Reports of Child Sexual Abuse in the Anglican Church of Australia' (2010) 6(2) *Ecclesiology* 183.

29 Ibid. See also *Final Report* (n 11) vol 16, bk 1, 12.

Governance Structures

With no separation of powers, the executive, legislative and judicial aspects of Church governance are vested exclusively in the person of the pope and in individual diocesan bishops. One consequence of this decentralised structure is that diocesan bishops have handled allegations of child sexual abuse and alleged perpetrators on their own terms, without any requirement that their decision making be subject to external review.

It appears that the extent of child sexual abuse has been further compounded by processes governing the appointment of Catholic Church leaders. Evidence from the Royal Commission suggests that candidates for leadership have invariably been chosen on the basis of their allegiance to specific aspects of church doctrine, even if they are otherwise ill-equipped to exercise leadership responsibility.[30]

Canon Law

There has long been a culture within Catholicism that the law of the Church – otherwise known as canon law – is effectively a 'law unto itself';[31] that is, a stand alone system of rules and codes of conduct that operate independently of the civil law. Technically, canon law establishes that clergy or religious who abuse children under the age of 18 will be 'punished with just penalties, not excluding dismissal from the clerical state'.[32] However, the emphasis in canon law on a 'pastoral approach' has meant that, in practice, dismissal from religious ministry is treated as a disciplinary measure of 'last resort'.[33] There is no concept in canonical thinking that child sexual abuse is a crime that needs to be reported to civil authorities and dealt with by the criminal courts. Instead, canon law treats child sexual abuse as a 'delict' against morals, that is, a moral

---

30 *Final Report* (n 11) vol 16, bk 1, 45.
31 Parkinson, 'Child Sexual Abuse and the Churches: A Story of Moral Failure?' (n 1) 129.
32 *Code of Canon Law* (n 4) canon 1395 § 2.
33 *Final Report* (n 11) vol 16, bk 2, 730.

offence, and a breach of the canonical obligation to observe celibacy.[34] According to the Royal Commission, this has led to a practice within the Catholic Church of administering canonical sanctions that are light on clerical offenders and rarely result in withdrawal from ministry, with the result that vulnerable children continue to be at risk.

Culture of Clericalism

Dr Thomas Doyle, a leading Catholic expert on child sexual abuse in the American church, characterised clericalism as 'a virus that has infected the Church'.[35] In a nutshell, clericalism is the idealisation of the priesthood, and by extension, the idealisation of the Catholic Church. Many Catholic institutions reflected a theological understanding that priests and other religious ministers undergo an 'ontological change' and attain a status of 'superiority' upon ordination.[36] The Commission found that clericalism was used by some bishops and religious superiors to justify cases of child sexual abuse, or worse, to deny that clergy and religious workers were capable of such acts. While sexual abuse of children was taking place, bishops and religious leaders exploited the clericalist mindset that 'Father knows best' to manipulate unsuspecting parents and dull the severity of abuse in the minds of victims.[37]

In view of the Commission's revelations, it is hardly surprising that there has been a strong commitment from governments to promote change within the Church in dealing with child sexual abuse matters.

II Mandatory Reporting in Australia After the Royal Commission

In total, the Royal Commission produced over 400 recommendations for child protection reform across culpable institutions. These

---

34 Ibid, 697.
35 Submission to the Royal Commission, Final Report ibid 613.
36 Ibid 619–21.
37 See Thomas Doyle, 'Roman Catholic Clericalism, Religious Duress, and Clergy Sexual Abuse' (2003) 51(3) *Pastoral Psychology* 189.

recommendations were wide-ranging, including improvements to reporting practices, amendments to the culture and governance structures of institutions, and an emphasis on informed decision making at the legislative level.

In Australian child protection law, there are three main statutory regimes under which an obligation to report child sexual abuse can arise.[38] These regimes, for which state and territory governments have individual legislative responsibility, include the following:

1   Mandatory reporting legislation ('child protection reporting')
2   Reportable conduct legislation ('employee conduct reporting')
3   Failure to report offences ('criminal offence reporting')

At first glance, it may appear that these different reporting requirements duplicate one another or at least overlap substantially. The position is, however, rather more complicated. Each scheme applies to different people, and the obligation to report arises in different circumstances. Furthermore, the relevant knowledge or suspicion that a person would need to have differs from one law to another. The Royal Commission presumably felt it was appropriate for the three regimes to operate in concurrent fashion.

Child protection reporting

By 2009, each state and territory across Australia had introduced mandatory reporting legislation in some form within its respective child protection statute.[39] Such legislation typically involves an obligation imposed on certain professionals to report to the child protection department concerns about the safety of a child arising from a range of

---

38   For a full taxonomy of the range of reporting obligations and duties to act to protect children, see Ben Mathews, 'A Taxonomy of Duties to Report Child Sexual Abuse: Legal Developments Offer New Ways to Facilitate Disclosure', (2019) 88 *Child Abuse & Neglect* 337.

39   For a comprehensive legislative history of mandatory reporting, see Ben Mathews, *Mandatory Reporting Laws for Child Sexual Abuse in Australia: A Legislative History* (Report, 2014), prepared for the Royal Commission into Institutional Responses to Child Sexual Abuse.

different possible sources of harm. The report is about *the child*, and so it is necessary to know, or for the department to be able from the information available to work out the name of the child.[40] In addition, the obligation to report only arises if the relevant concern is formed 'in the course of the reporter's employment'.[41] This raises some difficult questions around the extension of reporting requirements to religious ministers, given that the distinction between the professional and personal aspects of ministry is not always clearly defined. Priests, ministers and pastors, by whatever name they may be known, live out their ministries as members of a local community, and in particular, as leaders of a congregation within that community. The boundaries between professional and social interactions are difficult to identify in this context. To have dinner with a family in the congregation is, for instance, both a social and pastoral activity.

Notwithstanding this difficulty, the Commission recommended to state and territory governments that they amend mandatory reporting legislation to include ministers of religion as designated reporters.[42] The rationale behind this recommendation was that such persons, in the course of their ministerial roles, have frequent contact with children and are therefore in a position to both detect and prevent abuse from occurring.[43] This particular recommendation has not been contentious, even among religious organisations. The argument has been about the Commission's accompanying recommendation that no exception to the

---

40 See *Children and Young People Act 2008* (ACT) s 356(1)(c); *Children and Young Persons (Care and Protection) Act 1998* (NSW) s 27(2)(a); *Care and Protection of Children Act 2007* (NT) s 26(1)(a); *Child Protection Act 1999* (Qld) s 13E(2); *Children and Young People (Safety) Act 2017* (SA) s 31(1)(a); *Children, Young Persons and Their Families Act 1997* (Tas) s 14(2); *Children, Youth and Families Act 2005* (Vic) s 184(1); *Children and Community Services Act 2004* (WA) s 124B(1)(b).

41 See *Children and Young People Act 2008* (ACT) s 356(1)(d); *Children and Young Persons (Care and Protection) Act 1998* (NSW) s 27(2)(b); *Care and Protection of Children Act 2007* (NT) s 26(2)(a); *Child Protection Act 1999* (Qld) s 13E(3); *Children and Young People (Safety) Act 2017* (SA) s 31(1)(b); *Children, Young Persons and Their Families Act 1997* (Tas) s 14(2); *Children, Youth and Families Act 2005* (Vic) s 184(1); *Children and Community Services Act 2004* (WA) s 124B(1)(c)(i).

42 *Final Report* (n 11) vol 7, 100, recommendation 7.3(e).

43 Ibid 97–8.

reporting obligation be made for information disclosed during a religious confession.[44]

Table 1 indicates the states and territories which have implemented the Commission's recommendation to extend the class of mandated reporters to include ministers of religion.

Table 1 – Legislative Amendments to Mandatory Reporting Following the Royal Commission

Jurisdiction	Are Ministers of Religion Mandated Reporters?
NT	**Yes** (Section 26 of the *Care and Protection of Children Act 2007* (NT) imposes duty to report on 'any person')
NSW	**Yes** (Section 27(1)(c) of the *Children and Young Persons (Care and Protection) Act 1998* (NSW))
SA	**Yes** (Section 30(3)(e) of the *Children and Young People (Safety) Act 2017* (SA))
TAS	**Yes** (Section 14(1)(ja) of the *Children, Young Persons and Their Families Act 1997* (Tas))
WA	**Not yet** (Nb: *Children and Community Services Amendment Bill 2019* currently pending to (among other things) introduce mandatory reporting for ministers of religion)
VIC	**Yes** (Section 182(1)(ea) of the *Children, Youth and Families Act 2005* (Vic))
ACT	**Yes** (Section 356(1)(p) of the *Children and Young People Act 2008* (ACT))
QLD	**No**

Before the Royal Commission's final report was published, only South Australia expressly included ministers of religion as mandatory reporters,[45] although the relevant Northern Territory legislation extended the obligation to 'every person'.[46] Since the Commission released its Final Report, this situation has changed substantially. With the exception of Western Australia and Queensland, each jurisdiction in Australia now defines ministers of religion as a designated reporter group. It is likely that this situation will again change, with the Children and Community Services Amendment Bill 2019 (WA) having recently been read for

---

44 See generally *Criminal Justice Report* (n 10) pts III–VI, 202–7 [16.6.2].

45 *Children's Protection Act 1993* (SA) s 11(2)(ga).

46 *Care and Protection of Children Act 2007* (NT) s 26(1).

a second time in Western Australia's Legislative Council. If it passes, the Bill will amend the *Children and Community Services Act 2004* (WA) to introduce mandatory reporting of child sexual abuse for ministers of religion, among other changes. There will be no exemption in the WA law for information received as part of a religious confession, reflecting the approach already taken in other jurisdictions where ministers of religion are listed as mandatory reporters.[47]

It is important to note that in all the states and territories that have included ministers of religion as mandatory reporters under child protection legislation, the obligation to report applies to all forms of child abuse and neglect. This is because, typically, such legislation is framed in terms of defining the circumstances when a child is in need of protection and then mandating various professionals to report if they have a reasonable belief or suspicion that a child has such a need.[48] It follows that the duty to report extends to the full range of grounds on which a child may be deemed to require protective intervention. However, the Royal Commission's research and its conclusions on the value of reporting relate only to child *sexual* abuse.[49] This is because the Commission was constrained by its terms of reference. It acknowledged that different considerations would inevitably apply to reporting non-sexual forms of child abuse.[50]

The Royal Commission thought that some states would be reluctant

---

47 See, eg, *Children, Youth and Families Act 2005* (Vic) s 184(2A); *Children and Young People Act 2008* (ACT) s 356(2); *Children, Young Persons and Their Families Act 1997* (Tas) s 14(7). The NSW stance on the religious confession exemption is unclear, with the *Children and Young Persons (Care and Protection) Act 1998* (NSW) being silent on the point.

48 See, eg, *Children and Young Persons (Care and Protection) Act 1998* (NSW) ss 23, 27; *Children and Young People (Safety) Act 2017* (SA) s 31; *Children, Young Persons and Their Families Act 1997* (Tas) ss 3, 14.

49 Julie Dodds-Streeton and Jack O'Connor, *Implementation of Royal Commission into Institutional Responses to Child Sexual Abuse Recommendations regarding the Reporting of Child Sexual Abuse, with Implications for the Confessional Seal* (Analysis Report, 14 January 2019) 23.

50 *Criminal Justice Report* (n 10) pts III–VI, 211.

to expand mandatory reporting due to a fear of over-reporting.[51] It seems that the legislatures, in enacting such broad-ranging changes, were unconcerned about the detriments known to be associated with mandatory reporting laws generally, that the Commission itself recognised.[52] The well known risks of mandatory reporting are first, that a duty to report can impede disclosures of abuse by a child who knows the adult has an obligation to report; secondly, that in some situations trusted adults who promise to maintain confidentiality can more effectively assist the child to disclose when they are ready and to take protective measures in the meantime; and thirdly, that where a large number of professionals are required to report, child protection services may be overwhelmed by reports made 'just in case' where the reported risks are not sufficiently serious to warrant significant resources being expended in investigation and intervention.[53]

Employee conduct reporting

A second potential source of a reporting obligation arises from laws concerning 'reportable conduct'.[54] New South Wales ('NSW') has had such a law for some years. Owing to a recent amendment, the reportable conduct scheme in NSW currently requires the head of a designated entity to notify the Office of the Children's Guardian where there is 'reportable conduct' involving an allegation, substantiated misconduct or conviction of an employee of a kind that the law requires to be reported.[55] Typically, this arises where an allegation is made that an employee, working with children, has abused a child. The purpose is to ensure as far as possible that the allegation is properly investigated by the employing institution.

While the Commission recommended that state and territory

---

51 *Final Report* (n 11) vol 7, 94.
52 Ibid.
53 See generally Mathews and Bross (n 18)
54 See generally *Criminal Justice Report* (n 10) pts III–VI, 151 [16.2.2].
55 *Children's Guardian Act 2019* (NSW).

governments establish reporting requirements like in the NSW scheme, it did not address the issue of the seal of the confessional in this context. However, in the Australian Capital Territory ('ACT'), an amendment to the *Ombudsman Act 1989* (ACT) includes an obligation to report express assertions of reportable conduct made in a religious confession.[56] The amendment, which came into effect on 1 April 2019, renders an assertion reportable only if it relates to sexual abuse against a child or non-accidental physical injury to a child.[57] In practical terms, this means that if a priest is also a head of a designated entity and becomes aware of reportable conduct through receiving a religious confession, or a priest breaches the seal of the confessional and reports the matter to the head of the designated entity, then the confession becomes reportable under the Act. New South Wales has not adopted a similar reform.

Criminal offence reporting

In addition to the proposed amendments to mandatory reporting legislation and the reportable conduct scheme, the Royal Commission produced a Criminal Justice Report which recommended the introduction of a separate criminal offence for failure to report child sexual abuse.[58] The failure to report offence was designed to reach beyond existing prohibitive offences related to child sexual abuse by imposing a positive duty on third parties to report abuse to the police.[59] Although the Commission proposed a seemingly narrow offence aimed at individuals of a 'relevant institution', this is likely a reflection of the Commission's limited terms of reference, which related only to institutional child sexual abuse. A broader reporting culture was to be encouraged by lowering the threshold on the requisite state of mind not only to include knowledge or suspicions of child sexual abuse, but also

---

56   *Ombudsman Act 1989* (ACT) s 17EAB(3).
57   Ibid s 17EAB(2)(a)-(b).
58   *Criminal Justice Report* (n 10) pts III–VI, 213, recommendation 33.
59   *Royal Commission into Institutional Responses to Child Sexual Abuse* (Factsheet: Failure to Report Offence, 2017) 1.

suspicions that a reasonable person *ought* to have formed.[60]

Importantly, and consistent with its position on child protection reporting, the Commission specified that the obligation should extend to information given during, or in connection with, religious confession.[61]

At the time of writing, the 'failure to report' offence has been implemented into the criminal statutes of NSW, Victoria, the ACT, Tasmania and, most recently, Queensland.[62] These are listed in Table 2. The relevant offences broadly mirror the Royal Commission's recommended drafting, with several key departures. These mainly relate to the width of the reporter class, the kind of child abuse that will activate the reporting obligation, and the specific treatment of the confessional seal.

Table 2 – Criminal offence reporting by jurisdiction

Jurisdiction	Type of child abuse/maltreatment
NSW	Section 316A(1) *Crimes Act 1900* (NSW): An adult is criminally liable for concealing a '*child abuse offence*'.
TAS	Section 105A(2) *Criminal Code Act 1924* (Tas): A person is guilty of a crime if the person fails to report a reasonably held belief that an '*abuse offence*' has been committed against a child.
VIC	Section 327(2) *Crimes Act 1958* (Vic): A person is criminally liable for failure to disclose that a '*sexual offence has been committed against a child*'.
ACT	Section 66AA(1) *Crimes Act 1900* (ACT): A person commits an offence if the person fails to report that a '*sexual offence has been committed against a child*'.
QLD	Section 229BC *Criminal Code Act 1899* (Qld): An adult commits a criminal offence for failure to report belief of a '*child sexual offence committed in relation to a child*'.

As Table 2 shows, criminal offence reporting by clergy has been extended in NSW and Tasmania to a variety of forms of abuse or neglect. Section 316A of the *Crimes Act 1900* (NSW) establishes the criminal offence of concealing child abuse. The offence was created pursuant to the *Criminal Legislation Amendment (Child Sexual Abuse) Act 2018* (NSW) and commenced

---

60 *Criminal Justice Report* (n 10) pts III–VI, 213, recommendation 33(b).
61 Ibid 224, recommendation 35.
62 The Criminal Code (Child Sexual Offences Reform) and Other Legislation Amendment Bill 2019 (Qld) was passed on 8 September 2020.

operation on 31 August 2018. The offence attracts a maximum penalty of two years' imprisonment for an adult who knows, believes or reasonably ought to know that a child abuse offence has been committed against another person and who fails, without reasonable excuse, to notify a member of the NSW Police force as soon as it is practicable to do so.[63] The creation of a criminal offence based upon what someone ought to have known, but didn't, imports notions of negligence into the criminal law. The term 'child abuse offence'[64] is defined broadly and goes well beyond offences of a sexual nature. It extends, inter alia, to murder or manslaughter of a child, kidnapping, failure to provide the necessities of life and the offence of female genital mutilation. The definition in Tasmania is similarly broad.

There are variations between jurisdictions concerning the position in relation to a religious confession. In Victoria, s 327 of the *Crimes Act 1958* (Vic) provides that disclosures of child sexual abuse during religious confession are not exempt from the failure to disclose offence.[65] A similar approach has been taken in the ACT,[66] Queensland[67] and Tasmania,[68] with these jurisdictions also overriding statutory religious confession privilege.

By way of contrast, NSW law is silent on the issue. While the s 316A offence applies to all 'adults', it does not specifically deal with the situation where information of child sexual abuse is received during religious confession. The offence is committed unless the person who fails to report has a "reasonable excuse". Subsection (2) lists a number of grounds on which a person would have a reasonable excuse but subsection (3) provides this "does not limit the grounds on which it may be established that a person has a reasonable excuse for failing to bring information to the attention of a member of the NSW Police Force."

---

63 *Crimes Act 1900* (NSW) s 316A(1).
64 Ibid s 316A(1)(a).
65 *Crimes Act 1958* (Vic) s 327(7)(b).
66 *Crimes Act 1900* (ACT) s 66AA(3).
67 *Criminal Code Act 1899* (Qld) s 229BC.
68 *Criminal Code Act 1924* (Tas) s 105A(5).

This aspect of the NSW legislation was criticised by Greens' MLC, David Shoebridge, who condemned the state government and opposition for neglecting to incorporate a subsection that would have denied special protection to priests and other members of clergy for failing to disclose child sexual abuse.[69] The Greens' amendment would have filled this gap by specifically extending the duty to report to clergy members who receive child abuse information by way of confession.[70] Since the offence that was enacted includes no amendment to that effect, when an amendment was specifically proposed, it must be questioned whether Parliament intended to override confessional privilege. The principle of legality requires statutes to be interpreted on the assumption that Parliament did not intend to curtail fundamental rights and privileges without using clear language to that effect.[71] It may therefore be that there is no duty under s 316A to report a child abuse offence where the information came during confession. However, the matter is certainly not beyond doubt.

III The Interplay Between Legislative Reporting Requirements and Confessional Privilege Under the Uniform Evidence Law

The fact that a priest has a duty to report information obtained during a confession under any of the reporting laws discussed above does not mean that the priest is a compellable witness.[72] Various jurisdictions that have enacted the Uniform Evidence Law[73] have a statutory privilege in their *Evidence Acts* which ensures that priests are not compellable witnesses in relation to matters disclosed in confession. Section 127 of the *Evidence Act 1995* (NSW) is typical. It provides:

---

69 Paul Gregoire and Ugur Nedim, 'Sydney Criminal Lawyers', *NSW Passes Stronger Child Sexual Abuse Laws, But Priests Remain Protected* (Web Page, 21 June 2018).

70 Ibid.

71 *Momcilovic v The Queen* (2011) 245 CLR 1, 46–7 [43] (French CJ). See also *R v Secretary of State for the Home Department; Ex parte Simms* [2000] 2 AC 115, 131 (Lord Hoffmann).

72 Harman (n 5). See also Scrutiny of Acts and Regulations Committee, Parliament of Victoria, *Alert Digest* (Digest No 10 of 2019, 27 August 2019) 7.

73 The jurisdictions with statutory religious confession privilege are the Commonwealth, the ACT, NSW, the Northern Territory, Tasmania and Victoria.

A person who is or was a member of the clergy of any church or religious denomination is entitled to refuse to divulge that a religious confession was made, or the contents of a religious confession made, to the person when a member of the clergy.

The Royal Commission, in its Criminal Justice Report, did not recommend any abrogation of this evidential privilege. It wrote:[74]

We are not persuaded that it is necessary to provide an exemption from a failure to report offence because of the existence of an evidentiary privilege. We note that reporting obligations in respect of child sexual offences seek to prevent future harm to children, whereas evidentiary privileges prescribe how matters are to be dealt with in court proceedings.

While we believe that there should be no exemption for religious confessions from the operation of the failure to report offence, we make no recommendation beyond this in relation to the religious confessions privilege in Uniform Evidence Act jurisdictions more generally. To do so would go beyond our Terms of Reference. Some state or territory governments could, if minded, remove that privilege so that the fact and content of religious confessions is compellable as evidence in proceedings against, for example, perpetrators of child sexual abuse.

It seems that in the Uniform Evidence Law jurisdictions no changes have been made to the evidential privilege. There is, for example, no express legislative override of religious confession privilege under s 127 of the *Evidence Act 1995* (NSW) under any of the reporting laws in NSW. Section 105A(2) of the *Criminal Code Act 1924* (Tas) does refer to the privilege, but does not displace it:

Despite section 127 of the Evidence Act 2001, a member of the clergy of any church or religious denomination is not entitled to refuse to disclose information under subsection (2) on the grounds that the information was communicated to that member of the clergy during a religious confession.

---

74   *Criminal Justice Report* (n 10) pts III–VI, 223–4.

On its face, all this section means is that s 127 of the *Uniform Evidence Act*, which provides that the prosecution will not be able to compel the priest to give evidence, does not affect the priest's obligation to report abuse under s 105A of the *Criminal Code Act 1924* (Tas).

The position is different in Queensland, South Australia, and Western Australia because these jurisdictions do not recognise a statutory evidential privilege for religious confessions.

IV Implications of lifting the confessional seal

The mandatory reporting landscape in Australia has clearly changed considerably as a result of the legislative recommendations put forward by the Royal Commission. Most jurisdictions across Australia now have legislative mechanisms in place that require clergy to disclose information of child sexual abuse heard in the confessional, with penalties applicable for failure to do so.

The evidence base on which the Royal Commission relied for its recommendation was not strong. As previously stated, the Royal Commission heard evidence that the confessional was used as a forum for discussing child sexual abuse, both by children subject to abuse and by perpetrators of abuse.[75] According to its Criminal Justice Report, while the practice of religious confession is declining, disclosure is still a possibility. The claim that abusive Catholic priests use the confessional to disclose their crimes is also supported by John Cornwell in *The Dark*

---

75 See generally *Criminal Justice Report* (n 10) pts III–VI, 202–4 [16.6.2]. For victim disclosures of child sexual abuse, see Transcript of Proceedings, *Royal Commission into Institutional Responses to Child Sexual Abuse* (Case Study No 11, 29 April 2014) WA1604:25–5:1; Transcript of Proceedings, *Royal Commission into Institutional Responses to Child Sexual Abuse* (Case Study No 26, 14 April 2015) TC7316:39–7:26; Transcript of Proceedings, *Royal Commission into Institutional Responses to Child Sexual Abuse* (Case Study No 28, 20 May 2015, TC8265:13-27. For perpetrator disclosures of child sexual abuse, see Transcript of Proceedings, *Royal Commission into Institutional Responses to Child Sexual Abuse* (Case Study No 35, 24 November 2015) T13230:1–16.

Box.[76] Cornwell referred to some 1500 confessions of child sexual abuse allegedly made by defrocked priest Michael Joseph McArdle to a variety of confessors.[77]

On Keith Thompson's analysis, the veracity of these claims is doubtful. First, it was McArdle himself who testified to having confessed on so many occasions. Thompson suggests that this was in an effort to deflect blame for his crimes onto the Catholic Church and to seek mitigation of his sentence in the Brisbane District Court. Secondly, it is hard to imagine that 'thirty different priests over a twenty-five year period in a church that insists on frank disclosure of sin and restitution before absolution, would condone such grievous offending'.[78] Cornwell's further suggestion that religious confession privilege contributed to McArdle's recidivism has also been weakened by the infamous testimony of Gerald Ridsdale before the Royal Commission. He said that 'he never told anyone about his sexual abuse of boys, even during confession, because the "overriding fear would have been losing the priesthood"'.[79] This is also consistent with Dr Marie Keenan's observation that admitted abusers rarely disclose the 'whole story', making sure that anything they say is calculated to avoid further questions.[80]

---

76 John Cornwell, *The Dark Box: A Secret History of Confession* (New York, Basic Books, 2014).

77 For background context, see *R v McArdle* (2004) 144 A Crim R 151. The Court of Appeal expressed scepticism about McArdle's claim of self-rehabilitation and apparent ignorance of the severity of his offending.

78 Thompson, 'The Persistence of Religious Confession Privilege' (n 8) 446. See also *Criminal Justice Report* (n 10) pts III–VI, 204. McArdle's claim is difficult to reconcile with the assertions of multiple confessors that penitents simply do not confess to pedophilia: see, eg, Geoffrey Robinson, 'On Breaking the Seal of Confession', *Eureka Street* (Web Page, 23 November 2012); Transcript of Proceedings, *Royal Commission into Institutional Responses to Child Sexual Abuse* (Case Study No 50, 9 February 2017) T25109:26–30, T25110:47–1:1.

79 See Andrew Koubaridis and AAP, 'Vile Paedophile Gerald Ridsdale will Give Evidence At Royal Commission Today', *news.com.au* (Web Page, 27 May 2015).

80 Keenan (n 17) 162–4.

Previous consideration of the issue

The question of whether the privilege given to the seal of the confessional is an impediment to the work of child protection has, of course, been considered before. In Victoria, the *Betrayal of Trust* report specifically addressed the question whether there should be an exemption from the criminal offence for information provided during confession, stating that: '[t]he protection of children and the vindication of their rights is an overwhelming consideration. However, the central question is whether the removal of the exemption/privilege is likely to be of assistance in exposing offenders and bringing them to justice'.[81]

The Committee decided that the privilege against breaking the confessional seal should remain. The *Betrayal of Trust* report reflected sentiments that were echoed by the Australian Law Reform Commission ('ALRC') in its final report on *Evidence* in 1987. Although the ALRC recommended against a separate privilege for religious confession, the then President of the ALRC made an important dissenting remark. He observed that no jurisdiction providing a privilege for religious confessions 'has been heard to complain that the existence of the privilege has hampered law enforcement in any significant way.'[82] These remarks are significant because they tap into some of the contemporary practical concerns regarding abolition of the confessional seal. It is not clear that such a course will aid the detection of child sex abusers, in circumstances where the focus of reporting legislation is on *'encouraging reporting, rather than policing it'*.[83]

---

81 *Criminal Justice Report* (n 10) pts III–VI, 163, citing Family and Community Development Committee, Parliament of Victoria, *Betrayal of Trust: Inquiry into the Handling of Child Abuse by Religious and Other Non-Government Organisations* (Final Report, November 2013) vol 2, 500.

82 Australian Law Reform Commission, *Evidence* (Report No 38, 1987) [206], [213].

83 Mathews (n 39) 40 (emphasis added). Associate Professor Mathews identifies just six prosecutions in five Australian jurisdictions for failure to report under mandatory reporting duties.

Sacramental significance of confession

In his submission on the recently debated Child Sexual Offences Reform Bill in Queensland, the Catholic Archbishop of Brisbane, Mark Coleridge, explained the distinctly confidential nature of the confessional. He drew a distinction between confidential communications that form part of the 'internal forum' of the Church, and confidential exchanges associated with the sacrament of penance.[84] Confidential communications that take place in the internal forum—including, for instance, exchanges for the purpose of providing spiritual direction—are strict but not absolute. In contrast, the sacrament of religious confession attracts 'absolute and inviolable confidentiality'.[85] This position has the force of canon law, which explicitly provides that 'it is a crime for a confessor in any way to betray a penitent by word or in any other manner or for any reason'.[86] So significant is the imperative of confidentiality that 'a confessor who directly violates the Seal of Confession incurs an automatic excommunication from the [Catholic] Church'.[87]

In the recent debates concerning amendments to the *Criminal Code Act 1899* (Qld), Archbishop Coleridge explained the Church's teaching as follows:

> [t]he Church is not concerned so much about strict professional confidentiality or the internal forum as they might apply to confessors, but about the absolute confidentiality of the seal with its narrower application.[88]

He went on to explain the religious meaning of confession:

> The seal derives its meaning from a particular understanding of the

---

84 Mark Coleridge, Submission No 10 to Legal Affairs and Community Safety Committee, Parliament of Queensland, *Criminal Code (Child Sexual Offences Reform) and Other Legislation Amendment Bill 2019* (3 January 2020) 2.

85 Ibid. See also Seymour Moskowitz and Michael J DeBoer, 'When Silence Resounds: Clergy and the Requirement to Report Elder Abuse and Neglect' (1999) 49(1) *DePaul Law Review* 1, 8.

86 *Code of Canon Law* (n 4) canon 983 § 1.

87 Ibid canon 1388 § 1.

88 Coleridge (n 84) 3.

sacrament. It is God, not the priest, to whom the penitent comes to confess sin and receive absolution [...] The seal recognises the right of the sinful human being to approach God in complete freedom; and the seal is the guarantee of that freedom.[89]

It is sometimes claimed that the seal must be abolished in law because it is 'the linchpin of a culture of secrecy and cover-up in the Catholic Church'.[90] In response, the Archbishop clarified that the seal is the guarantee of a culture of full and frank disclosure that is quite the opposite of cover-up. To the extent that the Commission found perpetrators do utilise the confessional to disclose child sexual abuse, the abolition of the seal will almost certainly put an end to that possibility and remove any hope there might otherwise have been for the penitent to see the truth of their crime, stop the abuse and seek reconciliation with victims.[91]

While a priest has a canon law duty to 'keep absolute secrecy regarding the sins that his penitents have confessed',[92] the position with respect to disclosures made by a child victim was, until recently, less clear. Canon lawyers expressed varying views.[93] In response to a recommendation from the Royal Commission that it clarify this point,[94] the Holy See has now indicated that the obligation of strict confidentiality applies to 'the sins of both the penitent and others known from the penitent's

---

89 Ibid. See also Michael Quinlan, Submission to the Royal Commission into Institutional Responses to Child Sexual Abuse (Issues Paper No 11: Catholic Church Final Hearing, 2016) 29.

90 Coleridge (n 84) 4.

91 Ibid. See also Quinlan (n 7) 20; Frank Brennan, 'Breaking the Seal of the Confessional a Red Herring that will Not Save One Child', *Weekend Australian* (Web Page, 3 December 2016) 2–3 where it was suggested that with the seal intact, the occasional pedophile might find a 'listening ear to assist with the decision to turn himself in'.

92 *Catechism of the Catholic Church* (Libreria Editrice Vaticana, 2nd ed, 1997) [1467].

93 For a discussion on the broad view of the confessional seal, see, eg, Anthony Fisher, 'Safeguarding the Seal of Confession' (2018) 95(2) *Australasian Catholic Record* 131, 142, 146–7; Truth Justice and Healing Council, Submission in connection with Case Study 50: Final hearing into Catholic Church authorities in Australia – The Catholic Church: Then and Now (22 December 2016) 71. Cf narrow view of the confessional seal in Transcript of Proceedings, *Royal Commission into Institutional Responses to Child Sexual Abuse* (Case Study No 50, 9 February 2017) 25107:42–8:9, 25123:37–43.

94 *Final Report* (n 11) vol 16, bk 2, 872, recommendation 16.26(a).

confession.'[95] Nonetheless, the priest 'may, and indeed in certain cases should, encourage a victim to seek help outside the confessional or, when appropriate, to report an instance of abuse to the authorities'.[96]

The possibility has also been raised that perpetrators could be encouraged to make themselves known to civil authorities as a condition of their absolution.[97] The Catechism of the Catholic Church states that there are three preconditions to penance, these being contrition ('sorrow of the soul and detestation for the sin committed'), disclosure of sin (the 'confession' itself), and satisfaction ('positive action to make amends for sinfulness').[98] It was suggested by Bishop Geoffrey Robinson[99] and the Catholic Church in Victoria[100] that priests could—and indeed would—choose to 'withhold absolution and require any person making confessions of child abuse to relay that information to authorities, to receive absolution and forgiveness'.[101] Indeed, in its own recommendations to the Catholic Church, the Royal Commission encouraged the Australian Catholic Bishops Conference to consult with the Holy See about the possibility of amending canon law to so oblige priests.[102] Using this approach, canon and civil law requirements could be harmonised without significant interference in sacred ritual.[103] However, the Holy See has not been receptive to this recommendation. In its response to the Royal Commission, it said: '[s]ince repentance is, in fact, at the heart of this sacrament, absolution can be withheld only if

---

95 Holy See, 'Response of the Holy See to Particular Recommendations of the Royal Commission into Institutional Responses to Child Sexual Abuse' (26 February 2020) 7.

96 Ibid 8.

97 Fisher (n 93) 144–5.

98 *Catechism of the Catholic Church* (n 92) [1450].

99 Geoffrey Robinson, 'On Breaking the Seal of Confession' (n 78).

100 Catholic Church in Victoria, Submission to the Parliamentary Inquiry into the Handling of Child Abuse by Religious and Other Non-Government Organisations, *Facing the Truth: Learning from the Past: How the Catholic Church in Victoria has Responded to Child Abuse* (Report, 21 September 2012) 107.

101 Michael Guerzoni and Hannah Graham, 'Catholic Church Responses to Clergy-Child Sexual Abuse and Mandatory Reporting Exemptions in Victoria, Australia: A Discursive Critique' (2015) 4(4) *International Journal for Crime* 58, 70.

102 *Final Report* (n 11) vol 16, bk 2, 872, recommendation 16.26(b).

103 Guerzoni and Graham (n 101).

the confessor concludes that the penitent lacks the necessary contrition. Absolution then, cannot be made conditional on future actions in the external forum.'[104]

A religious-legal conundrum

It is disappointing that the Holy See has not taken the opportunity to moderate its teaching on the seal of the confessional in ways that would allow for some accommodation with state interests in the protection of children. Nonetheless, for the ordinary priest hearing confessions, the conflict between canon law and civil law is at least, entirely clear. The effect of 'failure to report' offences that give no exemption for religious confessions is to place clergy in the invidious position of having to negotiate conflicting obligations. On the one hand, priests will be bound by a law of the state which requires them to report confessions of child sexual abuse to public authorities. On the other hand, priests will be bound by a law of the Church prohibiting them from breaching the seal of confession. In short, when faced with a confession of child sexual abuse, the priest's subsequent action will either lead them to criminal punishment or excommunication.

In the face of conflicting canon law and civil law obligations, Catholic leaders have asserted that priests will likely maintain canonical allegiance, with some even saying they would 'prefer to go to jail' than break the seal of confession.[105] There is a tendency to misconstrue the allegiance to Church doctrine as somehow being morally negligent or incompatible with the welfare of children. Father Frank Brennan repudiates such claims and maintains that if anything is incompatible with child welfare, it is not the seal of confession itself but the laws that attempt to circumvent it. He suggests that the fixation with the

---

104 Holy See (n 95) 8.
105 See, eg, David Collits, Submission to the Royal Commission into Institutional Responses to Child Sexual Abuse (Issues Paper No 11: Catholic Church Final Hearing, 2016) 9; Brennan (n 91) 2; Fisher (n 93) 139–40; *Criminal Justice Report* (n 10) pts III–VI, 222–3.

confessional seal is a distraction from the real issues at play: '[k]ids will be better protected in future if we put to one side the furphy about the seal of the confessional and address the real questions about uniform mandatory reporting and clear guidelines for reporting any suspected serious crime'.[106]

The legislative changes appear futile without support from clergy. If those who are required to report believe they have a more compelling obligation that is in conflict with their civic duty, they will follow their conscience in this matter. That means, of course, that even if there were a confession by a perpetrator of child sexual abuse, the failure to report would be most unlikely to be disclosed.

Law is typically ineffective in achieving its ends without at least the majority of the population engaging in voluntary compliance. As Professor Tay once wrote: '[i]n all societies, it is often forgotten, law is not merely the utterance of power; it both represents and produces a significant degree of social consensus...Law thus stands halfway between violence and education, and partakes of both'.[107]

Laws abolishing the confessional privilege are just the utterance of power. They can have no educative effect if priests consider themselves to be bound to obey a higher power. Some laws can be efficacious in the absence of voluntary compliance, but this is only possible if there is a sufficient capacity for the discovery of offences. So speeding laws can be made effective without community acceptance if there are enough speed cameras, and particularly if they are both mobile and hidden. In contrast, there are no effective means of discovering failures to report abuse disclosed in the confessional. Neither the perpetrator nor the priest to whom a disclosure is made, and who fails to report it, will have any incentive to disclose the confession or failure to report. Each will be protected by the right not to incriminate themselves.

---

106 Brennan (n 91) 2.
107 Alice Tay, 'The Role of Law in the 20th Century: From Law to Laws to Social Science' (1991) 13(3) *Sydney Law Review* 247, 251–2.

The information disclosed in confession

Another impetus for the Commission's stance on religious confession was the view that leaving the privilege untouched would result in the loss of potentially significant evidence that would otherwise enable the prosecution of perpetrators in the Catholic Church.[108] However, this assumption is questionable.[109]

As one of us has previously argued, the 'case is quite weak for clergy to be required to report suspected child sexual abuse generally, if the objective is to identify sexually abused children and for the child protection authorities to respond accordingly'.[110] The legal duty to report would only arise where the priest had sufficient information to identify a perpetrator or child victim, as the case may be. The relevant reporting obligation in South Australia, for instance, is by name (and if known, the address) of *the child*.[111]

The problem is that to be able to report that a child is at risk, the child must first be identified. If a man admits to abusing his own daughter, then the priest will be able to identify the child if he can identify the person confessing. However, traditional confessions are given anonymously, and a person may choose to go to confession with a priest who does not know him personally, and would therefore not be able to put a name to a voice. If the person confesses to extrafamilial abuse, he may do so in vague terms giving no detail of the child or children involved.

Similar problems arise with criminal offence reporting obligations, but the requirements are different. The legal obligation to report criminal

---

108 *Criminal Justice Report* (n 10) 175.

109 See, eg, Robinson (n 99); Frank Brennan, 'Why I Will Break the Law Rather than the Seal of Confession', *Sydney Morning Herald* (Web Page, 15 August 2017); Helen Costigane, 'When Priests Hear about Sex Abuse in Confession, Should They Be Forced to Report It?' (Web Page, 30 July 2013) *America: The Jesuit Review*; Greg Craven, 'The Seal is Sacrosanct', *The Australian* (Web Page, 19 November 2012); Bill Uren, 'Seal of Confession Should Remain Inviolate' (Web Page, 7 December 2017) *Eureka Street*.

110 Parkinson, 'Mandatory Reporting of Child Sexual Abuse by Religious Leaders' (n 18) 305.

111 *Children and Young People (Safety) Act 2017* (SA) s 31(1)(a).

conduct is likely to be triggered only if the priest has knowledge in relation to *the perpetrator*.[112] In order for charges to be laid, the police would at the very least need to know or be able to find out by investigation, the victim, approximate dates of the offending, and the actus reus of specific, chargeable offences.

The confessional is not a forum for cross-examination, and a penitent cannot be required to clarify specific details regarding his or her sins. Dr Keenan's small-scale study[113] found that 'confessions' tended to be minimal on details and rarely contained sufficient information to 'invite guidance, counsel or reproof'.[114] Assuming details of the crimes and victims were not apparent from the reported terms of the confession, it is doubtful that the police would be able to support a prosecutor in adducing sufficient evidence to prove the case beyond reasonable doubt. This is especially so in jurisdictions where the priest is not a compellable witness due to the confessional privilege in s 127 of the Uniform Evidence Law.

For these reasons, Father Brennan is surely right to say that breaking the seal of the confessional is a 'red herring that will not save one child'.[115]

The Irish experience

This conclusion would seem to be supported by the Irish experience. In a nine-year investigation spanning from 2000 until 2009, the Ryan Commission was set up by the Irish government to study institutional child abuse since 1940. The Ryan Commission was also tasked with exploring the cause, nature and magnitude of any abuse uncovered, and recommending strategies to deal with the oppressive effects of

---

112 See, eg, *Crimes Act 1900* (NSW) s 316A(1)(b).

113 Keenan (n 17).

114 Thompson, 'The Persistence of Religious Confession Privilege' (n 8) 446, citing Keenan (n 17) 164.

115 Brennan, 'Breaking the Seal of the Confessional a Red Herring that will Not Save One Child' (n 91).

such abuse. In contrast to the Royal Commission in Australia, the Ryan Commission did not discuss religious confession privilege, nor make recommendations about its continued existence in the face of child protection needs.[116] It is not entirely clear why the Ryan Commission omitted this point from its final report, but Thompson surmises it was because the Irish evidence confirmed 'the intuitive expectation that child sex abusers do not confess their sins to clergy, and in consequence, that there would be no benefit to children in compelling the disclosure of past or future confessions'.[117]

Whatever the real reasons for the Ryan Commission's omission, the Irish government has since passed two laws which expand the duty to report child protection concerns. These are the *Criminal Justice (Withholding of Information on Offences against Children and Vulnerable Persons) Act 2012* and the *Children First Act 2015*. The former Act creates a criminal offence of withholding information relating to the commission of a serious offence— including a sexual offence—against a person under 16 years of age or a vulnerable person.[118] While it is not entirely clear how the duty interacts with clergy-penitent confidences, Thompson reflects some of the previously articulated concerns about whether Catholic priests would be able to identify information which would be of 'material assistance' to child protection authorities, as required by the legislation.[119]

A similar doubt is created by s 14(1) of the *Children First Act 2015*, which requires defined categories of persons to report that a 'specific child' has been harmed, is being harmed, or is at risk of being harmed. While clergy are mandated reporters under the Act, the requirement to know that a 'specific child' is or has been subject to harm arguably does not reach

---

116 Thompson, 'The Persistence of Religious Confession Privilege' (n 8) 457.

117 Ibid.

118 *Criminal Justice (Withholding of Information on Offences against Children and Vulnerable Persons) Act 2012* (Ireland) ss 2(1)–3(1) ('*Criminal Justice Act 2012*'). For a discussion of the Bill which predated the legislation, see 'Minister Shatter Announces Publication of Bill to Further Strengthen Child Protection', *Department of Justice* (Web Page, 25 April 2012).

119 *Criminal Justice Act 2012* (n 118) s 2(1)(b).

the generic confessions that Keenan says come to clergy from child sex abusers.[120] Moreover, with no prosecutions of clergy under either Act (for failure to report a confessional disclosure),[121] it seems clear that the Irish legislation is yet to demonstrate any beneficial effects.

V   Conclusions

English philosopher and jurist, Jeremy Bentham, observed that the secrets harvested by forcing clergy to report confessions would be fleeting. In consequentialist terms, people would stop confessing their sins as soon as their confidentiality was jeopardised. While Bentham was a sharp critic of the idea of privilege in general, he explained that religious confession privilege was justified on grounds of religious tolerance.[122] In his *Rationale of Judicial Evidence*, Bentham noted that society pays a cost by not recognising a priest-penitent privilege for religious confessions, especially when the alternative is to make priests testify about a confidential conversation using coercive means. Such coercion of ministers – whether in the form of a fine or imprisonment—would fuel public outrage, tarnish the legitimacy of government, and most certainly bring the justice system into disrepute.[123] Bentham wrote:

> The advantage gained by the coercion – gained in the shape of assistance to justice – would be casual, and even rare; the mischief produced by it, constant and extensive. ... this institution [confession] is an essential feature of the catholic religion, and ...

---

120 Thompson, 'The Persistence of Religious Confession Privilege' (n 8) 458, citing Keenan (n 17) 18–21.

121 For the difficulties involved in prosecuting failure to report offences generally, see Mathews (n 39). He identifies a pattern in under-prosecuting failure to report offences, and none of the cases he mentions relate to a confessional disclosure.

122 Michael Cassidy, 'Sharing Sacred Secrets: Is It (Past) Time for A Dangerous Person Exception to the Clergy-Penitent Privilege?' (2003) 44(4) *William & Mary Law Review* 1627, 1635.

123 Ibid.

the catholic religion is not to be suppressed by force.[124]

A coercive approach would not only fly in the face of religious liberty but may lead to a public sentiment that the secular state has punished clergy for simply observing their deeply held religious convictions.

The Royal Commission paid little attention to this downside of its recommendations. Nor did it properly address the slippery slope problem, as articulated by Father Bill Uren: '[i]f exceptions were to be made to identify paedophiles, it would be only a matter of time before exceptions would be sought for other crimes where recidivism is endemic'.[125]

Already, this is evident in the various state and territory enactments, some of which have extended reporting obligations to a range of other offences against children.

Church leaders are not the only ones concerned about setting this precedent. In its submission on the Child Sexual Offences Reform Bill, the Queensland Law Society expressed concern as to the possible repercussions for client legal privilege. It commented that the provisions are uncertain in their practical operation, particularly in terms of the requirement to report abuse to police upon attainment of a specific state of mind.[126] As drafted, these provisions 'mean that a legal practitioner who is approached for legal advice on the operation of these offences would be subject to the reporting obligation'.[127] Without express clarification in the Bill to exempt legal practitioners from the ambit of the duty, the Society expressed fears as to the longevity and stability of client legal privilege.

The changes to statutory reporting obligations – insofar as they bind

---

124 Jeremy Bentham, *Rationale of Judicial Evidence* (Garland Publishing, 1978) vol IV, 589–90.
125 Uren (n 109).
126 Queensland Law Society, Submission No 25 to Legal Affairs and Community Safety Committee, Parliament of Queensland, Criminal Code (Child Sexual Offences Reform) and Other Legislation Amendment Bill 2019 (7 January 2020) 3–4.
127 Ibid 2.

priests in the confessional – will not have the practical benefits that some scholars, child advocates and legislatures envisage. Arguably, not a single child will be saved from sexual abuse. Maybe that is no reason to reject the new laws, if of course, there are no countervailing factors. However, in a multicultural and multi-faith society, it is unwise for Parliaments to be so dismissive of religious liberty concerns. Law relies, for its efficacy, on the acceptance of the governed to a very considerable extent.

Placing priests in a conflict between their civil obligations and their faith, with the attendant risk of excommunication, creates a tension between church and state which has no countervailing benefit. It can only undermine respect for the law, encourage civil disobedience, and increase alienation between people of faith and the secular majority.

3

Monica Doumit

Formal and informal removal of legal protections for the confessional seal

Abstract

The Australian *Royal Commission into Institutional Responses to Child Sexual Abuse* recommended that state governments make amendments to existing mandatory reporting laws to remove legal protections for knowledge of child abuse obtained in the context of religious confession. It also recommended the creation of a new criminal offence of failure to report child abuse that did not include any exemptions for religious confession. The Catholic Church in Australia did not accept these recommendations, and the Holy See affirmed the inviolability of the seal of confession, even when abuse is confessed or disclosed in confession. This chapter outlines the moves by most Australian states and territories to abolish confessional privilege and considers some extra-legislative measures taken or threatened to coerce compliance with these laws.

Keywords:

Seal of the confessional – Religious Confession Privilege – Royal Commission into Institutional Responses to Child Sexual Abuse – mandatory reporting – child protection – criminal law

I Introduction

The scourge of the crime of child sexual abuse and its cover up in institutions generally, and in the Catholic Church specifically, led to a five year long Royal Commission into Institutional Responses to Child Sexual Abuse in Australia.

In public hearings and private sessions, as well as submissions and a review of literature relating to the Catholic Church, the Royal Commission identified a range of issues that may have contributed to the occurrence of child sexual abuse in Catholic institutions. Among these was the operation of the Sacrament of Confession,[1] which was examined in the Catholic Church final hearing, held in February 2017.

II Evidence before the Royal Commission relating to the Sacrament of Confession

There was limited evidence referred to in the Royal Commission's final report, handed down in December 2017, that suggested the operation of the Sacrament of Confession may have contributed to the occurrence of child sexual abuse in Catholic institutions.

With respect to the evidence of those directly involved in sacramental confession, the final report referred to the case of a perpetrator telling insurers and lawyers that he had made a full confession,[2] three survivors

---

1   *Royal Commission into Institutional Responses to Child Sexual Abuse* (Issues Paper No 11, 5 May 2016) 2.

2   *Royal Commission into Institutional Responses to Child Sexual Abuse* (Report of Case Study No 13, November 2015) 31.

testifying that they had disclosed the abuse to which they had been subjected during confession[3] and a former priest telling the Royal Commission that an abusive priest had used confession to trap him into silence.[4] None of these claims was tested by cross-examination.

In addition, Father Frank Brennan SJ gave anecdotal evidence of a woman who had emailed him to inform him that her abusive father 'went to confession regularly and went to priests who very readily forgave him'.[5] It was not clear from Father Brennan's evidence how the woman came to know the contents of her father's confessions or of the priests' responses.

The Royal Commission also received evidence from Irish psychologist Dr Marie Keenan, who conducted a study on clergy perpetrators of child sexual abuse. Dr Keenan reported that eight of the nine clergy who took part in the study confessed to the abuse. However, in another part of the same study not cited by the Royal Commission, Dr Keenan noted that clergy perpetrators of child sexual abuse did not confess their crimes in sufficient detail in confession to invite counsel, guidance or reproof.[6]

Based on this limited evidence, the Royal Commission made several recommendations that directly or indirectly affected religious confessions.

3   *Royal Commission into Institutional Responses to Child Sexual Abuse* (Final Report, 2017) vol 16, bk 2, 853.
4   Phil O'Donnell gave evidence that a victim had disclosed abuse at the hands of Father Victor Rubeo. This disclosure was not made within the context of confession. O'Donnell said that the victim then phoned Rubeo to tell him that he had reported the matter to O'Donnell and that, the following day, Rubeo visited O'Donnell in his home and 'dropped on his knees and went into the confessional mode, and I was a bit shocked, and I gave absolution... he had made sure that I couldn't speak to anyone': Transcript of Proceedings, *Royal Commission into Institutional Responses of Child Sexual Abuse* (Case Study No 35, 24 November 2015) 13230.
5   *Royal Commission into Institutional Responses to Child Sexual Abuse* (Final Report, 2017) vol 16, bk 2, 853.
6   Marie Keenan, Child Sexual Abuse and the Catholic Church: Gender, Power and Organizational Culture (Oxford University Press, 2012) 163–4.

A Recommendations of the Royal Commission

In terms of indirect affect on religious confessions, the recommendations included that state governments should make amendments to existing mandatory reporting laws[7] and create a new offence of 'failure to report'.[8]

Three recommendations were directly related to religious confession; two of these were generic in nature, and one specific to the Catholic Church.

Recommendation 7.4 provided: '[l]aws concerning mandatory reporting to child protection authorities should not exempt persons in religious ministry from being required to report knowledge or suspicions formed, in whole or in part, on the basis of information disclosed in or in connection with a religious confession'.

Recommendation 16.26 provided:

> The Australian Catholic Bishops Conference should consult with the Holy See, and make public any advice received, in order to clarify whether:
>
>> a. information received from a child during the sacrament of reconciliation that they have been sexually abused is covered by the seal of confession
>>
>> b. if a person confesses during the sacrament of reconciliation to perpetrating child sexual abuse, absolution can and should be withheld until they report themselves to civil authorities.

Recommendation 35 provided:

> Each state and territory government should ensure that the legislation it introduces to create the criminal offence of failure to report recommended in recommendation 33 addresses

---

7   *Royal Commission into Institutional Responses to Child Sexual Abuse: Final Report Recommendations* (Final Report, 2017) 17.

8   Ibid 100.

religious confessions as follows:

> a. The criminal offence of failure to report should apply in relation to knowledge gained or suspicions that are or should have been formed, in whole or in part, on the basis of information disclosed in or in connection with a religious confession.

> b. The legislation should exclude any existing excuse, protection or privilege in relation to religious confessions to the extent necessary to achieve this objective.

> c. Religious confession should be defined to include a confession about the conduct of a person associated with the institution made by a person to a second person who is in religious ministry in that second person's professional capacity according to the ritual of the church or religious denomination concerned.

Once implemented, these recommendations would have the effect of changing the existing exemption from mandatory reporting laws for information learned in religious confession. The recommendations would also ensure that new failure to report offences did not exempt knowledge gained or suspicions formed, in confession.

B Response from the Catholic Church

During Case Study 50 of the Royal Commission, each of the then-metropolitan archbishops confirmed that they agreed that priests and religious should be subject to mandatory reporting requirements, subject to an exception for the seal of confession.[9] In addition, the archbishops each expressed their support for a reportable conduct scheme to be rolled out in each state, consistent with the one currently operational in New South Wales.

---

9   Transcript of Proceedings, *Royal Commission into Institutional Responses of Child Sexual Abuse* (Case Study No 50, 26143).

Responding formally to the recommendations of the Royal Commission, the Australian Catholic Bishops Conference and Catholic Religious Australia did not accept Recommendation 7.4 and – as recommended – referred the issues raised in Recommendation 16.26 to the Holy See.[10] In July 2019, the Apostolic Penitentiary issued the *Note of the Apostolic Penitentiary on the Importance of the Internal Forum and the Inviolability of the Sacramental Seal*. It did not specifically address recommendation 16.26 but stated that the sacramental seal includes all the sins of both the penitent and others known from the penitent's confession and cannot be breached even if absolution is denied. In its response to Recommendation 16.26, the Holy See confirmed the note of the Apostolic Penitentiary as giving expression to the 'long-standing and constant teaching of the Church on the inviolability of the sacramental seal, as something demanded by the nature of the sacrament itself and thus deriving from Divine Law'.[11] The response went on to say, however, that a priest may and in certain cases, should, encourage a victim to seek help outside the confessional or report abuse to the authorities. The Holy See also confirmed that absolution cannot be made conditional on a penitent reporting themselves to civil authorities.

The Catholic Church's rejection of Recommendation 7.4 was not only based on Church law on the inviolability of the sacramental seal, but also because pastoral experience demonstrated that requiring priests to break the seal of confession might would be counterproductive in the goal of protecting children.

Archbishop of Perth, Timothy Costelloe, noted that the desire to abolish protections for the seal of confession was based on the erroneous presumption that the confessing of the sin of child abuse is common, that priests know the identity of the penitent, and that penitents are

---

10 Australian Catholic Bishops Conference and Catholic Religious Australia, 'Response to the Royal Commission into Institutional Responses to Child Sexual Abuse' (August 2018) 40–2.

11 Holy See, 'Response of the Holy See to Particular Recommendations of the Royal Commission into Institutional Responses to Child Sexual Abuse' (26 February 2020) 8.

very specific in the details disclosed in confession.[12]

Archbishop of Sydney, Anthony Fisher OP, observed that a change to the law that would require confessors to breach the seal of confession would be

> unjust, ineffectual and self-defeating: unjust because it is contrary to divine law and freedom of religion; ineffective because priests are willing to suffer civil sanctions rather than breach the seal of confession, and courts and the general population may well sympathise; self-defeating because it will ensure paedophiles never confess such matters and thus the (very rare) opportunity to counsel them to seek help from police, psychiatrists or others would be lost.[13]

He went on to say:

> Even were circumventing, circumscribing or breaking the seal in the ways proposed permissible, this would not serve to protect a single child: rather, it would help to ensure that such matters were never raised in confession. An opportunity would then be lost to counsel perpetrator or victim to do what is necessary to prevent recurrence. Without the seal, children would be less safe.[14]

The ineffectiveness of a law requiring the breaking of the sacramental seal was not only the Church's view; it was also the view of the Justice and Community Safety Directorate of the Australian Capital Territory, which issued an analysis report into the implementation of Royal Commission recommendations regarding the reporting of child sexual abuse, with implications for the confessional seal. The authors The Hon. Justice Julie Dodds-Streeton QC and Mr Jack O'Connor opined that:

> the imposition of an obligation to report child sexual abuse based on information obtained in or in connection with a religious confession is unlikely to result in many detections of, or successful prosecutions for, either child sexual abuse or breaches of the reporting obligation itself... Where sexual abusers of children are

---

12 Timothy Costelloe, 'Statement on the Seal of Confession' (5 December 2019) 2.

13 Anthony Fisher, 'Safeguarding the Seal of Confession' (2018) 95(2) *Australasian Catholic Record* 131, 147.

14 Ibid 150–1.

Roman Catholics who would otherwise attend confession, they will probably avoid confession altogether; or alternatively, they may exploit the potential under the rite of confession prevalent in Australia to confess anonymously and non-specifically, in order to avoid disclosures that will lead to their detection or oblige the priest to report.[15]

III Response from Australian States and Territories

Notwithstanding the limited evidence on which the Royal Commission's recommendations were based and the argument that a change in law would not achieve the goal of protecting children from harm or apprehending perpetrators of abuse, most Australian states and territories moved quickly to implement the recommendations regarding religious confession, and often did not confine the obligation of reporting to child sexual abuse.

For example, South Australia — the first state to abolish legal protections for religious confession — passed laws that require any actual or likely harm of a kind from which children are usually protected to be reported.[16] Harm is defined as 'physical harm or psychological harm (whether caused by an act or omission)' and includes on a non-limiting basis 'such harm caused by sexual, physical, mental or emotional abuse or neglect'. There is a carve out for emotional reactions such as distress, grief, fear or anger that are a response to the ordinary vicissitudes of life.[17]

Following this, the Australian Capital Territory, Tasmania, Victoria and Queensland passed similar laws, with each including imprisonment

---

15 Julie Dodds-Streeton and Jack O'Connor, *Implementation of Royal Commission into Institutional Responses to Child Sexual Abuse Recommendations regarding the Reporting of Child Sexual Abuse, with Implications for the Confessional Seal* (Analysis Report, 14 January 2019) 24 [89]–[90].

16 *Children and Young People (Safety) Act 2017* (SA) s 31.

17 Ibid s 18.

amongst the penalties for breach of mandatory reporting laws.[18] Western Australia has a similar bill tabled in Parliament.[19] However, a parliamentary committee examining the bill recommended that ministers of religion be excused from criminal responsibility for failing to report a reasonable belief that a child has been or is being sexually abused 'only when the grounds of their belief is based solely on information disclosed during religious confession'.[20] Notwithstanding the Committee's recommendation, both major parties have indicated an intention to abolish legal protections for the confessional seal.[21]

IV The Application of Mandatory Reporting Laws outside Religious Confession

In light of the rejection of Recommendation 7.4 by the Australian Catholic Bishops Conference and Catholic Religious Australia, as well as public statements from church leaders that indicate they will maintain the seal of confession irrespective of the changes in law,[22] there have been movements from governments to punish not only breaches of the mandatory reporting laws, but also any express or implied intention not to abide by them in the rare case that child harm is confessed or disclosed in the confessional.

The first example of such movements occurred in the Australian Capital

---

18   *Children and Young People Act 2008* (ACT) s 356; *Criminal Code Act 1899* (Qld) s 229BC; *Children, Young Persons and Their Families Act 1997* (Tas) s 14; *Criminal Code Act 1924* (Tas) s 105A; *Crimes Act 1958* (Vic) s 327.

19   Children and Community Services Amendment Bill 2019 (WA); Criminal Code (Child Sexual Offences Reform) and Other Legislation Amendment Bill 2019 (Qld).

20   Legislative Council Standing Committee on Legislation, Parliament of Western Australia, Children and Community Services Amendment Bill 2019 (Report, September 2020) 60.

21   Annabel Hennessy, 'WA Liberals Defy Powerbroker Nick Goiran to Support Child Sex Abuse Laws without Exemptions for Priests', *The West Australian* (Web Page, 15 September 2020).

22   See, eg, 'The sacredness of the sacramental seal.' *Archdiocese of Hobart* (Web Page, 11 August 2019); ABC Radio Melbourne, 'Melbourne Catholic Archbishop Peter Comensoli would Choose Jail over Breaking Confessional Seal', *ABC News* (Web Page, 14 August 2019).

Territory. At the same time as the mandatory reporting laws were amended in the Australian Capital Territory to remove protections for the seal of confession, changes were made to the education regulations that govern non-government schools to make provisional registration, registration and renewal of registration as a school contingent on compliance with Royal Commission recommendations.

In relation to each, the requirement is that

> A school must, through a representative of the non-government school sector, work with the Minister to implement the recommendations of the Royal Commission into Institutional Responses to Child Sexual Abuse.[23]

It has not yet been tested how this regulation will intersect with a Catholic school that takes students to the Sacrament of Confession during school hours, particularly if the confessor has either publicly stated that he will not break the seal of confession, or refuses to confirm to the Minister for Education that he will comply with the mandatory reporting laws as they pertain to confession. It is arguable that in such circumstances, a school will be asked to cease making the Sacrament of Confession available to students during school hours to acquire or maintain its registration.

It is important to note that in such a scenario, no breach of the mandatory reporting laws would need to occur for a school's registration to be threatened; such an outcome could occur merely on the basis of a stated intention of non-compliance. This is not the only example of how intended non-compliance can be punished, with no breach of a mandatory reporting law necessarily occurring.

On 15 October 2019, at a meeting of the Future Melbourne Committee for the City of Melbourne, Councillor Nicolas Frances Gilley tabled the following Notice of Motion:

---

23 *Education Regulation 2005* (ACT) ss 5A–5C.

1.   That the Future Melbourne Committee:

    1.1.   Commends the adoption in the Victorian Parliament of new laws which carry sentences of up to three years for workers in places of worship who fail to report cases of child abuse or mistreatment.

    1.2.   Notes with concern, reports in the media suggesting that some places of worship, as indicated by the Catholic Archbishop for Melbourne, will defy the laws as a means of protecting religious beliefs such as the confessional seal.

    1.3.   Reaffirms City of Melbourne's Goal as A City for People and one which seeks to create a safe, healthy and welcoming city for people of all ages including children

    1.4.   Requests management to undertake the following:

        1.4.1.   Immediately seek a public declaration of compliance with mandatory reporting laws from places of worship in the municipality;

        1.4.2.   Following the outcome of 1.4.1, ensure increased community awareness of those places of worship who fail to acknowledge compliance or do not respond to the request to affirm their commitment to comply with reporting requirements;

        1.4.3.   Seek legal advice as to further actions available to City of Melbourne to ensure compliance.[24]

In advance of the Committee meeting, Councillor Gilley stated that his proposal to 'ensure increased community awareness of those places of worship who fail to acknowledge compliance or do not respond to the request to affirm their commitment to reply with reporting requirements' could include the erection of 'great big signs' in front of churches, or writing on the pavement outside, warning that the safety of children

---

24 Future Melbourne Committee, Melbourne City Council, *Notice of Motion: Ensuring Safety of Children at Places of Worship in Our Municipality*, 66th mtg, agenda item 7.1 (15 October 2019).

could not be guaranteed within them.[25]

It is not only a public awareness campaign that the Committee considered, but imposing financial penalties as well. At the meeting, while discussing the motion, Councillor Stephen Mayne suggested that in addition to the motion, Melbourne City Council should consider taking a position of removing rates exemptions for church-owned properties 'as a further way that Council could put pressure on the Church to comply with the law'. Additionally, Councillor Rohan Leppert proposed that responses from places of worship be considered in future procurement decisions.[26]

Note that, in a similar fashion to the amendment to the *Education Regulations 2005* (ACT), these sanctions were proposed to be imposed without any evidence that the mandatory reporting law was being broken within churches or any other location by Catholic priests, or that mandatory reporting laws would ever be broken, given the overwhelming commentary from Catholic clergy that those who abuse children either do not go to confession or do not confess their crimes in sufficient detail to make a report useful.

The motion was not moved in the form tabled; but moved and passed by the Future Council Committee in the following form:

1.   That the Future Melbourne Committee:

    1.1.   Commends the adoption in the Victorian Parliament of new laws which carry sentences of up to three years for workers in places of worship who fail to report cases of child abuse or mistreatment.

    1.2.   Notes with concern reports in the media suggesting that some places of worship may defy the laws as a means of protecting religious beliefs, such as the confessional seal.

    1.3.   In light of the previous paragraph, requests management

---

25   Clay Lucas and Chris Vedelago, 'Council Motion Calls for Signs at Churches Warning of Dangers Within', *The Age* (Web Page, 15 October 2019).
26   'Future Melbourne Committee: Melbourne Town Hall: 15 October 2019' (Melbourne City Council, 15 October 2019).

to confirm with the Child Safety Commissioner if the new Safeguarding Children and Young People Framework will provide adequate standards and protection for young people and children.

1.4.   Reaffirms City of Melbourne's Goal as A City for People and one which seeks to create a safe, healthy and welcoming city for people of all ages including children.

1.5.   Requests management to report back to FMC on what the role of Local Government could be in seeking confirmation from places of worship that they will comply with mandatory reporting laws, and appropriately responding where this is not the case.[27]

Ultimately, legal advice received by the Council stated that it could not use its existing planning powers or pass new local laws to ensure compliance with state laws.[28]

The legal advice sought was limited to the role of local government in thus ensuring compliance with state laws; it remains to be seen whether a state government icould itself try to find alternate financial or other points of leverage to coerce compliance, or punish intended non-compliance.

V Crimes for which a Defence is Unavailable

Moves by state and local governments to allow punishment for an expressed intention to uphold church law have implications beyond those which affect churches or church-run institutions. There are also significant consequences for any Catholic priest or other minister of religion bound to the sacramental seal who is accused of having failed to comply with mandatory reporting obligations.

---

27 Future Melbourne Committee, Melbourne City Council, *Notice of Motion: Ensuring Safety of Children at Places of Worship in Our Municipality*, 66th mtg, agenda item 7.1 (15 October 2019) 7.

28 John Masanauskas, 'City of Melbourne Lacks Power to Out Churches over Mandatory Reporting of Child Abuse', *Herald Sun* (Web Page, 13 March 2020).

Naming the sacramental seal as 'inviolable', the Code of Canon Law provides 'it is absolutely wrong for a confessor in any way to betray the penitent, for any reason whatsoever, whether by word or in any other fashion'.[29] A confessor who directly violates the sacramental seal, incurs an automatic excommunication.[30] A priest accused of not reporting that he received information in the Sacrament of Confession that a child had been or was at risk of being harmed would not be able to proffer a defence, because the Code of Canon Law's prohibition on betraying the penitent in any way not only prevents him revealing what was said in confession, but also what was *not* said, and even whether the confession took place at all.

Mandatory reporting laws that include a penalty of imprisonment for breach, and which do not include an exemption for information learned within the religious confession breaks new and troubling legal ground because it creates a crime for which the accused is not able to offer a defence without violating his own religious beliefs in a way that would threaten his eternal salvation. The creation of an offence against which no defence can be made is a striking departure from principles of natural justice that require every accused to be afforded the opportunity to face and challenge their accusers. While this situation has not yet occurred in Australia, an illustrative example occurred in the US State of Louisiana, which also has mandatory reporting laws, but which include an exemption for religious confession.

Father Jeff Bayhi is a priest of the Catholic Diocese of Baton Rouge. It was alleged that on three occasions in 2008, 14 year old Rebecca Mayeux told Father Bayhi during the Sacrament of Reconciliation about abuse she was suffering at the hands of a parishioner, and that Father Bayhi 'responded she simply needed to handle the situation herself, because otherwise, 'too many people would be hurt'. Although it was clear that mandatory reporting of information learned in confession was not

---

29 *The Code of Canon Law: In English Translation* (Collins, 1983) canon 983 § 1.
30 Ibid canon 1388 § 1.

required, Father Bayhi and the Diocese of Baton Rouge were nevertheless sued for damage caused for failure to report, the case was still able to proceed with an interim court ruling that it was a mixed question of law and fact about whether the disclosure of abuse suffered by the penitent was confession per se, and thus covered by the exemptions to mandatory reporting laws.[31] During the case, Father Bayhi confirmed that he could not reveal the contents of the confession, nor whether it took place at all.[32]

The case against Father Bayhi and the Diocese of Baton Rouge, which was ultimately discontinued by the plaintiffs in 2019, with each party agreeing to bear their own costs for the nine years of litigation that had ensued,[33] illustrates the implications for the just conduct of litigation when a party is unable to challenge an accuser's version of events.

VI Conclusion

Laws that require the reporting of the harm or risk of harm to a child confessed or disclosed during religious confession have the potential to significantly impact religious institutions and individuals outside the context of confession itself, and even in circumstances where no breach of the mandatory reporting laws occurs. The extent of this impact is yet to play out in Australia. But it is clear that how it does play out will largely be in the hands of state governments and other authorities who may seek to coerce compliance through regulatory, financial or other penalties, or punish those who express an intention not to comply with the new laws. Some of these new laws will also place these matters in the hands of courts that will need to decide how to proceed in matters where an accused is left without a defence.

---

31 *Parents of Minor Child v Charlet*, 135 So 3d 1177, 1181 (Clark, Johnson and Knoll JJ, Hughes J agreeing at 1181, Guidry J agreeing at 1181) (La, 2014).
32 Joe Gyan Jr, 'Judge Dismisses Baton Rouge Catholic Diocese, Priest from Lawsuit involving the Confessional', *The Advocate* (Web Page, 22 February 2018).
33 Ibid.

Part II

Privacy, confidentiality and the seal of the confessional in Europe

4

Mario Ferrante

Religious confession privilege in Italy

Abstract

In Italy, the secrecy of confession practised in some religious denominations and especially in the [Roman] Catholic Church, is widely recognised. Indeed, it is so widely recognised that it is not perceived as a particular concession to religion, even less as a privilege, but rather as a right. This is due, in the first place, to the broad recognition of the right to religious freedom guaranteed by art 19 of the *Constitution of the Italian Republic 1948* ('*Italian Constitution*' or '*Constitution*')[1] which is a subjective and public right since it can be enforced against the state.

In other words, this protection of religious belief and action in the *Italian Constitution* denies that the state may limit religious confession and the secrecy of that confession by law or administrative act because confession is understood to be a part of worship.

Confessional secrecy is also protected by further specific guarantees.

---

1   Roughly translated, 'Anyone is entitled to freely profess their religious belief in
     any form, individually or with others, and to promote them and celebrate rites
     in public or in private, provided they are not offensive to public morality'.

For example, confession within the Catholic Church is also protected by art 4.4 of the *Villa Madama Agreement* ('*Accordo di Villa Madama*') of 18 February 1984 (implemented by Law No 121 of 25 March 1985) which provides that the clergy are not required to give magistrates or other civil authorities information about people or matters of which they become aware by reason of their ministry. Similar guarantees are provided to ministers of Jewish Communities and the Lutheran Church.[2] These additional guarantees of clerical secrecy even when information might be requested by the judicial authorities, is reiterated and extended to all ministers of religious denominations whose statutes do not conflict with the Italian legal system under art 200 of the *Code of Criminal Procedure* and art 249 of the *Code of Civil Procedure*. Thus, members of the clergy know that may can refuse to testify about anything they have learned because of their ministry in any criminal or civil court. But they also know that this confidentiality protection does not extend to anything they have learned as ordinary citizens or as mere friends of the people concerned and that it will be a judge's duty to make such an assessment if the source of their knowledge is ever questioned. Indeed, the obligation of confidentiality is taken so seriously that there are also provisions in the *Criminal Code* which make the disclosure of anything learned during confession a crime.[3]

Keywords:

Seal of the confessional – protection of religious freedom in Italy – religious confession privilege in Italian Constitution and Codes

---

2   Law No 101 of 8 March 1989 provides that ministers appointed by the Jewish communities and by their central union according to the bylaws ('*statuto*') of Italian Judaism 'are not required to give magistrates or other civil authorities information about people or matters of which they become aware by reason of their ministry': at art 3(1). And Law No 520 of 29 November 1995 provides that ministers appointed by the Evangelical-Lutheran Church in Italy 'are granted the right to maintain official secrecy about what they learn in carrying out their ministry: at art 4(3).

3   For example, breach of the confidentiality of Catholic confession is a crime under art 622 of the *Criminal Code*.

I Introduction

Even though the See of the Catholic Pope has been entirely separate from the Italian State since unification (1861–70), a strong connection between the Italian State and the Catholic Church remains. And that connection has become even more complicated recently because of strong immigration flows which have changed the Italian religious and social framework. For while there was no question that Italy was a majority Christian and even a Catholic country until the last twenty years, the consequence of the recent arrivals from many different religious traditions and particularly from Islamic countries, mean that the old Christian assumptions can no longer be taken for granted.[4]

These new social conditions have changed the way the Italian State interacts with all religions because national agreements with individual churches no longer cover all religious practices, and it is not always clear how the Italian juridical system should interact with religions when there are no specific legal instruments governing the relationship. Absent specific agreements, the courts are obliged to fall back on a law about freedom of religion that was passed during fascism in 1929 and which is still in force — the so called 'law on admitted cults'.[5]

While it is not possible here to review all the consequences of the way that the 1929 law operates in the absence of an agreement between individual church organisations and the state,[6] this chapter includes a brief analysis. That is because that legal context is essential in order to understand the reasons for the absolute respect guaranteed by Italian law for the confidentiality of confession and to appreciate the legal basis of the right of the clergy to refuse to disclose what they have heard from the faithful.

---

4   On this aspect see Pierluigi Consorti, *Diritto e religione: Basi e Prospettive* (Laterza, 2020).
5   Law No 1159 of 24 June 1929.
6   For further information see Francesco Finocchiaro, *Diritto ecclesiastico*, rev Andrea Bettetini and Gaetano Lo Castro (Zanichelli, 13th ed, 2020).

II Historical Analysis of the Relationship between Secular and Religious

Though there have been periods in Italian history when religion has been regarded as a private matter, there have also been periods where religion has been a very public matter and the Catholic Church has even been promoted by the State. However, the relationship between the churches and the Italian State is best characterised as one of coordination where laws are seen as governing a cooperative relationship.[7]

For the most part, that coordination is based on agreements between the State and the different religious organisations – and in particular the Catholic Church, as discussed below. These coordination agreements operate like contracts which regulate all the most relevant issues in order to avoid any possible conflict.

The reason various churches and the Italian State have signed these agreements is to define and regulate all aspects of their interaction. The coordination that results is seen to be different and better than formal separation of church and state because coordination anticipates that the churches and the State will work together to solve the problems of their constituents who are citizens and religious believers at the same time. And the reality is that an approach that coordinates the state and canon law that affects most citizens at the same time, works to avoid the conflicts which might otherwise occur. In other words, when church and state are separate, neither is interested in what the other determines and regulates. But under a concordat system, some of the most important matters of common interest (so called *res mixtae*) like legal entities and marriage, are regulated taking into account the needs of the other party and many problems are avoided for government, the church and ultimately for the people.

---

7   For a complete analysis refer to Marco Canonico, *I sistemi di relazione tra Stato e chiese* (G Giappichelli, 2nd ed, 2015).

A brief historical survey will explain why Italy has a concordat system. It developed as a consequence of the 'Risorgimento' period which led to the unification of Italy after 1870. On 20 September of that year, Rome was conquered by the Italian army and annexed to the Italian State as its new capital city. The juridical consequences of this act of war, was the *Debellatio* of the Pontifical State and the beginning of the Roman Question. Pope Pius IX declared himself a prisoner in the Vatican after he was forced to move to from the Quirinal Palace before the Italian king moved in. Today the President of the Italian Republic lives in that same building.[8]

In 1929, the 'Lateran Pacts' (named after the Lateran Palace in which they were signed) were concluded in three sections: a conciliation treaty, a concordat, and a financial convention.[9] Article 26 of the Conciliation Treaty resolved the Roman Question when it declared that 'the Roman Question [was] definitely and irrevocably settled and therefore eliminated, and recognise[d] the Kingdom of Italy under the Dynasty of the House of Savoy, with Rome as the capital of the Italian State'. The Italian State for its part, recognised the State of the Vatican City under the sovereignty of the Supreme Pontiff.

In the Concordat, several *res mixtae* were regulated. For instance, marriage was recognised as an institution with religious and civil effects, and from that moment on, it was called 'Concordat marriage'.

The last of the three protocols, the financial convention, set out the compensation that the Italian State had to pay the Pope and the Catholic Church in consequence of its takeover of Rome nearly sixty years previously.

---

8   Indeed, Italy tried to solve the Roman question one year later with the so called 'Legge delle Guarentigie pontificie' (Law No 214 of 13 May 1871) but this law was totally refused by the Pope because it was considered to be only a unilateral solution. Cf Carlo Cardia, *Risorgimento e religione* (G Giappichelli, 2011).

9   See Maria D'Arienzo (ed), *1929-2019 Novant'anni di rapporti tra Stato e confessioni religiose: Attualità e prospettive: Quaderno Monografico 1 – Supplemento Rivista* (Diritto e Religioni) XV, n 1-2020, Luigi Pellegrini.

The Lateran Pacts are international treaties and recognise that both parties have international legal personality.[10] Those Pacts have been updated and relations between the Italian State and the Catholic Church are now regulated by the by the *Italian Constitution* and the *Agreement for the revision of the Lateran Concordat* of 18 February 1984 which was implemented by Law No 121 of 25 March 1985.[11]

III The Constitutional Relationship of the Italian State and the Churches: The Change from an Established Church to Inclusive Secularism

The *Italian Constitution* included articles devoted to citizens' rights, freedom of religion and the relationship of the Catholic Church and the Italian State. Articles 7 and 8 regulate church/state relationships and the autonomy and freedom of churches, and art 19 safeguards individual and informal group freedom.[12] The *Constitution* was thus designed to protect

---

10 Being Italy a sovereign state, its juridical status was given for granted; on the other part it is important to understand why also the Holy See was considered the same way, even though the Pope since 1870, has not been a head of state. This is due to various reasons, starting with the fact that international law is based on customary law, and the international community from 1870 to 1929 (the international community in that period of colonialism was smaller than today) was composed mostly of states that were, if not Catholic, at least Christian. As a consequence, they respectfully regarded the Holy See, continuing to consider it as a subject of international law (ie the Pope continued to exercise his right of legation typical by a sovereign state). For this reason, when in 1929 Lateran Pacts were signed, no doubt arose whether they had to have a juridical nature by international treaty or not. The signing of the Treaty witnessed the birth of a new State, the Vatican City, represented by the Holy See. On this topic see Arturo Carlo Jemolo, *Chiesa e Stato in Italia. Dall'unificazione ai giorni nostri* (Einaudi, 1978).

11 See Salvatore Bordonali, *Problemi di dinamica concordataria*, in Mario Tedeschi (ed), *Il riformismo legislativo in diritto ecclesiastico e canonico* (Pellegrini, 2011).

12 Many other articles of the *Italian Constitution* assist in the protection of freedom of religion even though they have a general character. For instance, the right of assembly and association (art 18) and the right to freedom of expression and thought (art 21). Article 20 is particularly important because it regulates the juridical regime and insists that there is no distinction made between Catholic and non-Catholic religions. For example, it specifies that '[n]o special limitation or tax burden may be imposed on the establishment, legal capacity or activities of any organization on the ground of its religious nature or its religious aims'. On this topic see Mario Ferrante, *Enti religiosi/ecclesiastici e riforma del Terzo settore* (G Giappichelli, 2nd ed, 2019).

both individual and group freedom of religion. But there is no article that expressly establishes an Italian State Church.[13]

It is important to point out that the term secularism is never used in *Italian Constitution*. Nevertheless, by Sentence No 203 on 12 April 1989, the Constitutional Court established the so-called 'supreme principle of secularism'. But the Italian concept of secularism is completely different than French *laicité*. A good example of that difference is the absence of any requirement in Italian jurisprudence that the State must take a neutral attitude with regards to religion. On the contrary, the Italian State supports religion including economically. The Constitutional Court has thus called Italian secularism, 'positive secularism'[14] to distinguish it from French *laicité*.

We will now discuss some specific articles of the *Italian Constitution* which relate to religious issues (arts 7, 8 and 19).

By way of introduction, we observe that the pluralism safeguarded by the *Constitution* not only concerns the freedom of choice of individuals, but also the right of church organisations to exist, to organise, and to function autonomously without interference by the State. The Italian jurisprudential view is that church institutional freedom is essential to complete individual freedom of choice. That is because much individual freedom is exercised within religious institutions and would not be possible if the State did not guarantee the independence of the institutions within which much of that ideological, religious and political choice is exercised.

---

13 In the old monarchic Constitution (1848), Italy was a confessionist state in which the state religion was the Catholic one. According to the new Constitution, the Italian State is no longer confessionist but pluralist, as it relates on an equality level with all religions. It implies that the Italian state guarantees a series of rights, tax benefits, and public funding to all religions that, having all requirements, ask for them.

14 On the topic of French secularism see Jean-Pierre Chantin and Daniel Moulinet (eds), *La Séparation de 1905: Les hommes et les lieux* (Editions de l'Atelier, 2005); LV Méjan, *La separation des Eglises et de l'Etat: L'œuvre de Louis Méjan* (Presses universitaires de France, 1959); Maurice Larkin, *L'Eglise et l'Etat en France: 1905: La crise de la Séparation* (Privat, 2004).

A Article 7

We will first analyse art 7 of the *Italian Constitution* which exclusively refers to the relations between the Italian State and the Catholic Church. The reason why there is a specific article devoted to the Catholic Church resides in the historical importance that the Catholic Church has had in Italy.

Article 7 is divided into two paragraphs: '[t]he State and the Catholic Church are independent and sovereign, each within [its own sphere', and '[t]heir relationships are regulated by Lateran Pacts. Amendments to such Pacts which are accepted by both parties shall not require the procedure of constitutional amendments'.

The first paragraph of the article identifies the kind and level of the relations between Catholic Church and Italian State. This part of the article settles an ancient debate and explains that because the Catholic Church and the Italian State are two different entities, they each have a specific area of competence. The article makes clear that there is no kind of subordination between the two. In Italian Law, both of the two entities are considered 'independent'.

To strengthen this independence, the article repeats the idea behind the word 'independent' and states that both entities are separately 'sovereign'. The use of these two terms reinforces the autonomy explained above, as 'sovereignty' reinforces the idea of 'independence', but also reconfirms the latter. This separate 'independence' is confirmed by the identification of the separate spheres within which these two entities operate. Neither can interfere within the sphere of competence of the other. In other words, the Catholic Church is autonomous and omnicompetent in all its spiritual concerns, and the Italian State is separately competent in all the secular matters that come within its power. It is also important to underline that the term 'sphere' is wider than, and includes the legal system. Moreover, the recognition of the independence and sovereignty of the Catholic Church also confirms that its canon law is regarded as equal to the law of the Italian State, without any kind of mutual subordination.

The second part of this chapter is therefore focused on the relationship between the two entities. Though we have made clear that we are dealing with entities that govern two different spheres, we will now discuss some of the many points where they come into contact, because there are a lot of matters that are of common interest.

As we said earlier, the Catholic Church and the Italian State have many common interests. That is, many citizens of the Italian State are also members of the Catholic Church, and in order to optimise their freedoms under the law, the Church and the State have jointly established some rules which regulate common areas of interest. For this reason, the second part of the article, discusses the Lateran Pacts in more detail as those Pacts constitute a significant part of the common interest agreements between these parties.[15]

The last part of art 7 discusses the legal ways in which the Lateran Pacts can be modified. In essence, there are two methods of modification: the first is by concordat which involves the creation of separate new agreements; the other is by modification under art 7 of the *Constitution* using a procedure foreseen by art 138 of *Constitution*. In both cases, both parties must agree because as the *Constitution* states, agreements between church and state cannot be changed unilaterally. Unilateral modification would only be possible if the last part of art 7 were deleted.

The aforementioned *Villa Madama Agreement* of 18 February 1984 is an example of a modification of the original Lateran Pacts using the concordat method mentioned above. This Agreement takes its name

---

15 It is interesting, with this regard, to underline that in the Republican Constitution, which has been written by anti-fascists, there is mentioned an agreement signed by Mussolini himself. The communist party wanted to mention it because it was considered like a sign of continuity and reassurance for the Catholics and it preferred to avoid further changes. The Italian Constitution was issued shortly after the popular referendum that in 1946 abolished monarchy, so in that historical moment it was considered inopportune to reconsider also the status of Catholic Church.

from the fact that it was signed in a historical Italian 'villa' in accordance with the principle of alternating the venues.[16] The Italian State's respect for the Church's autonomy is also signified in the State's choice of its Ministry of Foreign Affairs as its representative agent in all Lateran Pact related matters.

While this 1984 agreement was not mentioned in art 7 of the *Constitution* because it did not exist when the *Constitution* was established, its integrity is safeguarded against possible unilateral modifications because art 7 secures not only the Lateran Pacts themselves, but any following modifications of them. Near the conclusion of the *Villa Madama Agreement*, art 13 also records that 'previous regulations and modifications of the Lateran Pacts [were] agreed upon by the parties, to reiterate that the autonomy of both parties has been preserved and that the guarantee against unilateral amendment is preserved in the 1984 Agreement. In reality, the 1984 *Villa Madama Agreement* only varied the original Lateran Pacts in two matters.[17]

B Article 8

We can now deal with art 8, which provides that all religious denominations are equally free before the law. Denominations other than Catholicism have the right to self-organization according to their own statutes, provided these do not conflict with Italian law. Their relations with the state are regulated by law, based on agreements with their

---

16   Pierluigi Consorti, '1984-2014: le stagioni delle intese e la terza età dell'art. 8, ultimo comma, della Costituzione' [2014] (1) *Quaderni di diritto e politica ecclesiastica* 91. The alternating venues principle symbolically assures that the continuing auton-omy of both parties is even respected in the choice of places where indepen-dent meetings are held so that neither party achieves superiority.

17   The most important modification concerns art. 1 of the Treaty, which estab-lished that the Italian state was still a 'Confessional State' and that Catholic religion was the religion of State (it was an anomaly of the Italian legal sys-tem, if we consider that in 1948 Italy adopted a new Constitution, inspired on this point by different principles from those of the previous one). As for the modifications to the Concordat, it is important to mention the introduction – through legislation derived from the 1984 agreement – of State funding to the Church called 'eight per thousand'.

respective representatives.

The second and third sentences of art 8, set out the constitutional position of religions other than the Catholic Church. They represent a significant change from the previous position where the Catholic Church was close to the established church of the Italian State. The first sentence expressly states that all religions are 'equally free before the law'. It is an important statement because even though it does not make all religions equal in fact, it establishes a principle of juridical equality between them.

We can better appreciate this provision by noting that according to the *Albertine Statute* (the previous *Italian Constitution*, issued in 1848), non-Catholic religions were merely tolerated. And while non-Catholic religions were paradoxically 'admitted' in 1929 during the fascist period, that terminology also indicates that non-Catholic religions were not treated as well as the Catholic Church which was the State religion.

While politics have prevented the passage of a new 'organic' constitutional law formally repealing the *Albertine Statute* and recognising religious groups whether they want their own concordat agreement with the Italian State or not, art 8 has significantly improved the legal status of non-Catholic churches in Italy.[18]

In the second sentence of art 8 it is stated that non-Catholic religions have the right, but are not compelled to be organised subject to their own statute, and to create an autonomous internal juridical system, provided that such system does not conflict with the Italian legal system.[19] Unlike the Catholic Church, this provision means that non-Catholic churches are subordinate to the Italian State, in the same way as other associations, foundations, or companies governed by internal statutes. Non-Catholic

---

18 See Fabiano Di Prima, *La mancata emanazione nell'Italia repubblicana di una legge "organica" solla libertà religiosa (il confronto col caso spagnolo)'* (2016) XXXII *Anuario de Derecho Eclesiástico del Estado* 879.

19 See. Giuseppe D'Angelo, '*La qualificazione giuridica del fatto religioso organizzato e la categoria «confessione religiosa»: Il tema del riconoscimento nella prospettiva di una legge generale*', in Giuseppe D'Angelo (ed) *Rigore e curiosità: Scritti in memoria di Maria Cristina Folliero* (Giappichelli, 2018).

churches are thus not treated at an international level as if they were sovereign states.

In practice, the third sentence in art 8 creates an intermediate level of non-Catholic church recognition by the Italian State.[20] This sentence allows religions with named representatives to conclude an agreement with the Italian State called an 'intesa' (memorandum of understanding) which formalises the status of their internal laws and acknowledges them under domestic public law. But once again, these agreements do not sound as treaties in international law. Under the Italian Constitution, while the corporate personality of minority religions can be recognised for domestic public law purposes, unlike the Holy See representing the Catholic Church, they cannot have international law juridical personality. That is because the Italian Constitution only contemplates that the State itself and the Catholic Church can make an international treaty.

We need to specify that neither the Italian State nor minority religions are compelled to enter into a concordat agreement. Nor is the Italian State obliged to sign any such agreement proposed by a minority religion because the Italian State retains its autonomy to make such agreements as mere political acts.[21] In practice, it is the Prime Minister who decides whether to sign such agreements with non-Catholic religions or not. And it is well known that the Prime Minister has refused to sign such agreements with representatives of Atheism (considered politically inappropriate) and that Muslims have not been able to enter into such an agreement because they do not have clear unified leading representatives.

Once such an agreement is signed, it is submitted as a draft law to the Italian Parliament to decide whether it should be approved or not.

---

20 See Salvatore Bordonali, 'La legge sui Culti ammessi, le Intese e l'esigenza di una legge comune sul fatto religioso' (2019) 66(3) Jus: Rivista di scienze giuridiche 149. [cf 7].

21 Cf Constitutional Court Sentence No 52 of 10 March 2016, according to which it is for the Council of Ministers to evaluate the opportunity to begin negotiations with the purpose of stipulating a bilateral memorandum of understating ('intesa') regulating mutual relations. That is because it is part of the discretionary political power of the Government that can be impugned only by the parliament.

However, the Parliament does not have the power to modify or amend such proposed agreements. The Parliament simply has a power of veto. If Parliament approves the resulting law, it can no longer be modified, unless a new agreement is signed. Under current interpretations of the third sentence in art 8 of the *Constitution*, unilateral modification is not possible. At present, the only way either party could unilaterally modify such an agreement in the future would be to amend art 8 of *Constitution* using the procedure provided by art 138 of *Constitution*.

Minority religions which do not have or do not want an agreement with the State, are subject to the 1929 law on 'admitted cults', subject only to the constitutional requirement in sentence one of art 8 that 'all religious denominations are equally free before the law'.[22]

We can thus visualise the relationship of the Italian State with religions as a pyramid whose vertex is represented by the Catholic Church. At a lower degree are all those religions that have an agreement recognised under art 8 of the *Constitution*, and at the bottom are the religions with no agreement at all.

C Article 19

Freedom of religion is guaranteed by art 19 of *Constitution*, according to which '[a]nyone is entitled to freely profess their religious belief in any form, individually or with others, and to promote them and celebrate rites in public or in private, provided they are not offensive to public morality'.

It is not only an individual right, but also a right against the State. That is because the *Italian Constitution* denies the government the authority to create any law or issue any direction that could limit this freedom, and art 8 confirms that any law or direction which purports to do so is

---

22 See Giancarlo Anello, *Organizzazione confessionale, culture e Costituzione: Interpretazione dell'art. 8 cpv. cost.* (Rubettino, 2007) 21 et seq.

invalid.[23]

The expression of freedom of religion as an individual subjective right in the *Italian Constitution*, makes it clear that all persons, citizens, foreigners, and even stateless persons can profess their own religion individually, or in association. They can also worship privately and in public and they are protected in their right to promote their faith. The essential content of the right to freedom of religion in Italy consists in ensuring that every individual can express his or her religious personality in a variety of ways, including by worshipping privately and in association with others, and by sharing his or her ideas with others in various ways including by informal discussion, by evangelism and in collective religious meetings.[24]

The only limit on the expression or practice of any religion is that its rites and other practices cannot be contrary to accepted principles of morality. This 'morality' limitation on religious practice has been interpreted to exclude only practices that offend common notions of sexual decency and honour.[25]

IV The Italian Idea of *Diritto ecclesiastico* (Ecclesiastical Law)

The following analysis will outline the general framework of the branch of Italian State law that deals with general religious beliefs and practices. It is multidisciplinary and crosses over all branches of law where issues

---

23 See generally Gaetano Catalano, *Il diritto di libertà religiosa* (Giuffrè, 1957).

24 Its content must be considered required by all the international treaties ratified by Italy, as, for instance, the article 9 of the 1950 *European Convention on Human Rights*, according to which:
Everyone has the right to freedom of thought, conscience and religion; this right includes freedom to change his religion or belief and freedom, either alone or in community with others and in public or private, to manifest his religion or belief, in worship, teaching, practice and observance. Freedom to manifest one's religion or beliefs shall be subject only to such limitations as are prescribed by law and are necessary in a democratic society in the interests of public safety, for the protection of public order, health or morals, or for the protection of the rights and freedoms of others.

25 See, eg, Vincenzo Pacillo, *Buon costume e libertà religiosa: Contributo all'interpretazione dell'art. 19 della Costituzione italiana* (Giuffrè, 2012).

of religious practice and belief can arise. Because constitutional, civil, administrative and criminal law can engage with religious issues, Italian ecclesiastical law has been called the 'halfway science'.[26] We explain Italian ecclesiastical law below using historical and comparative method.

Even though ecclesiastical law is rarely taught in universities elsewhere in the world, it is very important in Italy for social, political and jurisprudential reasons. Indeed, its significance is increasing because of growing tension between ideas of religious freedom and inclusion, mainly due to migration flows, which have transformed Italy from a largely Catholic and Christian society to a society that is religiously diverse.[27] While Italian diversity has previously been about ethnic differences, religious difference is now part of the diversity equation that cannot be ignored.

For this reason, some academics and other opinion leaders in Italy hope that an Act about religious diversity will be passed in the future. Such an Act would recognise the intersection of 'law', 'religion' and 'culture', and would create a regulatory system intended to mediate social conflicts in a way that engages all these elements of human character. An appropriately inclusive framework would both limit State action against minorities that do no harm, and would also recognise the contribution they make to the fabric of Italian society as a whole.[28]

V The Confidentiality of Confession according to Italian Legislation

Having outlined how religious belief and practice fit into the Italian legal system, we can now consider how Italian law treats the confidences which arise within churches.

---

26 See Mario Tedeschi, *Sulla scienza del diritto ecclesiastico* (Giuffrè, 2007) 10; Maria D'Arienzo, 'Nota del Curatore', in Maria D'Arienzo (ed), *Il diritto come 'scienza di mezzo': Studi in onore di Mario Tedeschi* (Luigi Pellegrini, 2017) xiii.

27 See, eg, Antonio Ingoglia and Mario Ferrante (eds), *Fenomeni migratori, Diritti umani e Libertà religiosa* (Libreriauniversitaria, 2017) *passim*.

28 Mario Ferrante, 'Diritto, religione, cultura: Verso una laicità inclusiva' (2017) 35 (November) *Stato, Chiese e pluralismo confessionale* 1.

It should first be recalled that each religious community has its own concept of church ministers, based on its own belief system and organisational model, so that the priestly function is not present in directly comparable ways in all religions.[29] By reason of their institutional duties, the clergy of many religious denominations, become aware of many intimate aspects of people's lives and beliefs. This is particularly true for Christian denominations that encourage the confession of sin and penance as is the case with the Catholic Church.[30]

---

29 See, eg, Angelo Licastro, *I ministri di culto nell'ordinamento giuridico italiano* (Giuffrè, 2005) 561 et seq; Matteo Carnì, 'I ministri di culto delle confessioni religiose di minoranza: Problematiche attuali' (2015) 19 (June) *Stato, Chiese e pluralismo confessionale* 1; Mario Deganello and Barbara Lavarini, 'Il segreto del ministro di culto come limite alla testimonianza penale', in Roberto Mazzola and Ilaria Zuanazzi (eds), *Aequitas sive Deus: Studi in onore di Rinaldo Bertolino* (G Giappichelli, 2011) vol II, 1331–2; Alessandro Diddi, *Testimonianza e segreti professionali* (Cedam, 2012) 185–8; Lucia Leoncini, 'Aspetti di rilievo processual penalistico nelle recenti intese tra lo Stato italiano e alcune confessioni religiose' (2013) 33(4) *Legislazione penale* 967, 980.

30 As far as the Catholic Church is concerned, on the basis of canon 983 § 1, it is absolutely not licit -- 'nefas est' -- for the confessor to betray in any way a penitent in words or in any manner and for any reason, meaning the sacramental seal is inviolable. With regard to the content of the seal, it includes 'all the sins of the penitent and of others known from the confession of the penitent, whether mortal or venial, whether hidden or public, insofar as they are manifested with regard to absolution and therefore known to the confessor by virtue of sacramental knowledge': Velasio De Paolis and Davide Cito, *Le sanzioni nella Chiesa: Commento al Codice di Diritto Canonico* (Urbaniana University Press, 2000) bk 5, 345. In addition, the circumstances of the sins and the names and sins of any accomplices fall within the scope of the seal. On the other hand, the interpreter, if there is one, and all others who have been informed of the sins of the confession in any way, are obliged to observe secrecy (canon 983 § 2). The penalties for infringements are very severe: excommunication *latae sententiae* reserved for the Holy See is inflicted in the case of direct violation of the sacramental seal (the revelation of both the sin and the person who committed it), which is the most serious penalty; while indirect violation is punished with an indeterminate and obligatory penalty *ferendae sententiae*, in proportion to the gravity of the crime (canon 1388 § 1). Finally, the interpreter and the other persons referred to in canon 983 § 2 who break the secret are punished with a just penalty, not excluding excommunication (canon 1388 § 2). By *ius canonicum* the priest is incapable of testifying to anything that has been revealed to him in sacramental confession, even if the penitent asks for it to be revealed (canon 1550 § 2 n 2). On this subject see Krzysztof Nykiel, 'Il sigillo confessionale e il segreto nella normativa canonica' (2019) 14(1) *Diritto e religioni* 15; Davide Cito, 'Trasparenza e segreto nel diritto penale e canonico' (2018) 107(3) *Periodica de re canonica* 513; Ulrich Rhode, 'Trasparenza e segreto nel diritto canonico' (2018) 107(3) *Periodica de re canonica* 465; Giuseppe Comotti, 'I delitti "contra sextum" e l'obbligo di segnalazione nel "motu proprio" "Vos estis lux mundi"' (2020) 32(1) *Ius Ecclesiae* 239.

The feelings, opinions and behaviour of individuals that are a direct expression of religious feeling or beliefs are protected in Italian law by a general principle of confidentiality. While the *Italian Constitution* does not include a specific article protecting the right to confidentiality, this can be derived by interpretation from arts 2 and 3 of the *Constitution*, where confidentiality is seen as one of the inviolable rights of man. But arts 13, 14 and 15 of the *Constitution* also provide support for the principle of confidentiality because it is part of the freedom of the individual and the home, where all forms of communication are protected from disclosure. When these indirect protections of confidentiality and privacy are connected with the interest of the individual believer in confidential communications with ministers of religion as part of the individual's right to religious freedom, it is unlikely that the Italian State would try to interfere with private religious communications except in very serious cases.

Indeed, because of the constitutional value extended to privacy in general and to religious confidentiality in particular, the only way these rights could yield in the face of other important values, would be if those other values were considered to outweigh them in accordance with the so-called 'balancing of values' jurisprudential principle that has been developed by the Italian Constitutional Court.[31] And while the protection of confidentiality may sometimes be outweighed by other

---

31 In Italian constitutional jurisprudence, the balancing of rights has been known and practiced for a long time, as an indispensable tool for the implementation of a pluralist Constitution, which embraces a 'dignitary' conception of rights, which differs – to use language well known in comparative law – from the 'libertarian' one, due to the fact that fundamental rights are never asserted in absolute terms, but are part of a complex constitutional tissue in which other rights and other constitutionally protected interests and goods can legitimately limit their scope. In the *Italian Constitution*, every right is always preached together with its limitation and, in this context, balancing is an interpretative and argumentative technique that allows for the necessary reasonable compromise of a plurality of competing constitutional interests. Indeed, as stated in Constitutional Court judgment No 264 of 2012: '[a]ll the fundamental rights protected by the Constitution are mutually complementary and it is therefore not possible to single out one of them as having absolute precedence over the others. Protection must always be systemic and not split up into a series of uncoordinated and potentially conflicting rules'. See, also, Constitutional Court judgment No 85 of 2013.

values, given the importance which is attributed to freedom of religion under the *Italian Constitution*, it is unlikely that any other value would be found to require the disclosure of any confidential knowledge acquired by a church minister in Italy.

So-called confessional secrecy is also protected at substantive and procedural law levels. As regards substantive law, art 622 of the *Criminal Code* which is entitled 'disclosure of professional secrets', requires the punishment of anyone who discloses knowledge of a secret obtained by reason of his status. Thus, if a minister of religion disclosed a confessional secret without just cause, or used that confidential information for his or her own benefit or for the benefit of others, that minister could be subject to criminal sanction particularly if there was harm to the person who entrusted the secret. But this obligation to respect confidences obtained by reason of ministerial status, does not extend to sensitive information obtained in other ways, as for example by chance, or through discussion with a friend. However, an alleged offence is only punishable on complaint by the injured party.[32]

Under procedural law, the first paragraph of art 200 of the *Code of Criminal Procedure*, states that 'ministers of religious denominations, whose statutes do not conflict with the Italian legal system cannot be obliged to testify about what they have known by reason of their ministry, office or profession, except in cases where they are obliged to report to the judicial authority'.[33] Ministers of religious denominations, therefore, have the right to abstain from any requirement to testify about professional secrets that come to them in their role as ministers of religion. Consistent

---

32 See Roberto Garofoli, *Manuale di diritto penale: Parte speciale* (Neldiritto Editore, 4th ed, 2017) vol 2, 782 et seq.

33 The faculty of abstention is implemented by means of a statement made orally at the hearing, when the judge admonishes the witnesses pursuant to Article 251 and, in any case, no later than the beginning of the testimonial examination. The legislator has not provided for an obligation on the part of the judge to warn the witness of the right to abstain. For a detailed analysis of the crime in question (false information) see, eg, Antonio Balsamo, *'Falsa testimonianza'*, in Giorgio Lattanzi and Ernesto Lupo (eds), *Codice penale: rassegna di giurisprudenza e di dottrina* (Giuffrè, 2005) vol 5 164 et seq; Giovanni Fiandaca and Enzo Musco, *Diritto penale (parte speciale)* (Zanichelli, 5th ed, 2012) vol 1, 381 et seq.

with the respect due to confidentiality and privacy generally under the *Italian Constitution*, this rule, also protects other 'types' of secrets (family, official, state, police) and is part of the evidential code that sets out the framework for discipline of testimony and how matters are proven in court.[34] Article 256 of the same Code which regulates what matters and documents are admissible in court, similarly prevents the admission of documents that would reveal professional secrets and provides that ministers of religion can refuse to hand over documents ordered by the judicial authorities by declaring in writing that the documents at issue concern confidential matters that arose in connection with their office or profession. The *Code of Civil Procedure* thus protects religious confessions whether they were expressed orally or were committed to writing and become documentary.[35]

Article 271 of the *Code of Criminal Procedure* also prohibits the use of interceptions relating to conversations or communications of ministers of religion 'when they concern facts known by reason of their ministry', unless they 'have testified on the same facts or have otherwise disclosed them'. The violation of the rule renders the evidence concerned inadmissible regardless of who raises the issue or when it is raised in the proceeding.[36]

Article 4 of the *Villa Madama Agreement* provides even more specific protection to confessional secrets within the Catholic Church. It states that 'ecclesiastics are not obliged to give magistrates or other authorities information on persons or matters of which they have become aware by reason of their ministry'. This international treaty extends well beyond testimony in court and protects church authorities and ministers from the revelation of any information held by the Church at all, however else

---

34 Article 249 of the *Code of Civil Procedure* expressly refers to the rules of the *Code of Criminal Procedure*, stating that '[t]he provisions of Articles 200, 201 and 202 of the *Code of Criminal Procedure* concerning the right of witnesses to abstain apply to the examination of witnesses'.

35 See Alberto Perlasca, 'La tutela civile e penale delle «notizie» apprese «per ragione del proprio ministero» come applicazione del principio della libertà religiosa' (1998) 11(3) *Quaderni di diritto ecclesiale* 284, 304 et seq.

36 *Code of Criminal Procedure* art 191.

it may have been discovered regardless of the technology and surveillance that may have been involved.

It should be noted that there are several similarities between art 200 of the *Code of Criminal Procedure* which protects confidentiality generally and art 4 of the *1984 Concordat* which protects the Catholic Church in particular. First, both authorise ministers of religion to abstain from giving evidence rather than prohibiting them from giving any particular evidence during the course of an established examination. This provision removes any doubt by preventing the commencement of an examination so that there is no possibility that confidential information might be disclosed accidentally. Previously, art 7 of the *Concordat of 1929* was more rigid and prevented only the admission of testimony that might reveal secrets.

However, there have been extended jurisprudential disputes as to whether the term 'ministers of religious confessions' in art 200 of the *Code of Criminal Procedure* and the term 'ecclesiastic' which is used in art 4 of the *Villa Madama Agreement* mean the same thing. That is, does this semantic difference mean that only Catholic priests are protected under art 4 of the *Villa Madama Agreement* (the *ius tacendi*), or does that protection extend to all Catholic clerics, consecrated persons and even some lay persons even if they are not ordained *in sacris*, if they are invested with certain 'ministerial functions'?[37] Given its exceptional nature, it seems preferable to read the *Villa Madama Agreement* rule more narrowly, limiting its scope to clerics who have care of souls and jurisdiction over the faithful.

The protection of the secrecy of office for ministers of the Catholic faith concerns not only the inviolability of the sacramental seal surrounding confession under canon 983 of the *Code of Canon Law*, but also – and this applies equally to ministers of religion of other religious denominations

---

37 See P M Pisani, '*Il processo penale nelle modificazioni del Concordato tra Italia e Santa Sede*', in Mario Pisani (ed), *Studi in memoria di Pietro Nuvolone* (Giuffrè, 1991) vol II ('*Problemi penalistici di varia attualità. Studi di diritto fallimentare: Altri studi di diritto penale dell'economia*') 149.

– to everything they have learnt in their role as ministers of religion.

On the other hand, what these persons may learn outside their clerical roles is not covered by the official secrecy provided in either the *Villa Madama Agreement* or the *Criminal* and *Civil Codes*. If a question were to arise before a judge as to whether the evidence at issue arose as a matter of professional confidence or not, the judge would have to decide whether the witness was justified in exercising her right to abstain from giving evidence or not.

In other words, as in the case of other professional secrets, the judge must be satisfied that there is a causal link between the information about which the cleric is called to testify and the exercise of his ministry. If the cleric only learned the information as an ordinary citizen or learned it because of a friendship unrelated to his ministry, the cleric will not be able to refuse to testify. The same is true if the information sought to be adduced in court were learned or perceived in an entirely occasional and fortuitous manner, or if the information was provided to the minister for the sole purpose of fraudulently abusing the guarantee of secrecy. In those cases, the minister would not be able to decline to testify either. It has also been concluded that even though paragraph I of art 200 of the *Code of Criminal Procedure* says that the protection of ministerial secrecy does not apply in cases where those ministers have an obligation to report to judicial authority, the obligation placed on private individuals to denounce crime[38] does not apply to ministers of religion if they learned that information professionally, and they can continue to refuse to disclose secrets even when the information has become public knowledge. However, under the second paragraph of art 200 of the *Code of Criminal Procedure*, if a judge has reason to doubt a declaration made by any person claiming exemption from giving testimony in court, he or she can question the exemption claim and order the witness to give evidence

---

38 See Paolo Tonini, *Manuale di procedura penale* (Giuffrè, 2012) 288.

if he or she finds the claim unfounded.[39]

Without wishing to overemphasise the point, despite the authority afforded to the concordat rules, we do not believe they would prevent a judge from checking on exemption claims even in a case involving Catholic priests. While such judicial examination would initially be limited to the external circumstances and would not involve an evaluation of the confessional secret itself unless the judge was satisfied that it was not obtained in professional circumstances, the possibility of such evaluation does dilute the strength of the protection. However, it may be expected that the exercise of such investigative powers by a state magistrate would be exercised with great care. That is because an investigation which extended beyond the 'simple ascertainment of the causal connection between learning of the information and the exercise of the profession' into the internal organisation of a religion, particularly if that religion were the Catholic Church, would be in flagrant contradiction of matters that

---

39 It should be recalled that the Italian State has concluded several agreements pursuant to art 8(III) of the *Constitution*: with the Churches represented by the 'Waldensian Table' (Law No 449 of 11 August 1984); with the Italian Union of the Adventist Churches of the Seventh Day (Law No 516 of 22 November 1988); with the Assemblies of God in Italy (Law No 517 of 22 November 1988); with the Union of Jewish Italian Communities (Law No 101 of 8 March 1989); with the Evangelical Lutheran Church in Italy (Law No 520 of 29 November 1995); with the Holy Orthodox Archdiocese of Italy and the Exarchate of Southern Europe (Law No 126 of 30 July 2012), with the Church of Jesus Christ of Latter-day Saints (Law No 127 of 30 July 2012), the Apostolic Church in Italy (Law No 128 of 30 July 2012); with the Italian Buddhist Union (Law No 245 of 31 December 2012); with the Italian Hindu Union Sanatana Dharma Samgha (Law No 246 of 31 December 2012); with the Soka Gakkai Italian Buddhist Institute (Law No 245 of 28 June 2016); with the Italian Hindu Union Sanatana Dharma Samgha (Law No 246 of 31 December 2012); with the Italian Buddhist Institute Soka Gakkai (Law No 130 of 28 June 2016) and with the association *Chiesa d'Inghilterra* (representing in Italy the Anglican confession 'Church of England') (Bill No 2060 of 2020). In some of them: see Law No 101 of 8 March 1989 art 3; Law No 520 of 29 November 1995 art 4; Law No 126 of 30 July 2012 art 3(2); Law No 127 of 30 July 2012 art 4(4); Law No 128 of 30 July 2012 art 3(2); Law No 245 of 31 December 2012 art 8(2); Law No 246 of 31 December 2012 art 8(2); Law No 130 of 28 June 2016 art 4(3). See also Giuseppe Dalla Torre, *Lezioni di diritto ecclesiastico* (Giappichelli, 6th ed, 2019).

are beyond scrutiny under the *Constitution*.[40]

It is also clear that in a State trial, no distinction can be made between information acquired in a sacramental confession and information obtained in ministry, since the rules protecting confidential religious communications in the *Code of Criminal Procedure* are addressed to ministers of all religious denominations and not only ministers of the Catholic Church, to which, almost exclusively, the *sigillum confessionis* pertains. It is therefore unlikely that religious confidences received professionally in non-Catholic churches will be treated less favourably than those received in confession in the Catholic Church, because such difference would be an invasion of privacy in breach of the religious equality that is now guaranteed under the *Constitution*. That is, to differentiate between the 'types' of secret obtained in different churches would dilute the safeguards that are intended under the *Constitution* for all churches. This is a crucial point.

Finally, like other professionals, members of the clergy are authorised but not obliged to always withhold information learned in confidence. As a matter of personal ethical conviction, a member of the clergy can decide according to his or her conscience, to breach confidence and give testimony voluntarily despite the obligation of secrecy to which he or she is bound pursuant to art 622 of the *Code of Criminal Procedure*. However, any such breach of confidentiality will expose the offender to the sanctions provided by both state and confessional law, and the possibility of civil suit by anyone claiming civil damage following unlawful disclosure of confidence.

---

40 See Geraldina Boni, 'Sigillo sacramentale, segreto ministeriale e obblighi di denun-cia-segnalazione: La ragioni della tutela della riservatezza tra diritto canonico e diritto secolare, in particolare italiano' [2019] (3) JusOnline 31.

VI Conclusion

We therefore affirm, in the light of the Italian historical and legal tradition, that the professional secrecy of priests exists not only for the benefit of the confidant and the priest, but also to relieve the priest of the criminal liability which he could incur under art 622 of the *Criminal Code* if he disclosed confidences reposed in him professionally. The rationale of art 200 of the *Code of Criminal Procedure* does not rest simply on the need to protect the professional from the risk of incrimination, or the confidant from a revelation that would cause him harm. The Constitutional Court has confirmed that professional confidentiality is also justified by the need to safeguard and balance constitutional rights which can be more important than the functional collection of testimonial evidence.[41] Sometimes constitutional balancing identifies values that are more important than the collection of evidence in a criminal investigation.[42]

Italian jurisprudence recognises that the inalienable dignity of a human individual includes both that person's character as a citizen and a believer. The State is obliged to take care of both of these parts of human personality. That is, the implementation of the entire religious freedom of the Italian people including her priests, insists that conscience and religious practice not be trampled upon and abridged to facilitate the passing investigative needs of those who prosecute the commission of crime.

It follows that any limitation of confessional secrecy to protect other important interests including the identification of criminal responsibility for heinous crimes including child sexual abuse, would undermine society's interest in confidentiality. Such limitation may also lead to the harassment of people who confess or confide in good faith and would create debilitating conflicts of loyalty for all ministers of religion. Such limitation would also destabilise the relationship between the order of the Church and that of the State set out in the *Constitution* and would

---

41 See Geraldina Boni, 'Giurisdizione matrimoniale ecclesiastica e poteri autoritativi della magistratura italiana' [2007] (September) *Stato, Chiese e pluralismo confessionale* 14.

42 See Constitutional Court, 8 April 1997, No 87 (1997) XLII *Constitutional Jurisprudence* 883, 883–9.

likely undermine the operation of its 7th article.[43] The limitation of judicial investigative powers caused by the recognition of religious confidentiality in Italian law is thus essential to the protection of the values expressed generally in the *Italian Constitution* and particularly the religious freedom which is granted by art 19.

---

43 See D Milani, *Segreto, libertà religiosa e autonomia confessionale: La protezione delle comunicazioni tra ministro di culto e Fedele* (Eupress FTL, 2008) 186; Angelo Licastro, 'Facoltà di astensione dalla testimonianza e «sacramentale sigillum»: Verso una ridefinizione dei confini del segreto ministeriale?' (2016) 33(3) *Quaderni di diritto e politica ecclesiastica* 901, 910.

5

Mark Hill QC and Christopher Grout

The seal of the confessional, the Church of England, and English law

Abstract

In the canon law of the Church of England, the seal of the confessional is described as inviolable: what is said during the course of the sacrament of penance cannot be disclosed. However, while the canon law may be tolerably clear, there is less clarity as to the extent to which state courts – particularly criminal courts – will uphold the doctrinal imperative of confidentiality. There is no legislative provision in England and Wales for the systematic protection of confidentiality arising from the sacrament of penance. This chapter considers the factors which would be engaged in the event that the seal of the confessional were to be scrutinised in the course of determining the admissibility of evidence in secular criminal proceedings. It is directed primarily at the unique position of clerics of the Church of England whose canon law is a part of English domestic law.

Keywords:

Seal of the confessional – Privilege – Church of England – Canon 113 of the Canons of 1603 – Police and Criminal Evidence Act 1984 (UK) – Article 9 of the European Convention on Human Rights

I Introduction

The sacrament of penance, or confession as it is frequently called, is a well-known and widespread practice within the western Christian church and beyond. In 'Principles of Christian Law',[1] a panel of experts recognises that: 'The seal of the confessional is inviolable, save as may be provided by the law of a church'.[2] The priest must maintain absolute secrecy about anything that a person discloses during the confession. Anything said by the person making their confession in this context should be said with openness before God, and therefore with complete confidence that it will not be repeated or disclosed by the priest under any circumstances.[3] The Church of England's position is to be found in the proviso to canon 113 of the Canons of 1603[4] which 'do straitly charge and admonish [the priest] that he do not at any time reveal and make known to any person whatsoever any crime or offence so committed to his trust and secrecy ... under pain of irregularity'.[5] This chapter seeks to evaluate the extent to which the seal of the confessional can truly be

---

1   Mark Hill and Norman Doe, 'Principles of Christian Law' (2017) 19(2) *Ecclesiastical Law Journal* 138.

2   Ibid 151.

3   This summary is lifted from Church of England, 'The Seal of the Confessional' (Interim Statement, 8 May 2019).

4   There was a wholesale redrafting of the Canons of the Church of England in the 1960s, leading to an entirely new 'code' being approved by the Convocations of Canterbury and York and receiving royal licence. It was intended to include a revised canon dealing with the seal of the confessional. However, advice was apparently received that a new canon in this form was unlikely to receive the royal licence, and, rather than risk a refusal, it was decided to retain the proviso to the old canon 113, whilst repealing the rest of the code of 1603. The reason why advice was given that the draft new canon might not receive the royal licence is that it was questioned whether it was in accordance with the law. The implication of the canon being passed in the absolute terms as drafted was that the clergy have the privilege of not being obliged to disclose information received in the confessional, if called to give evidence in court. It was thought that whilst that privilege might have existed in the past, the modern law of evidence had evolved without reference to it, and that it was, at the least, doubtful whether the privilege existed under the civil (as opposed to ecclesiastical) law. Rather than put the point to the test, it was decided to retain the status quo: see Church of England, *Report of the Seal of the Confessional Working Party* (March 2018) 31 [3.10.1] et seq.

5   Proviso to canon 113 of the 1603 Canons of the Church of England.

characterised as 'inviolable' in English law, with particular reference to the admissibility of evidence in secular proceedings of anything said or done in the course of the sacrament of penance. The discussion focuses on the Church of England[6] and the criminal law of England and Wales.[7]

II The Position of the Church of England

As Professor Norman Doe observes in his seminal work, *The Legal Framework of the Church of England*, 'The law of the Church of England provides for both public and private confession. Baptized persons have a canonical duty to make general confession in the liturgical services of the church, followed by absolution which can be pronounced only by a priest'.[8] In addition to this form of 'liturgical confession', an individual may make private confession to God in one of two ways; alone or in the presence of a priest in auricular confession.[9] Where the latter occurs, it must not be as a result of compulsion (by the priest) and no limit is placed on the frequency of confession sought by the person concerned.[10] As to the apparent inviolability of the seal of the confessional, the proviso to canon 113 of the 1603 Canons states:

> Provided always, that if any man confess his secret and hidden sins to the minister, for the unburdening of his conscience, and to receive spiritual consolation and ease of mind from him; we do not in any way bind the said minister by this our Constitution, but do straitly charge and admonish him, that he do not at any time reveal and make known to any person whatsoever any crime or offence so committed to his trust and secrecy (except they be

---

6 For convenience, save where the context indicates otherwise, references to 'the Church' are to the Church of England.

7 Cf the Roman Catholic position under canon 983 §1 of the 1983 *Code of Canon Law*, which reads: 'The sacramental seal is inviolable; therefore it is absolutely forbidden for a confessor to betray in any way a penitent in words or in any manner and for any reason'. See also John P Beal, James A Coriden and Thomas J Green (eds), *New Commentary on the Code of Canon Law* (Paulist Press, 2000).

8 Norman Doe, *The Legal Framework of the Church of England: A Critical Study in a Comparative Context* (Clarendon Press, 1996) 349.

9 Ibid 350. See also canon B29 of the Canons of the Church of England.

10 *Rector and Churchwardens of Capel St Mary, Suffolk v Packard* [1927] P 289, 301.

such crimes as by the laws of this realm his own life may be called into question for concealing the same), under pain of irregularity.[11]

An analysis of the proviso to canon 113 is important.[12] The minister who hears the confession is not 'at any time' to reveal to 'any person whatsoever' any 'crime or offence' imparted to him during the course of the confession. An exception exists insofar as 'they be such crimes as by the laws of this realm his own life may be called into question for concealing the same'. The exception appears to be a narrow one which compels the minister to reveal what he has been told if it is the type of crime concealment of which could itself constitute a criminal offence[13] for which the lawful punishment is execution. Whatever the position in 1603,[14] the death penalty in England and Wales has been abolished,[15] hence the exception is of no effect.[16]

---

11 This is the only segment of the 1603 Canons to survive the wholesale review and re-articulation of the Canons of the Church of England in the 1960s.

12 See the observations of Colin Podmore, 'The Seal of the Confessional in the Church of England: Historical, Legal and Liturgical Perspectives' (Speech, Bishop of Richborough's Initial Ministerial Education Session, 14 November 2016) 5 where he observed that the words 'this constitution' featured in the provisos of two other canons (LXIX and LXXVIII). He concludes:

It looks as if the proviso may have been drafted hastily as an after-thought, probably after discussion with the ministers of the Crown, and for that reason was not very precisely drafted. The sense must be that the permission given to the clergy in the main body of the canon to report the crimes of their people to the Ordinary does not apply in the case of sins disclosed in the confessional: at 5.

13 At the time, it was the offence of treason that was probably in mind, when the safety of the realm was in jeopardy.

14 There is some debate as to the precise position which pertained at this time. In Rupert DH Bursell, 'The Seal of the Confessional' (1990) 2(7) *Ecclesiastical Law Journal* 84, 88, the author comments that the exception contained within the proviso was 'new to the law and its meaning is obscure. Indeed it is possible that it has no meaning at all'. He notes that during the trial of Henry Garnet for complicity in the Gunpowder Plot, Sir Edward Coke, then Attorney-General, opined that the information that had come to Garnet's knowledge ought to have been disclosed at common law – it being *crimen laese Majestatis* – though no authority is cited for this proposition.

15 See especially *Murder (Abolition of the Death Penalty) Act 1965* (UK) s 1; *Crime and Disorder Act 1998* (UK) s 36.

16 Some argue that that the existence of the exception argues against the seal of the confessional being inviolable as the proviso to the 1603 canon specified a lawful circumstance in which it was required to be broken: see, for example, Christopher Grout, 'The Seal of the Confessional and the Criminal Law of England and Wales' (2020) 22(2) *Ecclesiastical Law Journal* 138, 140.

An *Act of the Convocation of Canterbury* of 1959[17] declared:

> That this House reaffirms as an essential principle of Church doctrine that if any person confess his secret and hidden sin to a priest for the unburdening of his conscience, and to receive spiritual consolation and absolution from him, such priest is strictly charged that he do not at any time reveal or make known to any person whatsoever any sin so committed to his trust and secrecy.

The *Act of Convocation* of 1959 makes express reference to the penitent seeking 'absolution', whereas this is implicit in the seventeenth century language of the proviso to canon 113. The *Act of Convocation* refers to any 'sin' so committed to the minister's trust and secrecy, whereas the proviso to canon 113 refers to 'any crime or offence so committed'. Little, if anything, turns on these minor differences: the language of the canon prevails due to its status as law, something which the *Act of Convocation* lacks.[18]

A Guidelines for the Professional Conduct of the Clergy

The Church of England has published *Guidelines for the Professional Conduct of the Clergy* (the '*Guidelines*'),[19] the primary aims of which are:

- to encourage the clergy – deacons, priests and bishops – to aspire to the highest possible standards of conduct throughout a lifetime of ministry;

- to identify certain basic minimum standards of behaviour;

- to seek to ensure the welfare and the protection of individuals and

---

17 For the status of Acts of Convocation as a matter of ecclesiastical law, see Mark Hill, *Ecclesiastical Law* (Oxford University Press, 4th ed, 2018) [1.34], citing *Bland v Archdeacon of Cheltenham* [1971] 3 WLR 706, 713: Acts of Convocation are considered 'guidelines for pastoral work, based on sound Anglican doctrine'. Such Acts are not law per se but have 'great moral force as the considered judgment of the highest and ancient synod of the province'.

18 *Bland v Archdeacon of Cheltenham* [1971] 3 WLR 706.

19 Church of England, *Guidelines for the Professional Conduct of the Clergy* (Church House Publishing, rev edition, 2015). Such guidelines are, at best, quasi-legislation or 'soft law', subservient to ecclesiastical law properly so defined: Mark Hill, *Ecclesiastical Law* (Oxford University Press, 4th ed, 2018) [1.34].

groups with whom the clergy work, and of the clergy and their families;

- to provide safe and effective boundaries for clerical ministry; [and]

- to encourage personal and corporate ministerial development.[20]

Section 3 of the *Guidelines* is headed 'Reconciliation', and paragraph 3.5 provides:

> A clear distinction must be made between pastoral conversations and a confession that is made in the context of the ministry of absolution. Where such a confession is to be made both the priest and the penitent should be clear that that is the case. If a penitent makes a confession with the intention of receiving absolution the priest is forbidden (by the unrepealed Proviso to Canon 113 of the Code of 1603) to reveal or make known to any person what has been confessed. This requirement of absolute confidentiality applies even after the death of the penitent.

The words 'forbidden' and 'absolute confidentiality' are unambiguous. The *Guidelines* are explicit that in circumstances where the penitent has disclosed a serious crime, the obligation on the priest is to require the penitent to report their conduct to the police or other statutory authority. If the penitent refuses, the priest 'should' withhold absolution.[21] Breaking the seal is not an option.[22]

---

20 Church of England, *Guidelines for the Professional Conduct of the Clergy* (Church House Publishing, rev edition, 2015) 1.

21 Ibid 7 [3.6].

22 Indeed, guideline 3.8 goes on to provide: 'However confidentiality extends far beyond the specific situation of the ministry of absolution. People have to be able to trust clergy with their stories, their fears, and especially their confidences. The duty of confidentiality relating to the ministry of absolution sets a standard for our ministry against which all other instances should be set and judged. Those to whom we minister must know that they can depend upon us not to disclose information which they have shared with us in confidence': Church of England, *Guidelines for the Professional Conduct of the Clergy* (Church House Publishing, rev edition, 2015) 7 [3.8].

B Report of the Seal of the Confessional Working Party

A working party was set up in 2014 by the Archbishops' Council with the aim of undertaking theological and legal work to enable the Archbishops' Council and the House of Bishops to review the purpose and effect of the unrepealed proviso to canon 113. The working party also considered whether the canon should be amended. Its report was published in March 2018.[23] The working party's legal analysis of the proviso to canon 113 concluded that a priest's duty of confidentiality under it was 'absolute'.[24] The report opined that

> It is the case that a priest of the Church of England is theoretically in a stronger position than any other claimant to a privileged status. All others rely on the ethics or rules of their profession; this includes Roman Catholic priests, because the Catholic Code of Canon Law has no legal status in England.[25]

The working party recognised the argument that 'whilst that privilege might have existed in the past, the modern law of evidence had evolved without reference to it, and that it was, at the least, doubtful whether the privilege existed under the civil (as opposed to ecclesiastical) law'.[26] There was, however, no discussion of the statutory framework that applies in secular proceedings.

III Two Common Misapprehensions

There are two common misapprehensions perpetuated by commentators on the seal of the confessional and it is important to identify these clearly before proceeding with this chapter. The first relates to the status of the canon law of the Church of England and the second derives from the failure to differentiate between the sacrament of penance and confidential communications more generally.

---

23 Church of England, *Report of the Seal of the Confessional Working Party* (March 2018).

24 Ibid 29 [3.8.4].

25 Ibid 31 [3.9.7].

26 Ibid 32 [3.10.4].

A The status of the Canon Law of the Church of England

As a consequence of its origins and history, the Church of England, uniquely amongst religious organisations in England, is established by law and regulated by primary legislation.[27] The ecclesiastical law of the Church of England is part of English law. In contrast, the internal regulation of other faith communities[28] is not the law of the land. The power to legislate by canon now vests in the General Synod.[29] Before 1970, it was exercised on a provincial basis by each of the Convocations of Canterbury and York.[30] The royal assent and licence is required for the making, executing and promulging of any canon, and no canon may be made which is contrary or repugnant to the royal prerogative, or the customs, laws or statutes of the realm.[31] The corollary to this latter proposition is that in the event that there is a conflict between a canon and a statute then the latter will prevail. This is a matter to which we will return later.

B General duties of confidentiality

There is an expectation that clergy will treat information imparted to them with discretion and that confidences will be respected. Paragraph 3.5 of the *Guidelines* expressly states that 'a clear distinction must be made between pastoral conversations and a confession that is made in the context of the ministry of absolution'. Paragraph 3.8 notes:

---

27 For a full discussion of the meaning and effects of establishment, see Mark Hill, *Ecclesiastical Law* (Oxford University Press, 4th ed, 2018) chs 1 and 2.

28 Including Sharia Law for Muslims, the Torah for Jews, the Roman Catholic Code of Canon Law and the various constitutions and governing instruments of other Christian traditions, see Norman Doe, *Comparative Religious Law: Judaism, Christianity and Islam* (Cambridge University Press, 2018).

29 *Synodical Government Measure 1969* (Church of England) s 1(1), (3), (5), sch 1 para 1, sch 2 art 6(a)(ii).

30 Ibid s 1(2). Canon H1(2) of the Canons of the Church of England preserves the right of the Convocations to meet separately for the purpose of considering matters concerning the Church of England and making provision for such matters by appropriate instrument.

31 *Submission of the Clergy Act 1533*, 25 Hen 8, c 19, ss 1, 3, applied by *Synodical Government Measure 1969* (Church of England) s 1(3).

However confidentiality extends far beyond the specific situation of the ministry of absolution. People have to be able to trust clergy with their stories, their fears, and especially their confidences. The duty of confidentiality relating to the ministry of absolution sets a standard for our ministry against which all other instances should be set and judged. Those to whom we minister must know that they can depend upon us not to disclose information which they have shared with us in confidence.

Much of the commentary on the seal of the confessional within the Church of England needs to be read with caution because (i) it fails to appreciate that the duty of non-disclosure is rooted in English law, not merely clerical practice and (ii) it wrongly elides the sacrament of penance with wider expectations of clerical confidentiality. Only when the sui generis position of Church of England clergy administering the sacrament of penance is fully understood can the matter be properly be addressed. Much academic comment and judicial observation is deficient because of the operation of either or both of these two misapprehensions.

IV Admissibility of Evidence in the Secular Courts

The competence and compellability of individuals to give evidence in secular criminal courts is uncontentious. Competence refers to the capability of an individual to appear before a criminal court as a witness. The matter is dealt with succinctly by virtue of s 53(1) of the *Youth Justice and Criminal Evidence Act 1999* (UK). It provides that '[a]t every stage in criminal proceedings all persons are (whatever their age) competent to give evidence.'

There are two statutory exceptions to this rule,[32] neither of which apply in respect of a priest. A witness is compellable if he or she

---

32 A person is not competent if it appears to the court that he is (i) unable to understand questions put to him as a witness and (ii) unable to give answers to such questions which can be understood. Further, a person charged in criminal proceedings is not competent to give evidence in the proceedings for the prosecution.

may lawfully be required to give evidence.[33] Most witnesses who are competent can be compelled to give evidence,[34] and their attendance at court can be secured by means of a witness summons.[35] Thus, a priest is competent to give evidence in criminal proceedings, is compellable to do so, and may be brought to court by means of a witness summons. The crucial question, however, is whether a Church of England priest may decline to answer specific questions about matters covered by the seal of the confessional. As Hill observes, 'An Anglican priest is in a different position from a priest of another denomination, since the duty of confidentiality which attaches to him is part of the law of the land'.[36]

In his article on this subject,[37] Grout quoted the foregoing excerpt

---

33 See 'Competence and Compellability', *The Crown Prosecution Service* (Web Page, 24 July 2018).

34 The only exception relates to spouses and civil partners who are only compellable to give evidence against their spouse or partner in limited circumstances. See also David Ormerod and David Perry (eds) *Blackstone's Criminal Practice 2019* (Oxford University Press, 2018) 2557: 'The general rule as to compellability is that all competent witnesses are compellable'. The exception for spouses and civil partners is to be found in s 80 of the *Police and Criminal Evidence Act 1984* (UK). Compellability appears to be a matter of common law, rather than statute.

35 Section 2 of the *Criminal Procedure (Attendance of Witnesses) Act 1965* (UK) provides that the Crown Court has the power to issue a witness summons where it is satisfied that (a) a person is likely to be able to give evidence likely to be material evidence, or produce any document or thing likely to be material evidence, for the purpose of any criminal proceedings before the Crown Court, and (b) it is in the interests of justice to issue a summons under this section to secure the attendance of that person to give evidence or to produce the document or thing. A person who, without just excuse, disobeys a witness summons is guilty of contempt of court and may be punished accordingly: at s 3. See also *R v Harish Popat* [2008] EWCA Crim 1921; David Ormerod and David Perry (eds) *Blackstone's Criminal Practice 2019* (Oxford University Press, 2018) 1857: 'The existence of "just excuse" will not be lightly inferred. Witnesses are required to submit even to very substantial inconvenience in their business and private lives'.

36 Mark Hill, *Ecclesiastical Law* (Oxford University Press, 4th ed, 2018) 156. Cf the position taken by Norman Doe, *The Legal Framework of the Church of England: A Critical Study in a Comparative Context* (Clarendon Press, 1996) 355 n 6: 'With regard to the Church of England ... the prohibition against disclosure is not strictly and clearly binding and could not therefore be presented as a duty arising under the law of the land'.

37 Christopher Grout, 'The Seal of the Confessional and the Criminal Law of England and Wales' (2020) 22(2) *Ecclesiastical Law Journal* 138.

from Hill and then ventured the following:

> Whilst it is unquestionable that canons form part of the law
> of the land[38] it is equally beyond doubt that where a canon
> contradicts the terms of a statute, the latter will prevail. As the
> Court of Appeal observed in *R v Dibdin*:
>
> > If there is anything in the Canons inconsistent with the
> > statute law the Canons are so far invalid and of no force
> > or effect.[39]
>
> Accordingly, insofar as there may be a conflict between Canon
> 113 and the statutes regulating criminal proceedings, the latter
> will prevail.

Grout did not identify the conflict which he perceived between canon 113 and what he styled 'the statutes regulating criminal proceedings'. In particular, he did not identify any statute law which purported to limit or remove the nature and scope of the seal of the confessional as articulated in the proviso to canon 113. What he said was this,

> Does there exist a conflict between Canon 113 and secular
> legislation? On the face of it, no, as nothing in Canon 113
> prohibits a priest, *per se*, from being called as a witness in criminal
> proceedings. The only time a conflict might arise is where,
> having been called as a witness, the priest is asked questions
> about what took place under the seal of the confessional.[40]

Hill's position is that the law concerning the seal of the confessional is supplemental to ([and] not in conflict with) the procedural provisions regarding the compellability of witnesses. A solicitor, for example, may be competent and compellable to give evidence, but can still refuse to answer questions which would breach legal professional privilege. The common law on the compellability of witnesses does not override the

---

38 In this regard see Mark Hill, *Ecclesiastical Law* (Oxford University Press, 4th ed, 2018) 13 n 27; Norman Doe, *The Legal Framework of the Church of England: A Critical Study in a Comparative Context* (Clarendon Press, 1996) 73 n 6.

39 [1910] P 57, 120. See also *Calvert v Gardiner* [2002] EWHC 1394 (QB).

40 Christopher Grout, 'The Seal of the Confessional and the Criminal Law of England and Wales' (2020) 22(2) *Ecclesiastical Law Journal* 138, 144.

long-established practice of protecting privileged communications between lawyer and client. Equally, the compellability of a priest to give evidence does not, without more, override the express legal obligation under Church of England canon law which makes the seal of the confessional inviolable. These are matters to be worked through in the exercise of judicial discretion. Grout's position is that matters relating to the competence and compellability of witnesses need to be considered in light of common law developments. As will be discussed below, the common law has consistently recognised the privileged nature of the relationship between lawyer and client; the same cannot be said in respect of priest and penitent.

V The Discretion to Exclude Evidence

In the briefest of footnotes in his practitioner text, *Ecclesiastical Law*, Hill comments in passing that 'it is likely that a trial judge would exclude evidence of a confession made to a priest',[41] citing ss 76, 78 and 82(3) of the *Police and Criminal Evidence Act 1984* (UK). Under that legislation, a 'confession' is defined as including 'any statement wholly or partly adverse to the person who made it, whether made to a person in authority or not and whether made in words or otherwise'.[42] Whilst this definition is sufficiently broad to encompass adverse statements made to a priest, the legislation is silent on the inviolable nature of the seal of the confessional.

Under s 76(1) 'a confession made by an accused person may be given in evidence against him in so far as it is relevant to any matter in issue in the proceedings and is not excluded by the court in pursuance of this

---

41 Mark Hill, *Ecclesiastical Law* (Oxford University Press, 4th ed, 2018) 156 n 27.
42 *Police and Criminal Evidence Act 1984* (UK) s 82(1).

section'.[43] The section is permissive in nature,[44] and is part of a suite of provisions contained in the 1984 Act designed to prevent misconduct by police officers in the investigation of crime. Thus, the exclusionary provisions speak of a confession being obtained by oppression, which would not be the case when a penitent voluntarily seeks the sacrament of penance.[45]

Section 78(1) of the *Police and Criminal Evidence Act 1984* (UK) is much more widely drafted and provides:

> In any proceedings the court may refuse to allow evidence on which the prosecution proposes to rely to be given if it appears to the court that, having regard to all the circumstances, including the circumstances in which the evidence was obtained, the admission of the evidence would have such an adverse effect on the fairness of the proceedings that the court ought not to admit it.

Section 78 is a broad discretionary power such that the Court of Appeal will not lightly interfere with its exercise by the trial judge.[46] Whilst the judge must have regard to 'all the circumstances', the test to be applied is whether or not the admission of the evidence would have an adverse effect on the 'fairness of the proceedings'. Grout points to instances where, notwithstanding the impropriety in the obtaining of the evidence,

---

43 The exclusionary provisions are where the confession was or may have been obtained (a) by oppression of the person who made it or (b) in consequence of anything said or done which was likely, in the circumstances existing at the time, to render any such confession unreliable: *Police and Criminal Evidence Act 1984* (UK) s 76(2). 'Oppression' is defined as including 'torture, inhuman or degrading treatment, and the use or threat of violence (whether or not amounting to torture)': *Police and Criminal Evidence Act 1984* (UK) s 76(8).

44 Note the use of the word 'may'.

45 The prospect of a priest coercing a penitent to confess is highly remote.

46 See *R v Jelen* (1989) 90 Cr App R 456; *R v Quinn* [1995] 1 Cr App R 480; *R v Dures* [1997] 2 Cr App R 247.

its admission may not affect the fairness of the proceedings,[47] including the Court of Appeal judgment in R v Quinn where Lord Lane CJ observed that

> The function of the judge in exercising his discretion under section 78 of the *Police and Criminal Evidence Act 1984* is to protect the fairness of the proceedings. Normally proceedings are fair if a jury hears all the relevant evidence which either side wishes to place before it.[48]

The third relevant section of the *Police and Criminal Evidence Act 1984* (UK) is s 82(3), which provides as follows that '[n]othing in this Part of this Act shall prejudice any power of a court to exclude evidence (whether by preventing questions from being put or otherwise) at its discretion.'

This section preserves the power of a court at common law to exclude evidence at its discretion, albeit it is less likely to arise in consequence of the operation of the statutory provisions introduced in 1984. At common law, the concern of the court focused on the interests of justice, and whether the prejudicial effect of the evidence outweighed its probative value.[49]

At this point, the two authors of this chapter find themselves in respectful disagreement. Grout puts his argument in the following terms:

> Accordingly, if a criminal court was considering whether or not

---

47 Christopher Grout, 'The Seal of the Confessional and the Criminal Law of England and Wales' (2020) 22(2) *Ecclesiastical Law Journal* 138, 147. As the Court of Appeal observed in *R v Chalkley* [1998] QB 848, 874: 'Just as the labelling of conduct as unlawful does not necessarily change its character for this purpose, nor does the application to it of the epithet "oppressive" automatically override the fundamental test of fairness in admission of evidence. Oppressive conduct, depending on its degree and/or its actual or possible effect, may or may not affect the fairness of admitting particular evidence. The test for the judge was what was fair "having regard to all the circumstances", and the single criterion for this court is the safety of the convictions'. The analogy with impropriety in obtaining evidence does not readily translate into considerations regarding English law on the inviolability of the seal of the confessional.

48 [1990] Crim LR 581, 582.

49 Of passing interest is *R v Griffin* (1853) 6 Cox 219, in which Alderson B stated that 'conversations' between a chaplain to a workhouse and a prisoner (which were not in the context of the sacrament of penance) 'ought not to be given in evidence'.

to exclude under this section evidence of a confession made to a priest, it is submitted that the objection of the priest - whether on canonical grounds or otherwise - would not be a relevant factor. Whilst the court would have regard to the 'circumstances' in which the evidence was obtained, the critical factor remains the fairness of the proceedings. It is difficult to see how the fairness of the proceedings could be adversely affected by admitting evidence which was not only relevant but also highly likely to be probative.[50]

Hill, on the other hand, is of the opinion that the matter cannot be disposed of quite as peremptorily as this. First, Grout refers to the 'objection' of the priest, but this is to mischaracterise the position. It is not merely a clerical objection,[51] but a clear provision of English law which compels the upholding of the inviolability of seal of the confessional. Secondly, and perhaps of greater significance, are the statutory human rights considerations which inform the exercise of judicial discretion, and which are not mentioned at all in Grout's analysis, still less applied. At the time the *Police and Criminal Evidence Act 1984* (UK) was drafted, procedural fairness was largely a matter of common law. Since the passing of the *Human Rights Act 1998* (UK),[52] public authorities (which include criminal courts) are under a statutory duty to comply with the provisions of the *European Convention on Human Rights*.[53] It follows that the Crown Court, when considering the admissibility of matters revealed in the sacrament of penance, would be acting unlawfully if it took a decision which was incompatible with a *Convention* right. The right to a fair trial is secured under art 6, but in addition art 9 provides as follows:

(1)   Everyone has the right to freedom of thought, conscience and

---

50 Christopher Grout, 'The Seal of the Confessional and the Criminal Law of England and Wales' (2020) 22(2) *Ecclesiastical Law Journal* 138, 147.

51 As might perhaps be the case of a Roman Catholic priest, or any cleric other than a priest of the established Church of England, for whom the obligation to observe the seal of the confessional is a primary obligation of English law.

52 *Human Rights Act 1998* (UK) s 6(1) provides: 'It is unlawful for a public authority to act in a way which is incompatible with a Convention right'; and s 6(3) continues 'In this section "public authority" includes ... a court or tribunal'.

53 *Convention for the Protection of Human Rights and Fundamental Freedoms*, opened for signature 4 November 1950, 213 UNTS 221 (entered into force 3 September 1953) ('*European Convention on Human Rights*').

religion; this right includes freedom to change his religion or belief and freedom, either alone or in community with others and in public or private, to manifest his religion or belief, in worship, teaching, practice and observance.

(2)   Freedom to manifest one's religion or beliefs shall be subject only to such limitations as are prescribed by law and are necessary in a democratic society in the interests of public safety, for the protection of public order, health or morals, or for the protection of the rights and freedoms of others.[54]

The suggestion that the established status of the Church of England precludes its various emanations[55] from relying on the freedom of religion provisions of art 9 was roundly rejected by the House of Lords in *Parochial Church Council of Aston Cantlow v Wallbank.*[56] A trial judge when considering an application to admit in evidence under the provisions of the *Police and Criminal Evidence Act 1984* (UK), matters revealed in a confession, will need to consider whether violating the seal of the confessional would be compatible with the rights of the priest, the confessor and the institutional Church of England[57] under art 9 of the *Convention.* There are no reported cases on the point,[58] but it would be a brave judge who directed the admission into evidence of matters covered by the seal of the confessional, as it could engage multiple violations of art 9, such a ruling being incompatible with the penitent's manifestation of his or her religion, the cleric's manifestation of his or her religion; and the freedom of the Church of England more generally to determine its worship, teaching, practice and observance.

Grout's response to this analysis is as follows. First, it is undoubtedly right to point to the sui generis nature of the Church of England, insofar as it is established by law and its ecclesiastical law forms part of the law of the land. Nevertheless, it is telling that even the working

---

54 Ibid art 9.
55 The Church of England itself has no juridic personality.
56 [2004] 1 AC 546.
57 The right is both individual and associational.
58 Hence the measured and tentative tone of the brief footnote in Mark Hill, *Ecclesiastical Law* (Oxford University Press, 4th ed, 2018).

party set up by the Archbishops' Council to report on the seal of the confessional was hesitant to attach much weight to this. It described the Church as being 'theoretically'[59] in a stronger position than any other claimant to a privileged status. It went on to cite the advice of the Legal Advisory Commission which had opined that 'if a priest with knowledge received in the circumstances described in canon 113 is summoned to give evidence in Court, he or she should seek legal advice, if possible, and should certainly claim privilege, even though this might not be upheld'.[60] Moreover, as noted above, the working party also recognised the argument that 'whilst that privilege might have existed in the past, the modern law of evidence had evolved without reference to it, and that it was, at the least, doubtful whether the privilege existed under the civil (as opposed to ecclesiastical) law'.[61]

It is unsurprising that both the working party and the Legal Advisory Commission were cautious in their approach to the alleged privileged status of things said during the sacrament of penance. Judicial utterances that do exist on the broader subject of privileged and confidential communications (the two being very different) tend to suggest that no such privilege exists.

As to art 9 considerations, Grout now accepts Hill's argument that the art 9 rights of the penitent, the priest, and the Church of England will be engaged in the event that a court is considering whether to admit evidence of things said during the course of confession. However, Grout suggests that if the proposed evidence is both relevant and probative, it would not be in the interests of justice to refuse to admit it simply because the various parties' art 9 rights are engaged. The freedom to manifest one's religion or beliefs is a qualified right and, as such, may be

---

59 Church of England, *Report of the Seal of the Confessional Working Party* (March 2018) 31 [3.9.7].

60 'Clergy: Confidentiality' in Legal Advisory Commission of the General Synod, *Legal Opinions Concerning the Church of England* (Church House Publishing, 8th ed, 2007) [33].

61 Church of England, *Report of the Seal of the Confessional Working Party* (March 2018) 32 [3.10.4].

limited in accordance with art 9(2) of the *Convention*. In the context of a criminal trial, the rights of the victim (or complainant) and witnesses also need to be considered, as does the wider public interest in ensuring that those who are guilty of criminal conduct are convicted following a fair trial. In Grout's view, it would be extraordinary if a judge permitted the Church of England to rely upon its 'theoretically' stronger position to argue against the admission of such evidence, an argument not open to other organised religions, no matter how well established their respective doctrines may be. Such nuances have no place in a modern system for the fair administration of criminal justice.

Hill welcomes Grout's concession that art 9 is engaged and would need to be considered,[62] but does not share the broad-brush manner in which Grout speculates a judge would dispose of the matter. It is inapt to dismiss the legal status of Church of England canon law as a mere 'nuance' nor to prioritise general criminal justice considerations over actual violations of the art 9 rights of priest and penitent to manifest their religion, not merely in accordance with their doctrinal belief but also in conformity with the law of the land. Grout also appears to overlook s 13 of the *Human Rights Act 1998* (UK) which provides:

> **13 Freedom of thought, conscience and religion**
>
> (1)   If a court's determination of any question arising under this Act might affect the exercise by a religious organisation (itself or its members collectively) of the Convention right to freedom of thought, conscience and religion, *it must have particular regard to the importance of that right.*
>
> (2)   In this section 'court' includes a tribunal.[63]

It would hardly be 'extraordinary', to adopt Grout's rhetoric, for judges to consider themselves constrained by the clear statutory duty to have particular regard to the importance of the exercise of the *Convention*

---

62 A consideration which did not feature in Christopher Grout, 'The Seal of the Confessional and the Criminal Law of England and Wales' (2020) 22(2) *Ecclesiastical Law Journal* 138, and to which no discussion was addressed.

63 (Emphasis added).

right to freedom of religion rather than to trivialize such right as a mere peccadillo or nuance. Hill's disagreement with Grout lies in the high-level absolutism in which Grout put his case in his original article, and (to a lesser degree) in the more mellowed manner in which it is now advanced. In the absence of transcripts from rulings where judges have addressed and determined these issues, it is impossible to express a concluded view upon the likely disposal. Hill still maintains that the issue is more complex than Grout appears to suggest, and that the matter is not amenable to the easy resolution or the hyperbolic language which Grout is inclined to adopt.

VI Privilege or Confidentiality?

As noted above, the proviso to canon 113 of the 1603 Canons was retained due a reluctance to test the proposition that the absolute terms of the proposed replacement canon would lead to clergy having a privilege not to disclose information imparted in the confessional. A dissonance was noted between the somewhat anachronistic content of canon 113 and the manner in which the modern law of evidence had developed.[64] But does the inviolability of the seal of the confessional, as expressed in the proviso to canon 113, create a legal privilege or a duty of confidence or some other form of legal protection to maters revealed during the sacrament of penance? As Bartlet observes:

> Unlike privilege, confidentiality does not in itself exclude evidence from being admissible in court, and a court may compel disclosure where it considers it necessary for the fair disposal of a case ... While it admits of exceptions, privilege offers far stronger protection against disclosure than confidentiality.[65]

Bartlet goes on to observe that

---

64 Church of England, *Report of the Seal of the Confessional Working Party* (March 2018) 32 [3.10.4], discussed above.

65 Michael Bartlet, 'Mediation Secrets "In the Shadow of the Law"' (2015) 34(1) *Civil Justice Quarterly* 112, 113.

Confidentiality is essential to a range of fiduciary relationships including the medical profession, the priesthood, a relationship between a journalist and his source and may give rise to equitable remedies. It is only in the case of the relationship between lawyer and client however where such confidences are exchanged in the context of a professional relationship that this is given the protection of privilege.[66]

That the relationship between lawyer and client is 'special' in this regard is recognised by case law; indeed, save where it has been waived by the client, the privilege is regarded as 'absolute'.[67] As for the priest-penitent relationship, as Elliott notes, 'there is a paucity of clear authority on the matter, but such as there is is against the existence of any privilege'.[68]

These observations, though weighty, need to be read with caution and applied with care. First, as already noted, many commentators fail to appreciate the unique nature of the seal of the confessional within the Church of England as a duty applied by English domestic law (as opposed to clerical practice). All too often, it is elided with Roman Catholic practice, which has no underpinning in English law (as opposed to canon law). In R v Hay[69] a Roman Catholic priest was committed for contempt of court after he declined to answer questions as to whom he had received a stolen watch from, saying that to do so would 'violate the laws of the Church, as well as the natural laws'.[70]

Secondly, the observations do not stop to ask why there is a paucity of authority, for which there is a simple answer. By the very nature of auricular confession, only two persons are present: the penitent and the

---

66 Ibid 115.
67 *Three Rivers DC v Bank of England (No 6)* [2005] 1 AC 610, 646 (Lord Scott). See also *R v Derby Magistrates Court Ex parte P* [1996] 1 AC 487.
68 DW Elliott, 'An Evidential Privilege for Priest-Penitent Communications' (1995) 3(16) *Ecclesiastical Law Journal* 272, 273. See also David Ormerod and David Perry (eds) *Blackstone's Criminal Practice 2019* (Oxford University Press, 2018) 2664: 'In the case of communications between priest and penitent, there is slender authority in favour of the existence of a privilege'.
69 (1860) 2 F & F 4.
70 Cited in Rupert DH Bursell, 'The Seal of the Confessional' (1990) 2(7) *Ecclesiastical Law Journal* 84, 92.

priest. It is highly unlikely that the penitent would disclose what was said, as this would be contrary to his or her interests; and it is equally unlikely that the priest would do so as the inviolability of the seal is so fundamental to their ministry. Based upon these observations, there is no basis to conclude definitively that there is no evidential privilege attaching to the sacrament of penance in the Church of England. The best that can be said is that the matter is yet to be authoritatively tested.[71]

The case of *R v Kent*[72] where a magistrate seemingly made no attempt to compel an Anglican clergyman who refused to disclose what had been said to him under the seal of the confessional attracted some media publicity. Lord Westbury, then Lord Chancellor, spoke in a debate in the House of Lords asserting:

> There can be no doubt that in a suit or criminal proceedings a clergyman of the Church of England is not privileged so as to decline to answer a question which is put to him for the purposes of justice, on the ground that his answer would reveal something that has been made known to him in confession. A witness is compelled to answer every such question.[73]

Westbury was speaking more as a politician that a lawyer, and his opinion has no legal authority, making no reference to the obligation on a priest, as a matter of English law, not to disclose matters arising during the sacrament of penance. Lord Denning MR in *Attorney-General v Mulholland*,[74] observed, but this was long before the *Human Rights Act 1998* (UK) came into force making freedom of religion a matter directly justiciable in domestic courts,

> The only profession that I know which is given a privilege from disclosing information to a court of law is the legal profession and then it is not the privilege of the lawyer, but of the client. Take the clergyman, the banker or the medical man. None of these is

---

71 Note the miscellany of cases cited by Rupert DH Bursell, 'The Seal of the Confessional' (1990) 2(7) *Ecclesiastical Law Journal* 84.
72 Cited in Bursell, ibid 93.
73 Ibid.
74 [1963] 1 All ER 767.

entitled to refuse to answer when directed to by a judge. Let me not be mistaken. The judge will respect the confidences which each member of these honourable professions receives in the course of it, and will not direct him to answer unless not only it is relevant but also it is a proper and, indeed, necessary question in the course of justice to be put and answered. A judge is the person entrusted, on behalf of the community, to weigh these conflicting interests — to weigh on the one hand the respect due to confidence in the profession and on the other hand the ultimate interest of the community in justice being done.[75]

In *X Ltd v Morgan-Grampian (Publishers) Ltd*,[76] an early case on press freedom, Lord Donaldson MR remarked:

It is sometimes said that the relationship between journalist and source is somehow akin to that between priest and penitent. Nothing could be further from the truth. The penitent comes to the priest for spiritual advice and guidance within a framework of a different and divine law.[77] If the penitent is breaking confidences, he does so in circumstances in which he knows that the priest will make no use of that breached confidence and that there will be no further publication. This is the antithesis of a 'confession' to a journalist which is made with the express or implied intention that there should be wider publicity than the source can himself achieve. If any secular relationship is analogous to that between priest and penitent, it is that between lawyer and client. That is sanctioned, both expressly and impliedly by Parliament, in the public interest of enabling every citizen to obtain advice as to his legal rights, obligations and liabilities without fear of the consequences. For my part, I do not doubt that Parliament would, if necessary, confer the same immunity upon priests, albeit for different reasons, but that is unnecessary because the judges traditionally do not require priests to break the seal of the confessional.[78]

---

75 Ibid 771.
76 [1990] 2 WLR 421.
77 Lord Donaldson may have been unaware that seal of the confessional in the practice of the Church of England is governed by English domestic law.
78 *X Ltd v Morgan-Grampian (Publishers) Ltd* [1990] 2 WLR 421, 430–1.

In *R v AR*[79] the Court of Appeal was addressing an appeal against sentence in relation to indictments which contained various sexual offences against children. Whilst reciting the facts, the Court observed that 'In July 2005 the appellant made a confession to a priest which resulted in the police being informed'.[80]

More recently still, on 4 February 2020, Lieven J gave judgment in *Lancashire County Council v E & F*, a family law case.[81] The case concerned an application by two elders of a congregation of Jehovah's Witnesses to set aside a witness summons, requiring them to provide certain information, on grounds of a religious duty of confidentiality. The mother had disclosed to the elders that the child had made allegations of child abuse against her father. Some years later, one of the elders notified the police of the mother's disclosure. The elders declined to provide any information that had been communicated to them in the course of confidential spiritual counselling without the express consent of the individuals involved. It was argued on their behalf that the elders were under a spiritual duty not to disclose confidential religious communications and that if such confidence is breached, individuals might no longer confide in their ministers. Lieven J rejected their submissions:

> [T]here is no evidence that the material sought through the witness summons was in any sense a confession or akin to a confession. It appears that the allegation of sexual abuse came to the elders' attention because the Mother reported it, not because the Father confessed to the elders, or sought spiritual counselling. The elders then carried out some form of investigation and met with the Father, probably on more than one occasion. It is possible that at some point the Father 'confessed', but I have no evidence this was the case. In any event, the investigation cannot itself amount to a confession. Therefore, to the degree that there is a duty of confidentiality in

---

79 [2009] EWCA Crim 1476.
80 Ibid [6]. The judgment does not record the denomination of the priest, whether the confession was sacramental, and how the matter came to the attention of the police. As events transpired, the priest was not required to attend Court and give evidence because the defendant pleaded guilty.
81 [2020] EWHC 182 Fam.

relation to a confession, which I am prepared to assume on the basis of R v Hay, but not decide, it would not arise here.[82]

The case did not concern the Church of England, nor the sacrament of penance. The judge characterised the relationship between ministers of religion and those who seek to confess, as giving rise to a duty of confidentiality, not a privilege. In reaching this conclusion, Lieven J relied upon a legal commentary accompanying the judgment in R v Hay which distinguished between things said during confession, and things said or done outside it. Even in cases where a duty of confidentiality may exist, Lieven J was not prepared to accept that the duty was an absolute one. She noted that respect for the elders' religious beliefs under art 9 of the *European Convention on Human Rights* was a qualified right and concluded that 'It could not be more obvious that a freedom to manifest ones religious beliefs must give way to the need to protect a child from sexual abuse'.[83]

VII Conclusion

It will be readily apparent that the question of the seal of the confessional in English law is a complex and contested matter. The canon law of the Church of England and the Roman Catholic Church both clearly and unambiguously state that the seal of the confessional is inviolable. Whether this gives rise to an evidential privilege or a duty of confidentiality which the secular courts recognise is a matter which has been the subject of debate for centuries. A priest of the Church of England is in a very different position from a priest of the Roman Catholic Church. The canonical prohibition on divulging what occurred during the sacrament of penance is, additionally, part of English domestic law to be applied by civil judges in state courts. Where canon law is in conflict with secular law, the latter prevails, but care should be taken when identifying genuine conflict, as opposed to overlay.

---

82 Ibid [39].
83 Ibid [45].

Whether the term 'privilege' is apt to describe the priest-penitent relationship is a matter on which commentators have expressed different views. Some opinions need to be discounted because commentators fail to discriminate between information imparted during the sacrament of penance and confidential clergy communications more generally. And few commentators recognise the exceptional position of the seal of the confession within the Church of England arising, as it does, from the express duty of non-disclosure being a matter of English law. Whether a Church of England priest can be forced to give evidence of matters revealed during the sacrament of penance is a matter on which the authors of this chapter disagree. Hill considers that a trial judge must carry out a careful balancing exercise, mindful of its duty to act in a manner compatible with art 9 of the *European Convention on Human Rights*. Grout contends that any art 9 considerations are outweighed by the greater need to ensure the fair and effective administration of criminal justice, in accordance with both the applicable legislation and basic common law principles. To which Hill responds that there can be no such generalized response because each matter is fact-sensitive, and they will fall to be determined on a case by case basis.

Many jurisdictions provide in their evidence and procedural codes for priest-penitent communications to be privileged and inadmissible in evidence: but there does not appear to be any appetite to adopt this course in England.[84] If anything, public pressure, in light of concerns over abuse of children by priests and others within organised religions, is likely to agitate for mandatory reporting of abuse confessed to priests. At present there is no relaxation of the seal in such circumstances.[85] Australia has passed legislation requiring priests to report child abuse revealed to them during confession and making it a criminal offence to

---

84 Although see the observations of the working party in this regard in its report.

85 The practice is to direct the penitent to self-report and to withhold absolution until that is done.

fail to do so.[86]

In the United Kingdom, the Independent Inquiry into Child Sexual Abuse is due to report in the latter part of 2020 on matters concerning the Church of England, and it is likely to make recommendations regarding the seal of the confessional. Those are awaited with interest. In the meantime, the current uncertainty will persist unless and until a direction given by a trial judge on the admissibility of evidence is reviewed in the Court of Appeal or Supreme Court, the prospect of which is vanishingly small.

---

86 The legal position in Australia is the subject of detailed consideration else-where in this volume.

6

Andreas Henriksen Aarflot

The seal of the confessional and the duty of confidentiality for priests – A comparison between the Church of Norway and the Church of Sweden

Abstract

This chapter explores and compares the duties of confidentiality and evidential privilege for priests in the Churches of Norway and Sweden. The Norwegian confidentiality obligation is superseded by a duty to avert certain criminal offences. The duty of confidentiality in Sweden is considered to be absolute, although Swedish priests may also be obliged to prevent certain criminal offences. The chapter also explores recent developments.

Keywords:
Seal of confession – duty of confidentiality – privilege – mandatory reporting – duty to avert crimes – Church of Norway – Church of Sweden

I Introduction

'Confession in our churches is not abolished', reads the introduction to Article XXV of the Augsburg Confession.[1] Indeed, Luther recognised penance or confession as one of the three sacramental signs which

---

1   *Augsburg Confession of 1530*, art XXV.

manifested the promises of the Gospel.[2] Nevertheless, in legal terms, the Reformation led to what Norman Doe describes as 'the juridical abandonment of obligatory private auricular confession' for many of the emerging churches of the Reformation. However, Lutheran churches still retain confession as a voluntary facility.[3] Lutheran confessional texts, which are part of the doctrinal basis of the Church of Norway and the Church of Sweden, include provisions about confession.[4] Confession and absolution generally have a place in the liturgy of Lutheran churches, but provision often exists for private confession to a priest[5] as well.[6]

As Grout explains, a vital part of private confession is that it will allow a person to confess his or her sins in complete openness to God, so that they may receive absolution and forgiveness for their sins from God through the priest.[7] To facilitate such openness, priests from various Christian traditions have generally had a duty to keep information from confessions confidential.[8] The obligation of the priest to keep information from confessions secret is known as the 'seal of the confessional'.[9]

---

2   John Witte Jr, *Law and Protestantism: The Legal Teachings of the Lutheran Reformation* (Cambridge University Press, 2002) 58.

3   Norman Doe, *Christian Law: Contemporary Principles* (Cambridge University Press, 2013) 265, 267–8.

4   *Augsburg Confession of 1530*, arts XI, XXV; *Luthers lille katekisme* [*Luther's Small Catechism*] in Arve Brunvoll and Kjell Olav Sannes (eds) *Den norske kirkes bekjennelsesskrifter* [*The Church of Norway's Confessional Texts*] (Lunde forlag, 2017) pt IV. Cf *Kong Christian den Femtis Norske Lov 1687* [King Christian V's Norwegian Code of 1687] bk 2, ch 1 ('Norwegian Code'); *Kirkeordning for Den norske kirke 2019* [Church Order of the Church of Norway 2019] s 1; *Kyrkoordning för Svenska kyrkan* [The Church Order of the Church of Sweden] ch 1, s 1; see also Andreas Henriksen Aarflot, 'A Lutheran perspective', in Norman Doe (ed), *Church Laws and Ecumenism – A New Parth for Christian Unity* (Routledge, 2021) 120.

5   This chapter uses the term *priest*, rather than *pastor*, to describe the Lutheran ministers. This is because *priest* is the closest translation of the title used by the Churches of Norway and Sweden, '*prest*' and '*präst*'. In the Norwegian and Swedish contexts, *pastor* usually refers to a minister of a free church. In the worldwide Lutheran context, *pastor* or *minister* are more commonly used to describe Lutheran ministers.

6   Doe (n 3) 267.

7   See Christopher Grout, 'The Seal of the Confessional and the Criminal Law of England and Wales' (2020) 22(2) *Ecclesiastical Law Journal* 138, 138.

8   See *Principle* VII.5.2 in Mark Hill and Norman Doe, 'Principles of Christian Law' (2017) 19(2) *Ecclesiastical Law Journal* 138, 151; Norman Doe (ed), *Church Laws and Ecumenism: A New Path for Christian Unity* (Routledge, 2021) 281.

9   See, eg, Grout (n 7) 138.

Recent reports from Australia, the USA, and the United Kingdom have raised the issue of whether Churches should retain the seal of the confessional or introduce forms of mandatory reporting of child sexual abuse.[10] This chapter will explore how the law of the Church of Norway and the Church of Sweden address this issue.

This chapter will compare the understanding of the seal of the confessional and the duty of confidentiality for priests in the two churches. In both the Church of Norway and the Church of Sweden, priests are bound by a duty of confidentiality to protect both confessional secrets and secrets received through certain other parts of their pastoral ministry. At the same time, the churches want to ensure that they do not provide a cover for illegal activity, in particular when it comes to harm to children. Yet, there are differences. Priests in the Church of Norway are covered by duties of confidentiality prescribed by both the state and the church, whereas the duty of confidentiality for priests in the Church of Sweden is prescribed by the church. The Norwegian confidentiality obligation is superseded by a duty to avert certain criminal offences. The duty of confidentiality in Sweden is considered to be absolute, although Swedish priests may also be obliged to prevent certain criminal offences.

The chapter will start by looking at the seal of the confessional and duty of confidentiality for priests in the Church of Norway. It will first outline the rite of confession, the duties of confidentiality for priests, exceptions from the duty of confidentiality, including the obligation to avert certain criminal offences, and the corresponding evidential privilege of priests. Secondly, it will consider recent developments and debates concerning questions of confidentiality and mandatory reporting in the Church of Norway. Because any Christian may hear confessions in the Church of

---

10 *Royal Commission into Institutional Responses to Child Sexual Abuse* (Final Report, 2017) vol 16, bks 1–3; *Independent Inquiry Child Sexual Abuse: The Anglican Church* (Investigation Report, October 2020); *Independent Inquiry Child Sexual Abuse: The Roman Catholic Church* (Investigation Report, November 2020); Marci A Hamilton, Stephanie Dallam and Sabine Glocker, *Survey and Analysis of the Written Child Protection Policies of the 32 U.S. Roman Catholic Archdioceses* (White Paper, 1 October 2020).

Norway, the law relating to confessional confidentiality for laypersons will also be explained briefly. The chapter then goes on to look at the same questions with regard to the Church of Sweden. Finally, the two churches will be compared and evaluated against the *Statement on Principles of Christian Law* (2016) principles regarding confession, before the chapter will be concluded with a summary of its findings.

II The Seal of the Confessional and Duty of Confidentiality for Priests in the Church of Norway

A Confession in the Church of Norway

With the Reformation, confession as a rite was continued in the Norwegian Church, both in law and later in the liturgical books of the church.[11] Supreme Court Justice Motzfeldt explained in 1844 that 'private confession has ... not had the same significance in the Protestant church as in the Catholic church; in our church, it is almost only a preparation to the Communion'.[12] Although the Church of Norway recommends to allow for the possibility to conduct private confession in connection with the Principal Service, private confession is rare.[13] A priest or another Christian may hear confession.[14]

At the ordination of priests, the ordinands make ordination vows where they, inter alia, promise to care for each individual in pastoral care and in

---

11 *Ordinatio ecclesiastica regnorum Daniae et Norwegiae et ducatuum Sleswicensis Holt-satiae* (etc) 1537 [The Church Order of the Realms of Denmark and Norway and the Dutchies of Schleswig and Holstein (etc) [of 1537]; *Danmark og Norges Kirke-Ritual af 1685* [Denmark and Norway's Church Ritual of 1685]; *Alterbok for Den norske kirke 1920* [The Altar Book for the Church of Norway of 1920] (Norway); *Kongelig resolusjon av 8 oktober 1920* [Royal Decree of 8 October 1920]; *Kongelig resolusjon 1 november 1985* [Royal Decree of 1 November 1985] (Norway).

12 Ulrik A Motzfeldt, *Den norske Kirkeret* [The Norwegian Church Law] (Johan Dahl, 1844) 184.

13 *Den norske kirke / Den norske kyrkja, Gudstjeneste med veiledninger / Gudsteneste med ret-tleiingar* [Church of Norway, Service with Guidance] (Eide forlag, 2020) 353.

14 This follows from the General Instructions on Confession 2, cf *Alminnel-ige bestemmelser for skriftemål* / General Instructions for Confession. See also Ivar Ramvi and Gunnar Stålseth, *Kirkelig håndbok* [Ecclesiastical Handbook] (Nomi forlag, 2nd ed, 1972) 57.

confession.[15] Priests have a duty to comply with the ordination vows and to administer sacraments to members, including confession.[16]

B Duty of Confidentiality for Priests

Because the Church of Norway has been a state church until recently, there has historically not been a separation between the law of the state and the law of the church, as the Church was considered to be the official religion of the state.[17] This means that most of the legal provisions relating to the seal of the confessional and the duty of confidentiality have, until recently, been laid down by state-made law. After the changes made to the *Constitution* in 2012 and legislative reforms effective from 2017 and 2021, it may be argued that the Church of Norway is no longer a state church, but a church established by law.[18]

Priests in the Church of Norway have been obliged by several duties of confidentiality prescribed by law. Historically, King Christian V's *Norwegian Code 1687*, which was in force until 25 October 1991,[19] held that:

> The priest must not without the loss of his benefice, reveal what someone has confessed to him in secret confession unless it could be about treason, or misfortune, which could be avoided by the priest's revelation; and the name of the penitent should, as far as

---

15 *Gudstjenestebok for Den norske kirke* [Service Book for the Church of Norway] (Verbum forlag, 1992) vol 2. Other parts of the ordination liturgy, including the declaration of assent, is translated into English in *Together in Mission and Ministry: The Porvoo Common Statement with Essays on Church and Ministry in Northern Europe: GS 1083* (Church House, 1993) 192.

16 *Tjenesteordning for menighetsprester* [Order on the Ministry of Parish Priests ss 5, 11.

17 Until its amendment in 2012, art 2 of the *Kongeriket Norges Grunnlow av 1814* [*Constitution of the Kingdom of Norway 1814*] stated that '[a]ll inhabitants of the Realm shall have the right to free exercise of their religion. The Evangelical-Lutheran religion shall remain the official religion of the State. The inhabitants professing it are bound to bring up their children in the same'.

18 Aarflot, 'A Lutheran perspective' (n 4), 125.

19 *Lov 20 desember 1985 nr 102 om opphevelse av en del foreldede lovbestemelser* [Act of 20 December 1985, Act No 102, Repealing Some Statutory Provisions] (Norway); *Lov 18 desember 1987 nr 100 om endring i lov 20 desember 1985 nr 102 om opphevelse av en del foreldede lovbestemmelser* [Repealing Some Statutory Provisions (Amendment) Act 1987, Act No 100] (Norway); *Kongelig resolusjon 25 oktober 1991* [Royal Decree of 25 October 1991] (Norway).

possible, be kept secret.[20]

Priests who broke the duty would also face criminal charges.[21] However, the prohibition against revealing information did not apply to the cases where the priest had a statutory duty to avert criminal offences, as this chapter will explore.[22]

The new *Penal Code 2005* has continued this principle in s 211.[23] Thus, a priest in the Church of Norway 'who illicitly reveals or fails to prevent others from gaining access to or knowledge of secrets confided to them ... in connection with their position or assignment' will risk a penalty of a fine or imprisonment.[24] The same provision also covers certain other professionals and their assistants, such as priests or leaders in other registered faith communities, and lawyers. 'Secrets confided to' the priests cover the seal of the confessional, but also extends to other secrets confided to the priest in connection with the priest's pastoral ministry. This duty is commonly referred to as the *professional* duty of confidentiality.[25]

The Norwegian Supreme Court has explained that the purpose of this professional duty of confidentiality: 'is that people must be able to seek professional treatment, help or advice from professionals covered by the provision, without the information they provide in this connection being

---

20   Norwegian Code 1687 (n 4), bk 2, ch 5, art 19. This provision was in force until 25 October 1991.

21   See, eg, *Almindelig borgerlig Straffelov 1902* [Penal Code 1902] (Norway) ss 121, 144. See also Henrik S. Broch, *Norsk kirkeret* [Norwegian Church Law] (Aschehoug, 1904) 57–8.

22   Penal Code 1902 (n 22) s 139. See also Absalon Taranger, *Norsk kirkeret: forelæsninger ved det praktisk-teologiske seminar* [Norwegian Church Law: Lectures at the Practical-Theological Seminary] (Cammermeyer, 1917) vol 2, 110–1.

23   The last amendments of the Act were passed by the *Storting* and received royal assent on 19 June 2020, 4 December 2020, and 5 March 2021. Cf *Lov 19 juni 2020 nr 91 om endringer i straffeloven mv. (avvergingsplikt, utenomrettslig tvangsekteskap, diskrimineringsvern, skyting mot politiet mv.)* [Penal Code (Amendment) Act of 19 June 2020]; *Lov 4 desember 2020 nr 135 om endringer i straffeloven mv. (avvergingsplikt, utenomrettslig tvangsekteskap, diskrimineringsvern, skyting mot politiet mv.)* [Penal Code (Amendment) Act of 4 December 2020]; *Lov 5 mars 2021 om endringer I lov 20 mai 2005 nr 28 om straff* [Penal Code (Amendment) Act of 5 March 2021].

24   *Lov om straff (straffeloven) 2005* [Penal Code 2005] (Norway) s 211.

25   Norwegian: '*yrkesmessig taushetsplikt*' or '*kallsmessig taushetsplikt*'.

disclosed or passed on'.[26] Because the same section also regulates lawyer-client-confidentiality, Supreme Court Justice Skoghøy has explained that the provision of the code builds on the right to respect for private and family life according to art 8 of the European Convention on Human Rights.[27] Convictions concerning lawyer-client confidentiality in the European Court of Human Rights support this understanding.[28] Under Norwegian law, this applies equally to the other professions mentioned in s 211, including priests.[29]

When they were civil servants, priests in the Church of Norway also had an administrative duty of confidentiality relating to information received in the course of their duties concerning an individual's personal affairs, or commercial secrets.[30] A breach of the duty could be sanctioned by criminal courts.[31] The administrative duty of confidentiality was an additional duty, partly overlapping with the professional duty of confidentiality pursuant to s 211 of the *Penal Code 2005*. In 2017, priests were transferred from the civil service to become employees of the church.[32] However, statutory law still obliged priests to keep this duty until 1 January 2021.[33] From 1 January 2021, the *Church of Norway Act* was repealed and succeeded

---

26 Rt 2010 s 1638, 33.

27 Jens Edvin A Skoghøy, '*Advokaters taushetsplikt og de korresponderende bevisforbud i tvisteloven § 22-5 og straffeprosessloven § 119*' (2013) 13 (2) *Tidsskrift for strafferett* 166, 167–9; *Convention for the Protection of Human Rights and Fundamental Freedoms*, opened for signature 4 November 1950, 213 UNTS 221 (entered into force 3 September 1953) art 8 ('*European Convention on Human Rights*').

28 See, eg, *Altay v Turkey (No 2)* [2019] Eur Court HR 276; *Campbell v United Kingdom* [1992] Eur Court HR 41.

29 Skoghøy, (n 27), 167–8.

30 *Forvaltningsloven 1967* [The Public Administration Act 1967] (Norway) s 13. As this duty of confidentiality follows is prescribed by the Public Administration Act, this duty may be called an *administrative* duty of confidentiality (*forvaltningsmessig taushetsplikt*), to separate this duty from the *professional* duty of confidentiality pursuant to s 211 of the Penal Code 2005 (*yrkesmessig taushetsplikt*).

31 Section 209 of the Penal Code 2005 makes it a criminal offence to breach the duty of confidentiality by revealing 'information in respect of which he/she has a duty of confidentiality pursuant to statute or regulations, or exploits such information with intent to obtain an illicit gain for himself/herself or for other persons'.

32 Lisbet Christoffersen, 'Towards Re-Sacralization of Nordic Law?', in Marius Timmann Mjaaland (ed), *Formatting Religion: Across Politics, Education, Media, and Law* (Routledge, 2019) 187.

33 *Kirkeloven 7 juni 1996 nr 31* [The Church of Norway Act 1996] s 38.

by the *Faith Communities Act 2020*, adopted by the *Storting* (Parliament), and the Church Order of the Church of Norway, adopted by the General Synod.[34] After this date, it is the Church Order which prescribes that the same duty is continued.[35] However, as of 1 January 2021, a breach of the administrative duty of confidentiality prescribed by the Church Order will not be considered a criminal offence,[36] unlike a breach of the duty of professional confidentiality under the *Penal Code*. Instead, a breach of the duty prescribed by the Church Order can be enforced internally through disciplinary measures, under tort law, or by general provisions on the violation of privacy.[37]

Until 2019, a provision in the liturgical law of the church stated that: '[t]he priest has ecclesiastical authority to receive confession and have a *legally unconditional duty* of confidentiality. Also others who receive confession must remain silent about what they have heard in the confession'.[38]

Article 16 of the *Constitution* gave the King-in-Council the royal prerogative to make legislation for the Church of Norway in the form of 'ecclesiastical ordinances', including provisions about liturgy and service

---

34 *Trossamfunnsloven 24 april 2020 nr 31* [Faith Communities Act 2020] (Norway) s 23. Cf *Kongelig resolusjon 24 april 2020* [Royal Decree 24 April 2020] (Norway); Church Order for the Church of Norway.

35 Church Order for the Church of Norway, s 42.

36 This is the opinion of the National Council of the Church of Norway. Cf Kirkerådet, *Høring – endringer i kirkeordningen og enkelte andre regler* [National Council, Consultation – Draft Amendments to the Church Order and Certain Other Rules] (2020) An exception applies to Church's burial administration, which still must follow the Public Administration Act according to its section 1.

37 Section 267 of the Penal Code 2005 (n 24) states that 'any person who by public communication violates the privacy of another person shall be subject to a fine or imprisonment for a term not exceeding one year'.

38 *Kronprinsregentens resolusjon 26 oktober 1990 nr 880* [Crown Prince Regent's Decree of 26 October 1990, No 880] (Norway); Crown Prince Regent's Decree of 19 October 1990 (Norway) appendix, also incorporated in *Gudstjenestebok for Den norske kirke* [Service Book for the Church of Norway] 87 (emphasis added).

books, and this provision was part of such an ordinance.[39] 'A legally unconditional duty of confidentiality' would suggest that the seal of the confessional could not be broken in the Church of Norway according to the provision. The provision was, however, amended by the General Synod in 2019.[40] The reason why will be explored in the following sections.

C Exceptions from the Duty of Confidentiality

In some cases, a priest is bound by law to report information to authorities or avert certain criminal offences, notwithstanding any duty of confidentiality. According to s 196 of the *Penal Code 2005*, 'any person who fails to report or seek to avert by other means a criminal offence or the consequences thereof at a time when this is still possible and it appears certain or most likely that the act has been or will be committed' risks the penalty of fines or imprisonment for up to one year.[41] Before 2010, the duty required 'reliable knowledge' of the offence, a higher threshold than what 'appears certain or most likely'.[42] This duty 'applies regardless of any duty of confidentiality'.[43] The provision lists 52 serious criminal offences, including treason, terrorism, homicide, sexual assault, sexual

---

39 Until its amendment in 2012, art 16 of the Norwegian constitution read as follows: '[t]he King ordains all public church services and public worship, all meetings and assemblies dealing with religious matters, and ensures that public teachers of religion follow the norms prescribed for them'. See Aarflot, 'A Lutheran perspective' (n 4), 120–1. It was a constitutional requirement that at least half of the members of the Council of State were members of the Church of Norway, as only those who were members could participate in the ecclesiastical decisions cf the former art 12 second paragraph and art 27 second paragraph.

40 After the constitutional changes in 2012, which removed the King's role in church affairs, Aarflot explains that the statute recognises that the General Synod have an inherent liturgical authority: see Aarflot, 'A Lutheran perspective' (n 4), 121–2. The decision of the General Synod is reported in the *Report of Proceedings of the General Synod of the Church of Norway* (2019) 196–200 ('*Report of Proceedings (2019)*').

41 Penal Code 2005 (n 24) s 196, first paragraph.

42 *Prop 116 L (2009–10) Endringer i domstolloven (ekstraordinære valg til lekdommerutvalgene m.m.) og straffeloven 1902 (avvergingsplikt)* [Court of Justice and Penal Code of 1902 (Amendment) Bill, No 116 of 2009–10] (Norway) 17 ('*Prop 116 (2009–10)*').

43 Penal Code 2005 (n 24) s 196, first paragraph.

assault on children under 14 years of age, aggravated sexual activity etc with a child between 14 and 16 years of age.[44] Breach of the duty to avert is not penalised in certain circumstances, eg if the duty cannot be carried out without exposing the person with the duty, his or her next-of-kin, or an innocent person to a charge or indictment or risk to life, health or welfare.[45]

The provision is forward-looking: If a person confesses to having killed another person 20 years ago, and the priest is convinced that there is no risk of repetition, the duty of confidentiality applies. In such a case, the priest is expected to help the penitent report the crime to the authorities but must keep silent if the penitent will not do so. The priest must be convinced that 'it appears certain or most likely' that a criminal act will be committed.[46] There is, however, one circumstance where the priest may reveal information about such a confession: namely to prevent an innocent from being indicted or convicted of a criminal act punishable by imprisonment for a term of more than one year.[47]

If the conditions for acting under the principle of necessity or self-defence according to ss 17 or 18 of the *Penal Code* are met, the duty of confidentiality may also be set aside.[48] The exact extent of how far necessity may set aside the duty of confidentiality has, however, not been tried by the courts.[49] In general, there have been few cases tried relating

---

44 Ibid.
45 Ibid s 196, first paragraph. However, this exemption does not apply if the offended is a minor and the person who fails to avert is the child's parent, stepparent, foster parent or another who has daily care for children: cf fourth paragraph.
46 Ibid s 196, first paragraph.
47 Ibid s 226.
48 Ibid ss 17–8. See Morten Holmboe, *Tale eller tie - om plikt til å avverge alvorlige lovbrudd og uriktige domfellelser* [To Speak or to Remain Silent: On the Duty to Avert Serious Criminal Offences and Incorrect Convictions] (Gyldendal Akademisk, 2017) 32, 204.
49 Holmboe (n 48) 32, 204.

to the duty to avert criminal offences.[50]

Under Norwegian law, a priest may be released from both the professional and the administrative duty of confidentiality by the penitent.[51] This is equivalent to the rule in the Church of England.[52]

D The Corresponding Evidential Privilege

Information protected by the priest's professional duty of confidentiality is generally not admissible as evidence in court unless the penitent consents to it.[53] An exception is made for a situation where 'the statement is needed to prevent an innocent person from being punished' (penalised).[54] The same evidential privilege applies to civil court proceedings.[55] It also applies to written evidence: In 2008, the Agder Court of Appeal ruled that the police could not go through a priest's seized computer, as it would breach the evidential privilege.[56] However, the Court of Appeal found that the court itself could access the material

---

50 A notable exception is the Supreme Court case HR-2017-824-A (Norwegian citation standard after 2016), in which a man witnessed a criminal offence resulting in death, without alerting authorities at a time where it was still possible to avert the consequences of the offense (the death). The Supreme Court convicted the man to 8 months of prison.

51 Section 211 of the Penal Code 2005 speaks of 'illicitly' revealing 'secrets'. If the penitent consents, it is no longer illicit or secret. Section 13a(1) of the Public Administration Act clarifies that '[t]he duty of secrecy pursuant to section 13 shall not prevent ... information from being made known to those it directly concerns or to others, insofar as those to whom the duty of secrecy is owed consent thereto'.

52 See, eg, Judge Rupert DH Bursell, 'The Seal of the Confessional' (1990) 2(7) *Ecclesiastical Law Journal* 84, 109.

53 'Without the consent of the person entitled to the preservation of secrecy, the court may not receive any statement from priests in the Church of Norway ... about anything that has been confided to them in their official capacity ... The prohibition no longer applies if the statement is needed to prevent an innocent person from being punished': cf *Straffeprosessloven* 1902 [Criminal Procedure Act 1902] (Norway) s 119.

54 Ibid s 119, third paragraph.

55 'The Court cannot hear evidence from priests in the Church of Norway ... about something that was confided to them in their professional capacity': cf *Tvisteloven* 2005 [Disputes Act 2005] (Norway) s 22-5(1).

56 RG 2008 s 1025.

to examine if the computer contained confidential material.[57] The privilege only applies to the information and notes from the priest. In 2008, the Supreme Court considered whether a recording of a presumed confidential conversation between a prison chaplain and two inmates could be admitted as evidence in a case relating to attempted homicide. Based on the merits of the case, the Supreme Court found that although the chaplain could not admit evidence from the conversation according to s 119, the duty of confidentiality did not extend to the other inmate present who made the recording.[58]

E Recent Developments

In 2016, Revd Kjartan Leer-Salvesen published a study where he found that priests to a limited degree would report issues to the police or the Child Welfare Service in cases where they were obliged by law to do so.[59] The priests he interviewed explained this partly with reference to their duty of confidentiality.[60] Based on his findings, Leer-Salvesen recommended in 2018 that in addition to the duty to avert certain criminal offences, the Church of Norway should introduce a duty to report to child welfare services when they are concerned about a child.[61]

The Bishop of Hamar, the Right Revd Solveig Fiske, endorsed Leer-Salvesen's recommendation and raised the issue of reporting to child

---

57 RG 2008 s 1025.

58 Rt. 2009 s 1526, 20-32.

59 Kjartan Leer-Salvesen, 'På tilliten løs? En studie av læreres og presters skjønnsutøvelse i spenningen mellom taushetsplikt, meldeplikt og avvergeplikt' [Endangering the Trust? A Study of Teachers' and Clerics' Use of Discretion in Matters of Confidentiality and Mandatory Reporting] (PhD Thesis, University of Agder, 2016) 143–4. Revd Leer-Salvesen is an ordained priest in the Church of Norway who currently works as a professor at the Institute of Social Work of Volda University College.

60 Ibid 189–92.

61 Kjartan Leer-Salvesen, 'Hvor mange liv er tilliten verdt?' ['How Many Lifes is the Trust Worth?'] (2018) 122 (2) *Kirke og Kultur* 95.

welfare services at the General Synod in 2018.[62] A public debate followed.[63] The issue was later debated, in various ways, in the Bishops' Conference, in the National Council[64] and in the General Synod.[65] The Bishops' Conference discussed the issue over the course of several meetings and decided to take an initiative to introduce mandatory reporting.[66] According to the *Child Welfare Act 1992*, 'public authorities shall of their own initiative provide information to the municipal child welfare service when there is reason to believe that a child is being mistreated at home or subjected to other forms of serious neglect', 'notwithstanding the duty of confidentiality'.[67] The Bishops' Conference's initiative would expand the duty to report to include not only public authorities, but also priests and other church employees, thus setting aside the priest's duty of confidentiality in such cases.[68]

The National Council of the Church of Norway brought draft legislation to the General Synod in 2019 to change the provision on the duty of

---

62 Bishop Solveig Fiske held a speech in the General Debate of the General Synod, which was not minuted, but she repeated her comments in a newspaper article later: Solveig Fiske, *'Ingen oppheving av taushetsplikten'* [No Repealing of the Duty of Confidentiality], *Vårt Land* (Web Page, 2 May 2018).

63 Kjartan Leer-Salvesen, *'Når taushet er svik'* [When silence is betrayal], *Vårt Land* (Web Page, 2 May 2018), ‹http://www.verdidebatt.no/innlegg/11725132-nar-taushet-er-svik›; Martin Enstad, *'Taushetspliktens grenser'* [The Limits of the Duty of Confidentiality], *Vårt Land* (Web Page, 2 May 2018); Ingrid Løining Ørum, *'Regelforvirring om taushetsplikt'* [Confusion About the Rules on the Duty of Confidentiality], *Vårt Land* (Web Page, 3 May 2018).

64 The National Council (*Kirkerådet*) is the executive body of the General Synod of the Church of Norway, consisting of a lay moderator, the Presiding Bishop and 15 other members elected by the General Synod: cf Church Order of the Church of Norway, s 29.

65 Protokoll fra Bispemøtet februar 2019 [Minutes from the Bishops' Conference February 2019]; Protokoll fra Bispemøtet oktober 2019 [Minutes from the Bishops' Conference October 2019]; Protokoll fra Kirkerådet januar 2019 [Minutes from the National Council January 2019]; *Report of Proceedings (2019)* (n 40).

66 Minutes February 2019 (n 65); Minutes October 2019 (n 65).

67 *Barnevernloven 1992* [Child Welfare Act 1992] (Norway) s 6-4. A governmental bill is currently before the Norwegian Parliament (*Stortinget*) with a proposal for a new law replacing the *1992 Child Welfare Act*, but the proposal will not make substantial changes to this duty: cf *Prop 133 L (2020–1) Lov om barnevern (barnevernsloven) og lov om endringer i barnevernloven* [Bill No 133 (2020–1) Child Welfare Bill and Child Welfare (Amendment) Bill] 418–9.

68 Minutes February 2019 (n 65); Minutes October 2019 (n 65).

confidentiality relating to confession as 'legally unconditional'.[69] The General Synod adopted the amendments, clarifying that the priest's duty of confidentiality is a duty the priest has according to current regulations.[70] Matters of a doctrinal character must be referred to the Bishops' Conference before the General Synod considers them, and the Bishops' Conference has a suspensive veto in such cases.[71] However, the draft legislation did not go through this procedure; the amendment was not considered to be a matter of a doctrinal character.[72] Instead, the National Council argued that the provision was 'hardly compatible with the exceptions that apply' according to the current legislation, but that the proposed amendment would bring the text into accordance with the current legislation.[73] No theological arguments relating to the seal of the confessional are found in the explanatory document from the National Council, nor in the report of the Revision Committee to the General Synod.[74]

The Bishops' Conference's initiative to include church employees among the persons who have a duty to report concerns to the child welfare services according to the *Child Welfare Act* has, at the time of writing, proven fruitless.[75] The Government published a new Child Welfare Bill in April 2021, without any mention of the church.[76] It is unlikely that the

---

69 Kirkerådet, *Endringer i regelverk vedtatt av Kirkemøtet: KM 10/19* [Miscellaneous Provisions (Amendment) Rules] (1 April 2019).

70 *Report of Proceedings* (2019) (n 40) 200 [tr author]. The full text of the amendment was: '[t]he priest has ecclesiastical authority to receive confession. Both the priest and any others who receive confession, have a duty of confidentiality in accordance with current regulations'.

71 Aarflot, 'A Lutheran perspective' (n 4), 122. This previously followed from s 2-4 of the *Kirkemøtets forretningsorden* [Standing Orders of the General Synod] but was from 1 January 2021 elevated from the Standing Orders to the Church Order for the Church of Norway: at s 28.

72 This is not explicitly said in any document, but the follows from the explanatory notes from the National Council: cf Kirkerådet (n 69); *Report of Proceedings* (2019) (n 40) 196–200.

73 Kirkerådet (n 69).

74 Kirkerådet (n 69); *Report of Proceedings* (2019) (n 40) 196–200.

75 May 2021.

76 *Prop 133 L (2020–1) Lov om barnevern (barnevernsloven) og lov om endringer i barnevernloven* [Bill No 133 (2020–1) Child Welfare Bill and Child Welfare (Amendment) Bill].

bill will be amended to extend the duty to report to church employees.

F A Conflict Between the General Instructions on Confession and Statutory Law?

In the literature, writers generally portray the old provision in the *General Instructions for Confession* as something the Church of Norway has made by mistake,[77] where 'the Church of Norway has in its *General Instructions on Confession* formulated that 'the priest has ... a legally unconditional duty of confidentiality',[78] thus giving an 'erroneous notions of the duty of confidentiality', contrary to the law of the land.[79] However, it was the Crown Prince Regent-in-Council, in the function as the highest body of the Church of Norway, who made the provision in 1990.[80] This complicates the matter, as the King-in-Council according to the *Constitution* used to have exclusive competence to make ecclesiastical ordinances under art 16.[81] This exclusive competence could not be infringed upon by parliamentary decisions.[82] In 1987, the Supreme Court heard a case on the relationship between the *Storting's* power to legislate and the King's power to make ecclesiastical ordinances.[83] In the case, there was a conflict between a provision of the *Church Order Act 1953* and an ecclesiastical ordinance adopted pursuant to art 16 of the

---

77 Leer-Salvesen (n 59) 131.

78 Ingrid Løining Ørum, *Presters taushetsplikt - innhold, grenser og rettslige konsekvenser* [Priests' Duty of Confidentiality — Content, Limits and Legal Consequences] (LLM dissertation, Universitetet i Oslo, 2018) 9.

79 Kjartan Leer-Salvesen and Pål Morten Andreassen, 'Taushetsplikt, meldeplikt og avvergeplikt i Den norske kirke' [The Duties of Confidentiality, Reporting and Averting Crimes in the Church of Norway] (2017) *Tidsskrift for Sjelesorg* 166, 167, 183

80 Aarflot, 'A Lutheran perspective' (n 4), 120-1; Crown Prince Regent's Decree of 26 October 1990 (n 39).

81 Johs Andenæs, *Statsforfatningen i Norge* [The Constitution of Norway] (Tano Aschehoug, 8th ed, 1998) 241-2. The Crown Prince Regent conducts 'the Government as the temporary executor of the Royal Powers' when the King is absent or ill according to art 41 of the Norwegian Constitution.

82 See Andenæs (n 81) 241-2, Johs Andenæs and Arne Fliflet, *Statsforfatningen i Norge* [The Constitution of Norway] (Universitetsforlaget, 11th ed, 2017) 357-8.

83 Rt. 1987 s. 473.

Constitution.[84] The Supreme Court ruled that the ecclesiastical ordinance would prevail, as art 16 gave the King-in-Council a royal prerogative.[85]

Therefore, it is a simplification to state that the Church of Norway had made an 'erroneous' description of the duty of confidentiality in the *General Instructions for Confession*, as it was a legislation approved by the Crown Prince Regent-in-Council. It is instead a conflict between two norms, where the authority of the King-in-Council's exclusive competence stood against the authority of the *Storting's* general competence as legislator. While a 'legally unconditional duty of confidentiality' would suggest that the duty was not conditional on anything, the duty to avert according to s 196 of the *Penal Code*, 'applies regardless of *any* duty of confidentiality'.[86] Through an amendment of the *Penal Code* in 2010, this was clarified by the *Storting*.[87] In the preparatory works, the Ministry of Justice explained that this meant *any* duty of confidentiality, 'regardless of the legal basis for the duty of confidentiality'.[88] This would clearly include the duty of confidentiality according to the *General Instructions*, as well. It is also worth noting that the senior civil servant responsible for the decree from 1990, has later maintained that the seal of the confessional has not been absolute since the Reformation.[89] As the General Synod amended the provision in 2019, this point is only of academic interest. The current provision states that '[b]oth the priest and any others who receive confession, has a duty of confidentiality in accordance with

---

84 *Lov 29 april 1953 nr 1 om Den norske kirkes ordning* [Church Order Act 1953] (Norway) s 32b; *Kongelig resolusjon 16 september 1977* [Royal Decree 16 September 1977] (Norway).

85 *Rt. 1987 s. 473*. For a discussion of the decision see Jens Edvin Andreassen, 'State and Church in Norway' (1992) 36 *Scandinavian Studies in Law* 13; Jens Edvin A Skoghøy, *Konge, rikskirke og lokalmenighet* (Universitetsforlaget, 1989).

86 Penal Code 2005 (n 24) s 196 (emphasis added).

87 *Lov 25 juni 2010 nr 47 om endringer i domstolloven (ekstraordinære valg til lekdommerutvalgene m.m.) og straffeloven 1902 (avvergingsplikt)* [Court of Justice and Penal Code 1902 (Amendment) Act 2010] (Norway).

88 Prop 116 (2009–10) (n 42) 17.

89 Ole Herman Fisknes, '*Informasjonsstrøm, offentlighet og taushet*' [Information Flow, Publicity and Confidentiality] (1996) 13(2) *Halvårsskrift for praktisk teologi* 36, 37; Ole Herman Fisknes, '*Presters taushetsplikt*' (2006) *Inter Collegias* 30, 30. Ole Herman Fisknes, a governmental lawyer, was the Director-General of the Department of Church Affairs of the Ministry of Culture and Church Affairs until 2008.

current regulations in force'.[90]

G Duty of Confidentiality for Other Christians Hearing Confessions

As mentioned, confession in the Church of Norway may be heard by a priest or another Christian.[91] This raises the following question: How does the law regulate the secrecy of a confession heard by another Christian than the priests? The answer depends partly on what function the person hearing the confession has. Deacons, catechists, cantors and other church employees are bound by the administrative duty of confidentiality prescribed by the *Church Order*.[92] The same applies to 'any person rendering services to' the Church in connection with 'any matter disclosed to him in the course of his duties'.[93]

In addition, if a person may be considered an *assistant* to the priest, the professional duty of confidentiality according to s 211 of the *Penal Code 2005* also applies to the assistant. Professor Morten Holmboe explains that if the person hearing the confession is meant to seek advice from the priest, he or she becomes an assistant to the priest, and he or she will then be covered by extension by the same duty as that of the priest.[94] However, if the person hearing the confession is asked by the penitent not to share the information with anyone, not even the priest, the person hearing the confession will not act as the priest's assistant, and thus not be covered by the priest's professional duty of confidentiality.[95]

As any Christian may hear a confession, it is not clear that every Christian may be said to render services to the church by taking the confession. The *General Instructions for Confession* previously contained a provision stating that '[a]lso others who receive confession, must remain silent

---

90 *Alminnelige bestemmelser for skriftemål 2* [General Instructions for Confession 2] (1977, as amended in 2019).
91 Ibid.
92 Church Order of the Church of Norway s 42.
93 *Public Administration Act 1967* (Norway) s 13.
94 Holmboe (n 48) 200.
95 Ibid.

about what have been confessed in the confession' until 2019, when it was amended.[96] After the amendment, the provision only states that they have 'a duty of confidentiality in accordance with current regulations in force'.[97] This means that a lay Christian may hear a confession without being covered by a duty of confidentiality prescribed by either the church or the state. This suggests that the amendment in 2019 created a *lacunae legis*. However, the practical consequences are limited, as there are no sanctions available for any breaches of the duty prescribed by the general instructions.[98]

Despite the above, Holmboe explains that a person who reveals private information received in confession to the public, may face criminal charges for having violated the privacy of another person by public communication.[99] Additionally, infringement of privacy may also entail liability under tort law.[100] A practical implication is that the evidential privilege does not apply. However, the court may exempt the witness from testifying about something received in confession according to s 121 of the *Criminal Procedure Act 1902* and s 22-5 of the *Disputes Act*.[101]

III The Seal of the Confessional and Duty of Confidentiality for Priests in the Church of Sweden

A Confession in the Church of Sweden

Anyone belonging to the Church of Sweden has a legal right to participate in the rite of confession.[102] The *Church Order* explains that:

> Confession consists of two main elements: the confession and the

---

96 General Instructions for Confession 2 (n 90), before its amendment in 2019.
97 Ibid.
98 In fact, ecclesiastical ordinances may not create any legal rights or duties as such: see *Prop 55 L (2015–6) Endringer i kirkeloven* [Bill No 55 Church of Norway (Amendment) Bill], 55.
99 Holmboe (n 48) 199, citing Penal Code 2005 (n 24) s 267.
100 *Skadeerstatningsloven 1969* [Act of 13 June 1969 relating to Compensation in Certain Circumstances] (Norway).
101 Holmboe (n 48) 199.
102 *Kyrkoordning for Svenska kyrkan 1999* [Church Order of the Church of Sweden], ch 17, s 2.

announcement of forgiveness (absolution) on behalf of Jesus Christ. In the confession, which is normally preceded by a conversation, the penitent confesses his or her guilt and sin. In the absolution, the priest pronounces God's forgiveness personally to the penitent. Jesus Christ carries the burdens of the penitent.[103]

Confession may only be heard by a priest.[104]

B Duty of Confidentiality

The *Church Ordinance 1571* included provisions about secret confession.[105] An amendment from 1575 imposed a duty of confidentiality on the priest, with loss of benefice and prohibition from ministry for life as punishment for revealing secrets from confession.[106] In 1686, the *Riksdag* (Parliament) adopted a *Church Act*, which made breaching the seal of the confessional a capital offence.[107] The capital offence was repealed in 1889 and replaced by the punishment of prohibition for life.[108]

The duty of confidentiality relating to confession was gradually extended by customary law to include individual pastoral conversations.[109] However, the *Instrument of Government 1974* introduced a requirement for an explicit statutory provision in order for a duty of confidentiality to be considered a legal duty.[110] The General Synod of the Church of Sweden discussed in 1975 the impact of the Instrument of Government on the

---

103 Ibid ch 21, preamble.
104 Ibid ch 21, s 2.
105 *Swenska Kyrkoordningen 1571* [Swedish Church Order 1571].
106 Kyrkostyrelsen, Svenska Kyrkan, *Ett skyddat rum — tystnadsplikt i Svenska kyrkan (SKU 2010:3)* [A Protected Space — Duty of Confidentiality in the Church of Sweden (SKU 2010:3)] (2010) 42–3 ('SKU 2010:3').
107 *1686 års kyrkolag* [The Church Act of 1686] (Sweden) ch VII § II.
108 *1889 års lag om straff för ämbetsbrott för präst* [Act on Punishment for Misconduct by the Priest of 1889] (Sweden), cited in SKU 2010:3 (n 106) 43.
109 Tystnadspliktkommittén [Committee on the Duty of Confidentiality], *Tystnadsplikt och yttrandefrihet. Betänkande av tystnadspliktskommittén: SOU 1975: 102* [Duty of Confidentiality and Freedom of Expression: SOU 1975:102] (Report, 1975) 308–9 ('SOU 1975:102'); SKU 2010:3 (n 106) 44–6; *Lag (1979:926) om tystnadsplikt för präst inom svenska kyrkan* [Duty of Confidentiality for Priests of the Church of Sweden Act (1979:926)].
110 Chapter 2 § 1 of the *1974 års regeringsform* [Instrument of Government 1974] (Sweden) lists freedom of speech as a constitutional right, which can only be limited by statute according to ch 8 of that Instrument of Government.

priest's duty of confidentiality. The *Church Act 1686*, which was still in force (as amended), contained provisions about a duty of confidentiality applying to confession, but not to the cure of souls.[111] The Synodical Church Law Committee held that the duty of confidentiality had applied to the exercising of the cure of souls as a legal custom, but that the new *Instrument of Government* had made it impossible to claim a continued duty of confidentiality for the cure of souls, and had thus, in effect, abolished the customary rule.[112] The General Synod, therefore, petitioned the Government to consider legislation to provide for a statutory basis for the duty of confidentiality for the cure of souls.[113] After some consideration, the *Riksdag* passed an Act in 1979 on the Duty of Confidentiality for Priests of the Church of Sweden, which stated that '[a] person who is ordained a priest in the Church of Sweden has a duty of confidentiality with regard to what he has experienced in individual confession or in pastoral conversations in general'.[114]

The *Church Act 1686* remained in force, though subject to a series of amendments, until 1992 when the *Riksdag* adopted a new *Church Act*.[115] The duty of confidentiality was, however, substantially transferred and continued in ch 36 of the new *Church Act 1992*, with a minor amendment in 1997.[116] The amendment clarified what was covered by the duty of confidentiality, additionally to confessions, by changing changing

---

111 SOU 1975:102 (n 109) 308.

112 *Kyrkolagutskottets betänkende nr 12 (1975 års kyrkomöte)* [Church Law Committee Report No 12 to the General Synod of 1975], cited in SOU 1975:102 (n 109) 308.

113 SKU 2010:3 (n 106) 45.

114 'Den som är prästvigd i svenska kyrkan har tystnadsplikt i fråga om det som han har erfarit under enskilt skriftermål eller under själavårdande samtal i övrigt': Duty of Confidentiality for Priests of the Church of Sweden Act (1979:926) (n 109).

115 See Frank Cranmer, 'The Church of Sweden and the Unravelling of Establishment' (2000) 5(27) *Ecclesiastical Law Journal* 417, 419. Cranmer translates the Act of 1686 (n 107) as the Church Code, whereas this chapter translates it as the Church Act; both translations are equally valid. See *Kyrkolag (1992:300)* [Church Act (1992:300)] (Sweden) ch 36; *Lag (1992:301) om införande av kyrkolagen (1992:300)* [Act (1992:301) on the Enactment of the Church Act (1992:300)] (Sweden) s 2 No 1 and No 26.

116 Church Act (1992:300) (n 115) ch 36; *Lag (1997:300) om ändring i kyrkolagen (1992:300)* [Church (Amendment) Act (1997:300)] (Sweden). Cf *Prop 97 (1996–7) Prästers tystnadsplikt* [Bill No 97 (1996–7) on Priests' Duty of Confidentiality] (Sweden) ('Prop 97 (1996–7)').

'pastoral conversations in general' (*själavårdande samtal*) to individual cure of souls (*enskild själavård*).[117] Individual cure of souls was defined as 'a secluded personal meeting between a priest and a confident (or a couple confidents with a common problem they want to discuss together with the priest)'.[118] As the priests where obliged to keep their duty of confidentiality according to law, they could, at the time, receive criminal sanctions for breaching their duty of confidentiality.[119]

The legal status of the Church of Sweden changed radically over night from 31 December 1999 to 1 January 2000, when the church separated from the state.[120] In advance, the *Riksdag* adopted the *Faith Communities Act 1998* and the *Church of Sweden Act 1998*.[121] These statutes, which came into effect on 1 January 2000, are often described as Acts separating state and church in Sweden.[122] Norman Doe explains that priests of the Church of Sweden used to be subject to a rule of confidentiality, which was abolished in 2000, in connection with the separation.[123] It is correct that the statutory rule was abolished, but the General Synod adopted its own *Church Order* in 1999, where the duty of confidentiality for priests was substantially transferred to the *Church Order*.[124] The difference is that the duty is enforced internally by the church, rather than externally by

---

117 Prop 97 (1996–7) (n 116). Note that the expression 'individual cure of souls' is the term employed by eg Lars Friedner, 'Church and State in Sweden', in Gerhard Robbers (ed), *State and Church in the European Union* (Nomos, 3rd ed, 2019) 647; Per Hansson, 'Complaints about Priests in the Church of Sweden 2001–2013' (2017) 4 *Scandinavian Journal for Leadership and Theology* 1, 10. It is also possible to translate the concept as 'individual pastoral care'.

118 '*Med enskild själavård avses i första hand själavårdande samtal som sker under avskildhet i ett personligt möte mellan en präst och en konfident (eller flera konfidenter med ett gemensamt problem)*': Prop 97 (1996–7) (n 116).

119 Cf *Brottsbalken 1962* [Criminal Code of 1962] (Sweden) ch 20, s 3.

120 Cranmer (n 115); Frank Cranmer, 'Church/State Relations in Scandinavia', in RM Morris (ed), *Church and State in 21st Century Britain* (Palgrave Macmillan, 2009) 146.

121 *Lag (1998:1593) om trossamfund* [Faith Communities Act 1998] (Sweden); *Lag (1998:1591) om Svenska kyrkan* [Church of Sweden Act 1998] (Sweden).

122 Friedner (n 117) 647.

123 Norman Doe, *Law and Religion in Europe: A Comparative Introduction* (Oxford University Press, 2011) 135.

124 Church Order of the Church of Sweden, ch 31, s 9.

criminal courts.[125]

Under the current *Church Order*, priests have a duty of confidentiality concerning information received in confession and conversations relating to individual cure of souls.[126] The promise to keep the duty of confidentiality is part of the ordination vows of priests.[127] If a priest is found guilty by the Diocesan Chapter of having breached his or her duty of confidentiality, the Diocesan Chapter may impose one of the following penalties, first, prohibition from exercising ordained ministry for life, secondly, probation, that is to say, a term of three years in which the priest must not repeat any disciplinary offences to avoid being prohibited from exercising ordained ministry for life, or thirdly a written warning.[128]

The Doctrinal Commission has explained that the priest's duty of confidentiality is fundamental to the identity of both the priest and the church.[129] The duty of confidentiality for priests is considered to be *absolute*.[130] Anna Trônet explains that the absolute duty of confidentiality in Sweden has its source in the confession, and that the seal of the confessional is often explained by the fact that the confession of sins does not take place before the priest, but before Christ, and because Christ does not reveal what has been said, the priest cannot and must not do

---

125 This was confirmed by Minister of Culture Marita Ulvskog in an answer on 18 April 2002 to a written question from Swedish MP Tuva Skånberg: cf Marita Ulvskog (18 April 2002), Svar på skriftleg fråge 2001/2002: 1006 om tystnadsplikten för präst og biskop (Answer to written question 2001/2002: 1006 about the duty of confidentiality for priests and bishops), available from ⟨https://www.riksdagen.se/sv/dokument-lagar/dokument/skriftlig-fraga/tystnadsplikten-for-prast-eller-biskop_GP111006⟩, assessed 21 December 2020.
126 Church Order of the Church of Sweden, ch 31, s 9.
127 *KsSkr 2011-7 Tystnadsplikt m.m.* –– *Kyrkostyrelsens skrivelse* [Report from the Church Board on Duty of Confidentiality etc (KsSkr 2011-7)] 9.
128 Church Order of the Church of Sweden, ch 31, s 12.
129 The Doctrinal Commission of the Church of Sweden made this statement in a report to the General Synod in 1996: 'Prästens tystnadsplikt är identitetsmässigt grundläggande både för prästen och kyrkan': *Lāronämndens ytrande 1996:15* [Doctrinal Commission Statement 1996:15].
130 Biskopsmötet [The Bishops' Conference], *Tystnadsplikt och sekretess i Svenska kyrkans arbete* [Confidentiality and Secrecy in the Work of the Church of Sweden], (Biskopsmötet [The Bishops' Conference], 2nd ed, 2004) 21–4.

so either.[131] This is also expressed in the *Church Order* in the introduction to pt XII.[132]

A priest in the Church of Sweden may not disclose confidential information even if the penitent waives the seal of the confessional.[133] This is equivalent to the rule in the Roman Catholic Church.[134]

Priests are additionally bound by a duty of confidentiality according to the collective agreement between the Church of Sweden's Employer's Association and the church unions: '[a]ll employees have a duty of confidentiality regarding information received in parish work ... regarding personal and sensitive information if it is not clear that the information can be disclosed'.[135]

C A Duty to Avert Criminal Offences?

After an amendment in 2011, the *Church Order* prescribes that if anyone becomes aware of suspected child abuse, through church activities, they are obliged to report this immediately to the social services.[136] This provision applies to priests, deacons, church employees and volunteers alike.[137] However, this only applies to a priest if he or she has become aware of the information outside of confession or individual cure of souls.[138]

---

131 Anna Trönet, 'Prästens tysnadsplikt', in Leif Nordenstorm (ed), *Med god ordning och efter Guds vilja* (Artos & Norma bokförlag, 2019) 451.

132 Church Order of the Church of Sweden, pt 12.

133 Biskopsmötet (n 130).

134 *The Code of Canon Law: In English Translation* (1983) canon 983 § 1. See also a commentary in Canon Law Society of Great Britain and Ireland, *The Canon Law: Letter & Spirit: A Practical Guide to the Code of Canon Law* (Veritas, 1995) 535.

135 *Svenska kyrkans avtal 17* [Church of Sweden's Collective Agreement 17] 107.

136 Church Order of the Church of Sweden, ch 54, s 13a. It is a requirement that the suspected abuse is of a character that would oblige the social services to intervene for the protection of the child.

137 Gunnar Edqvist et al, *Kyrkoordning för Svenska kyrkan 2018 med kommentarer och angränsande lagstifting* [Church Order of the Church of Sweden 2018 with Commentaries and Related Legislation] (Verbum, 2018) 793.

138 Church Order of the Church of Sweden, ch 54, s 13a.

A breach of the duty by clergy and church employees may be followed by disciplinary sanctions, but volunteers do not face any sanctions according to the internal church-made law.[139] However, leading Swedish ecclesiastical lawyers have explained that the duty to report provides 'a clear signal both about how the Church of Sweden believes participants in church activities should behave in these situations, and how the church views the child's value'.[140] Even though there is a limited possibility for the church to enforce or sanction non-compliance for volunteers, the provision sends a signal.[141]

If a person in confession or individual cure of souls speaks of harmful or criminal acts and there is a risk of repetition, the priest is expected to use the opportunities available to stop the harmful behaviour, eg by making the person take responsibility for his/her actions, or by trying to persuade the person to turn him/herself in.[142] However, if a priest is made aware of a plan to commit a criminal offence, the priest has an obligation to warn the person threatened by the crime or contact the police or other authorities, but without revealing the identity of the penitent.[143] In 1992, the Government confirmed that priests would fulfil their duty to avert the crime by following such a course.[144] Such actions to avert crimes are not considered as breach of absolute confidentiality.[145]

D The Corresponding Privilege of Confidentiality

Although the duty of confidentiality for priests now follows from the internal law of the Church of Sweden, there are still some remnants of this duty in the form of an evidential privilege of confidentiality

---

139 Edqvist (n 137) 794.
140 Ibid.
141 Ibid.
142 SKU 2010:3 (n 106), 99–100, 104.
143 Ibid; Hans Gustaf Frederik Sundberg, *Kyrkorätt* [Church Law] (Frenckells-ka Tryckeri, 1948) 234; Maria Lundqvist Norling, *Offentlighet och tystnadsplikt i Svenska kyrkan* [Openness and Duty of Confidentiality in the Church of Sweden] (Verbum, 2007) 66–7.
144 *Prop 85 (1991–2) Ny kirkolag* [Bill No 85 (1991–2) New Church Act] (Sweden) 94–7.
145 SKU 2010:3 (n 106) 99–100, 104; Trônet, (n 131) 451.

according to both criminal and civil procedure law. A priest in a faith community or a person in such a community with a position similar to a priest, cannot testify in criminal and civil proceedings in Swedish courts about anything (s)he has heard during confession or individual cure of souls.[146]

E Recent Developments

After the separation of church and state in 2000, the Bishops' Conference published a pastoral letter on their interpretation of the duty of confidentiality in the Church, which it later amended in 2004.[147] However, some unclarity remained, especially with regard to whether church employees would be bound to report suspected child abuse.[148] This led to the 2008 appointment of a committee tasked with reporting on the legal and theological understanding of the duty of confidentiality and recommending legislative amendments to the General Synod. The committee published its report in 2010.[149] Based on its recommendations, the General Synod adopted some amendments to the *Church Order* and the *Service Book* in 2011. The previously mentioned amendment that introduced the duty for church employees and volunteers to report issues to the social services was adopted.[150] At the same time, the General Synod also adopted some clarifications to the rules in the *Church Order*, and the ordination liturgy was amended to include a vow to 'follow our Church's Order, observe the duty of confidentiality that applies to a priest, and realise your calling with Christ as a model'.[151] However, the General

---

146 *Rättegångsbalken 1942* [Procedure Code 1942] (Sweden) ch 36, s 5. See also Friedner (n 117) 654.

147 Biskopsmötet (n 130).

148 SKU 2010:3 (n 106) 23.

149 SKU 2010:3 (n 106).

150 *Report of Proceedings of the General Synod of the Church of Sweden* (2011) 64–5 ('*Report of Proceedings (2011)*').

151 From the Service book, cited in Edqvist et al (n 137) 389.

Synod underlined that the duty for priests should remain absolute.[152]

Anna Trônet explains that 'overall, the priest's absolute duty of confidentiality has a strong position in the Church of Sweden and the Swedish society'.[153] She also explains that unlike in England, Australia, and the United States, there has not been any debate about limiting the absolute duty of confidentiality in the Swedish Church in order to introduce mandatory reporting.[154] This must be understood in light of the priest's obligation avert serious crimes.

IV Comparison

In this section, the two churches will be compared and considered in light of the *Statement on Principles of Christian Law* (2016) on confession. A panel of experts agreed on this statement of principles of Christian law common to the Catholic, Orthodox, Anglican, Lutheran, Methodist, Reformed, Presbyterian, and Baptist traditions.[155]

Although the churches of Norway and Sweden are both Evangelical-Lutheran churches, it seems clear that they have different understandings of both the seal of the confessional and of the duty of confidentiality attached to the exercise of ministry.

Confession may only be heard by a priest in the Church of Sweden. In the Church of Norway, the matter is somewhat different. Although it is specifically mentioned that the priest has ecclesiastical authority to hear confessions, suggesting a preference for the priest, confession may

---

152 *Kyrkomötets tillsyns — och uppdragsutskotts betänkande 2011:1 — Tystnadsplikt m.m.* [Report 2011:1 from the Standing Committee on Oversight and Mission of the General Synod on the Duty of Confidentiality] 7, 11; *Report of Proceedings (2011)* (n 150) 64–5.

153 Trônet (n 131) 448, 464.

154 Ibid.

155 Hill and Doe (n 8); Doe (n 8). On confession, they agreed that 'a church may practise private confession and absolution in the presence of an ordained minister to the extent that this is permitted by the law of that church' (*Principle* VII.5.1), that 'the seal of the confessional is inviolable, save as may be provided by the law of a church' (*Principle* VII.5.2), and that 'a duty of confidentiality attaches to the exercise of ministry to the extent provided by law' (*Principle* VII.5.3).

also be heard by another Christian. *Principle* VII.5.1 suggests a preference for 'the presence of an ordained minister' at private confession and absolution. However, this is nuanced by the fact that the church 'may practise' private confession 'to the extent permitted by law'.[156] If the law of the church permits it, this can be interpreted to open for the possibility of practising private confession by someone other than an ordained minister.

For both churches, the duty of confidentiality applies both to the seal of the confessional, as well as to certain other parts of the exercise of the priest's ministry; that is, secrets confided to them in connection with their position or individual cure of souls, respectively. This is in line with *Principle* VII.5.3. In addition to the duty of confidentiality attached to their role as a priest, both churches have a duty of confidentiality attached to every church employee (including priests) relating to personal information received.

In the Church of Sweden, both the Doctrinal Commission, the Bishops' Conference and the General Synod have underlined the theological significance of the priest's duty of confidentiality relating to confession and individual cure of souls, underlining that it is absolute or inviolable. In the Church of Norway, priests have a duty of confidentiality relating both to the seal of the confessional, as well as to other secrets confided to them in their exercise of ministry. However, in Norway, the duty of confidentiality is superseded by their duty to avert certain planned criminal offences. In other words, the duty of confidentiality is inviolable, save as provided by the law in connection with the duty to avert criminal offences, cf *Principle* VII.5.2.

Even though the duty of confidentiality is absolute for the Swedish Church, priests have an obligation to avert planned crimes, eg by giving a warning or reporting it to the authorities. Unlike in the Church of Norway, where the priest may reveal the penitent's identity if it is necessary to avert a crime, priests in the Church of Sweden are prohibited from

---

156 *Principle* VII.5.1 in Hill and Doe (n 8); Doe (n 8).

revealing the identity of the penitent. If a person confesses to an already committed crime, including homicide, and there is no risk of repetition, priests in both churches are duty-bound to keep it confidential.

In Norway, a priest may be released by the duty of confidentiality by the penitent. This rule is equivalent to the rule in the Church of England.[157] In Sweden, the priest may not disclose confidential information even if the penitent waives the seal of the confessional.[158] This rule is equivalent to the rule in the Roman Catholic Church.[159]

After the separation of church and state in Sweden in 2000, the duty of confidentiality became part of the internal law of the Church of Sweden, and not part of state law. In Norway, the duty of confidentiality according to the *Public Administration Act* has been transferred from being an obligation under state law to being an obligation under internal church law, while the professional duty of confidentiality attached to priests, is still prescribed by state-made law.

With the exception of the conflicting texts of the *General Instructions for Confession* and the *Penal Code* in Norway, which was a conflict between two state-made laws, until resolved in 2019, there has been little conflict between state-made law and church-made law on confidentiality in both countries. Rather, the state-made laws strengthen and facilitate church law and the understanding of the churches on confidentiality.

In both Sweden and Norway, priests have an evidential privilege according to state law. Neither criminal or civil courts may call upon priests to testify about information learned during confession or individual cure of souls, in Sweden, or secrets learned in connection with their profession, in Norway. Some scholars have described certain remnants of privileges from the time of establishment as the *vestiges of*

---

157 See, eg, Bursell (n 52) 109.
158 Biskopsmötet (n 130).
159 *The Code of Canon Law: In English Translation* (1983) canon 983 § 1. See also a commentary in Canon Law Society of Great Britain and Ireland, *The Canon Law: Letter & Spirit: A Practical Guide to the Code of Canon Law* (Veritas, 1995) 535.

establishment.[160] While one might think that this privilege was such a vestige in Norway and Sweden, this is not the whole story. The evidential privilege is not unique to the two former state churches, but also applies to priests and religious leaders of other faith communities in both countries.[161] Especially in Norway, the professional duty of confidentiality relating to 'secrets confiding to them' applies equally to priests in the Church of Norway and religious leaders of other registered faith communities. In Sweden, on the other hand, the privilege applies to information received during confessions and individual cure of souls. It therefore primarily applies to Christian faith communities who subscribe to confession and individual cure of souls, rather than to non-Christian religions that do not practice confession.

One possible explanation for the difference between the churches could be the different ways the Reformation was introduced into Norway and Sweden. The Reformation in Denmark and Norway was introduced by royal decree in 1537.[162] In fact, with the *Norwegian Code 1687*, the concept of 'church' even disappeared from law.[163] In Sweden, on the other hand, the Reformation was officially introduced at the Uppsala Synod of 1593. Duke Charles and the Synod of the church jointly decided to declare Sweden as Lutheran by adopting the Augsburg Confession as the confessional foundation of the Church of Sweden.[164] Thus, in Norway, the church became part of the King's civil service, the bishops became the King's advisers, and there were no autonomous church

---

160 Thomas Glyn Watkin, 'Vestiges of Establishment: The Ecclesiastical and Canon Law of the Church in Wales' (1990) 2(7) *Ecclesiastical Law Journal* 110; Norman Doe, 'The Constitution of the Church', in Norman Doe (ed), *A New History of the Church in Wales: Governance and Ministry, Theology and Society* (Cambridge University Press, 2020) 85; Norman Doe, 'The *Welsh Church Act 1914*: A Century of Constitutional Freedom for the Church in Wales?' (2020) 22(1) *Ecclesiastical Law Journal* 2, 6–9.

161 *Procedure Code 1942* (Sweden) ch 36, s 5; *Criminal Procedure Act 1902* (Sweden) s 119.

162 Niels Valdemar Vinding, 'State and Church in Denmark', in Gerhard Robbers (ed), *State and Church in the European Union* (Nomos, 3rd ed, 2019) 87–108.

163 Christoffersen (n 32) 175.

164 Trygve R Skarsten, 'The Reception of the Augsburg Confession in Scandinavia' (1980) 11(3) *Sixteenth Century Journal* 87. Skarsten explains that the Lutheran reformation came gradually to Sweden from 1527 onwards, but it was only at the Uppsala Synod of 1593 that Sweden officially was declared as Lutheran.

institutions.[165] In Sweden, by contrast, the church kept its internal, hierarchical administrative structure with the archbishop, synod and diocesan chapters.[166] As this gave the Swedish church a more autonomous position, it may have allowed the church to retain its understanding of the seal of the confessional as absolute, closer to the previous Catholic understanding. In Norway, on the other hand, where the King was the head of both the church and the state, matters of the state may have triumphed over the absolute seal of the confession. Indeed, as we have seen, King Christian V's *Norwegian Code of 1687* mentions 'treason' as an exception from the duty.[167]

Both churches have recently taken steps to facilitate and strengthen mandatory reporting, although the Church of Sweden has made exceptions for the priest's absolute duty of confidentiality. In Norway, church leaders have emphasised the importance of mandatory reporting for the safeguarding of children.

V Conclusion

This chapter has explored the duty of confidentiality in the Church of Norway and the Church of Sweden. Both churches offer private confession. Confession may be heard by a priest in both churches, and by any other Christian in the Church of Norway, cf *Principle* VII.5.1.

In both churches, the priest's duty of confidentiality originated from the seal of the confessional, but was extended to include other, specific parts of their pastoral ministry, cf *Principle* VII.5.3. The duties of confidentiality have been extended from the seal of the confessional but have otherwise remained more or less constant even though both churches have been subject to significant changes in the relationship between church and

---

165 Lisbet Christoffersen, 'Church Autonomy in Nordic Law', in Lisbet Christ-offersen, Kjell Å Modéer and Svend Andersen (eds), *Law & Religion in the 21st Century – Nordic Perspectives* (Djøf Publishing, 2010) 577.
166 Ibid.
167 Norwegian Code 1687 (n 4) bk 2, ch 5, s 19.

state. State-made law still regulates evidential privilege in both churches, and priests in the Church of Norway are covered by a professional duty of confidentiality prescribed by state law. At the same time, both churches have adopted internal church law imposing a duty of confidentiality on priests and others. While the former, state-made law may be enforced by the state, the internal church law may only be enforced internally by the church. Although both churches are Evangelical-Lutheran, they have different understandings of both the seal of the confessional and the duty of confidentiality attached to the exercise of ministry. In the Church of Sweden, the priest's duty of confidentiality relating to confession and individual cure of souls is considered absolute. In the Church of Norway, by contrast, the duty of confidentiality is not considered absolute: It may be set aside by law.

The duty of confidentiality covering both the seal of the confessional and individual cure of souls or secrets, is inviolable, save as provided by law, cf *Principle* VII.5.2. Priests in the Church of Norway have a statutory duty to avert certain crimes that supersedes their duties of confidentiality, and the church seems to value the prevention of future harm more than the duty of confidentiality. For instance, the Bishops' Conference has taken the initiative to strengthen mandatory reporting. Although the Church of Sweden underlines that the priest's duty of confidentiality is absolute, priests still have a duty to avert criminal offenses and prevent future harm, either by warning the person threatened by the crime or by reporting future crimes to the authorities. Such prevention of future harm is, however, not recognised as something that undermines the absolute duty of confidentiality.

On first sight the differences between the churches in Norway and Sweden seem substantial, due to the different emphases put on the duty of confidentiality as *absolute*. Upon further inquiry, however, we have seen the two churches are more similar. While they both offer a protected space for anyone seeking spiritual guidance and forgiveness, through their priest's confidentiality, they also act to prevent future harm. This is because both churches acknowledge the need to safeguard children, and over the last years they have both taken steps to strengthen this safeguarding.

7

Stephen Farrell

Sacerdotal privilege and the seal of the confessional in Irish law

Abstract

The seal of the confessional in the Irish common law has developed significantly since Irish independence. The leading case of *Cook v Carroll* saw a widening of the scope of the privilege attaching to disclosures made to a priest. Recent attempts by the Irish parliament to introduce mandatory reporting would seem to override the privilege attaching to the seal of the confessional, though this has yet to be tested in court.

Keywords:

Sacerdotal privilege – Seal of the confessional – Cook v Carroll [1945] Ir Rep 515 – Criminal Justice (Witholding of Information on Offences Against Children and Vulnerable Persons) Act 2012

'Practically, while Barristers and Judges are gentlemen the question [of a court compelling a priest to break the seal of the confession] can never arise. I am told it has never arisen in Ireland in the worst of times'.[1]

---

1   Coleridge, defence counsel in *R v Kent* (1865) in a letter he wrote subsequently to Mr Gladstone. The letter is to be found in E Hartley Coleridge, *Life and Correspondence of Lord Coleridge* (1904) vol II, 364, quoted in JR Lindsay, 'Privileged Communications: Part I: Communications with Spiritual Advisers' (1959) 13(2) *Northern Ireland Legal Quarterly* 160, 164–5.

I The Common Law and its development in Ireland

A The Classical Common Law Position

In general, a witness is bound to answer all relevant questions put to him or her, and will be guilty of contempt of court if he or she refuses to do so.[2] There are limited exceptions to this rule where a person may enjoy a privilege from being compelled to answer a question or produce a document.[3] The generally accepted view is that prior to the Reformation, the common law recognised a sacerdotal privilege whereby a priest could not be compelled by a court to reveal what he had been told during confession.[4] Following the Reformation new canons were promulgated for the Church of England in 1603.[5] Canon 113 dealt with the issue of the seal of the confession and concludes with the words:

> Provided always, That if any man confess his secret and hidden sins to the Minister, for the unburdening of his conscience, and to receive spiritual consolation and ease of mind from him; we do not any way bind the said Minister by this our Constitution, but do straitly charge and admonish him, that he do not at any time reveal and make known to any person whatsoever any crime or offence so committed to his trust and secrecy, (except they be such crimes as by the laws of this realm his own life may be called into question for concealing the same) under pain of irregularity.[6]

Thus it would seem that the sacerdotal privilege continued through the reformation into the laws of the Church of England if not entirely without alteration. The words in brackets do seem to form an exception

---

2   Declan McGrath, *Evidence* (Thompson Round Hall, 2005) 521. See, eg, *R v Duchess of Kingston* (1776) 1 Leach 146; 168 ER 175.

3   For instance, legal professional privilege: see *Anderson v Bank of British Columbia* (1876) 2 Ch D 644.

4   See Michael James Callahan, 'Historical Inquiry into the Priest-Penitent Privilege' (1976) 36 *Jurist* 328; McGrath (n 3) 612; Judge Rupert DH Bursell, 'The Seal of the Confessional' (1990) 2(7) *Ecclesiastical Law Journal* 84; Lindsay (n 1) 169–71; Martin O'Dwyer, 'A Matter of Evidence: Sacerdotal Privilege and the Seal of Confession in Ireland' (2013) 13 *University College Dublin Law Review* 103.

5   For a full treatment of the position in England, past and present, see Mark Hill and Christopher Grout, 'The Seal of the Confessional, the Church of England, and English Law' in chapter 5 of this volume.

6   *The Canons of the Church of England: Canons Ecclesiastical Promulgated by the Convocations of Canterbury and York in 1964 and 1969* (SPCK, 1969) xii.

to the rule but its scope is uncertain as mere concealment of an offence was not itself a capital offence.[7] It has been interpreted to mean that the privilege should not apply to confessions of high treason,[8] though there seems little justification for the proposition and the view taken by Bursell is persuasive that this was based on a misreading of the canon by Sir Edward Coke.[9]

More recent consideration of the principle by the courts has been sporadic. The privilege is rarely in issue, by virtue of the fact that confessions are secret neither the priest nor penitent are likely to acknowledge that a confession has been made. For a Roman Catholic priest it would result in an automatic excommunication[10] and for the penitent in a criminal trial the drawbacks are obvious. The paucity of case law combined with the fact that many of the comments taken to be expressions of the law are obiter dicta combine to mean that the case law does not establish a clear uniformity of principle. It has been noted that 'there does not seem to be an English case in the past 150 years in which the matter has been fully argued or fully considered'.[11]

In *Broad v Pitt*, Best CJ stated obiter

> The privilege does not apply to clergymen since the decision the other day in *Gilham*. I, for one, will never compel a clergyman to disclose communications, made to him by a prisoner; but if he chooses to disclose them, I shall receive them in evidence.[12]

This personal reluctance of Best CJ to compel a cleric to divulge communications made to him by a prisoner does nothing to strengthen the principle in law. However, it ought to be noted that Best CJ misread

---

7   Bursell (n 4) 88 n 46.
8   See, eg, GD Noakes, 'Professional Privilege' (1950) 66(1) *Law Quarterly Review* 88, 94, 101; Lindsay (n 1) 160; *R v Garnet* (1606) 2 How St Tr 217; *A-G v Briant* (1846) 15 M & W 169; 153 ER 808.
9   Bursell (n 4) 88.
10   *The Code of Canon Law: In English Translation* (Collins, 1983) canon 1388 § 1. See also Alex Stenson, 'Penalties in the New Code: The Role of the Confessor' (1983) 43(2) *Jurist* 406.
11   Lindsay (n 1) 161.
12   (1828) 3 Car & P 518; 172 ER 528.

R v Gilham.[13] That case did not concern the seal of the confessional at all. Rather, *Gilham* was a convicted murderer whose execution was stayed to allow the court to consider whether certain confessions he made to his gaoler and a magistrate after his meeting with a chaplain ought to have been read in evidence. No confession made to the chaplain was in issue and the chaplain divulged nothing to the court, nor was the question whether the chaplain could be compelled so to do considered or decided upon.

A sacramental confession was in issue in *R v Hay*,[14] a case concerning the larceny of a watch. At the defendant's trial a Roman Catholic priest from whom the police had possession of the watch refused to divulge from whom he had received the watch as he had 'received it in connexion with the confessional'. Hill J noted that the priest was not being asked to divulge anything he was told in confession simply from whom he had received the watch. The priest refused on the grounds that this would implicate the penitent and would violate the laws of the Church. He was committed for contempt. It has been argued that the judge impliedly admitted that a privilege exists in relation to confession by drawing the distinction between what was said to the priest in confession and the identity of the person from whom he received the watch.[15] In reality, the judge simply tried to persuade the priest that the distinction could be made and thus the priest might not be violating the law of the church in the way he feared.

Subsequent considerations of the seal of the confessional have been obiter. *Wheeler v Le Marchant*[16] concerned legal professional privilege. Sir George Jessel MR said that '[c]ommunications made to a priest in the confessional on matters perhaps considered by the penitent to be more

13   (1828) 1 Mood CC 186; 168 ER 1235.

14   (1860) 2 F & F 4; 175 ER 933.

15   Lindsay (n 1) 163; Bursell (n 4) 92, quoting a note to *R v Hay* made by the reporter WF Finlayson: 1860) 2 F & F 4; 175 ER 933, 934 n (a), 936 n (a).

16   (1881) 17 Ch D 675.

important even than his life and fortune, are not protected'.[17]

Lord Denning was the source of adverse obiter dicta in two cases. In *McTaggart v McTaggart*[18] he said 'the probation officer has no privilege of his own in respect of disclosure any more than a priest, or a medical man, or a banker'.[19] In *Attorney-General v Mulholland*[20] he said

> Take the clergyman, the banker or the medical man. None of these is entitled to refuse to answer when directed by a judge. Let me not be mistaken. The judge will respect the confidences which each member of these honourable professions receives in the course of it, and will not direct him to answer unless not only is it relevant but also is a proper and, indeed, necessary question in the course of justice to be put and answered.[21]

The general tenor of the authorities is clearly against recognising a privilege in relation to priest-penitent communication. One case which leant the other way was *Ruthven v De Bour* when Ridley J told counsel 'you are not entitled to ask what questions priests put in the confessional or the answers given'.[22] It is uncertain on what this assertion was based. The problem that remains is that the issue has not been properly considered by the courts for over a century and a half and the previous cases do not adequately make clear whether their reluctance to apply the privilege to clergy extends to the confessional.

B The Development of the Principle in Ireland

The only Irish case against recognising the privilege relating to the seal of the confessional is the early case of *Butler v Moore*[23] where Smith

---

17   Ibid 681.
18   (1949) P 94.
19   Ibid 97 (Denning LJ).
20   [1963] 2 QB 477.
21   Ibid 489–90 (Lord Denning MR).
22   (1901) 45 Sol J 272.
23   (1802) It is not fully reported: see Lindsay (n 1) 165; Bursell (n 4) 96.

MR refused to recognise the privilege claimed by a Roman Catholic priest because he received 'confidential communications made to him in the exercise of his clerical functions'. It is unclear whether or not the case relates to the confessional. Two subsequent pre Irish independence cases clearly recognise sacerdotal privilege in relational to the confessional. Re Keller[24] concerned a priest who refused to answer a question relating to a bankrupt's affairs on the ground that he came to possess the information based solely on his being a priest.[25] The information was not communicated during confession, though the priest felt 'bound in honour' not to answer and was committed for contempt. Though obiter, Boyd J said that he was willing 'to protect any witness . . . from being obliged to answer any question in reference to anything received in confidence in the confessional'.[26] In Tannian v Synott[27] the issue of sacerdotal privilege was again considered in obiter dicta. The case concerned slander. A priest had been consulted 'as a clergyman', not in confession, but in conversation in the street. Palles CB stated, obiter, that he would not expect the priest to depose to anything connected, directly or indirectly, with confession.

II Cook v Carroll

The most important Irish case in this area is *Cook v Carroll*.[28] Consideration of this case renders unavoidable a few words on the trial judge, Gavan Duffy J of the Irish High Court. Gavan Duffy J was a devout Catholic, a committed nationalist, and a keen diviner of many unforeseen legal consequences brought by the recognition of the special position of the Roman Catholic Church in art 44.1.2 of the *Bunreacht na hÉireann 1937 (Irish Constitution)*. Though now repealed, the section was said to have

---

24 (1887) 22 LR Ir 158.
25 Ibid 160–1.
26 Ibid 159.
27 (1903) 37 Ir L T 275.
28 [1945] Ir Rep 515.

'had very little impact on the interpretation of law, if one excepts the highly individual and independent judgments of Gavan Duffy J'.[29]

> Perhaps the most striking of the innovatory judgements which he based on his conceptions of the place of the Christian and Catholic faith in the Irish tradition and the Irish Constitution is the judgement which added a new category to the communications which a witness is privileged from being obliged to disclose.[30]

The case concerned the parish priest of Ballybunion, the Revd WJ Behan, who had been called as a witness in a seduction action, and who claimed privilege. He was found to be guilty of contempt and fined. The plaintiff to the seduction action appealed to the High Court and again the priest was called as a witness and again claimed privilege. The facts are straightforward. Carroll, a married man, was accused by Cook of being the father of her as yet unborn child. Anxious to avoid scandal Carroll went to see their parish priest. The priest then sent his car to collect Cook that he might interview both parties at his residence. He spoke to both together that he might 'induce the delinquent (seducer or calumniatrix) to make proper amends'.[31] In court Cook claimed Carroll had at that meeting admitted paternity, a claim he denied. The priest was asked to divulge what had been said. He refused and Gavan Duffy J reserved the question whether or not the priest was guilty of contempt.

Though ample precedent existed to form at least a starting point for his consideration, Gavan Duffy J dismissed the treatment of the issue at common law. He conceded that 'apart from the sacrament of penance, no sacerdotal privilege was recognised in an Ireland dominated by English legal precedent for its common law'.[32] However, the judge did not feel

---

29 GW Hogan and GF Whyte (eds), *JM Kelly: The Irish Constitution* (LexisNexis Butterworths, 4th ed, 2004) 2031. The editors go so far as to consider the judgments of Gavan Duffy J in their own section.

30 Ibid 2039.

31 *Cook v Carroll* (n 28) 118 (Gavan Duffy J).

32 Ibid 117. See also *Re Keller* (n 24); *Tanniam v Synnott* (n 27).

at all bound to follow the existing decisions as

> it would be intolerable that the common law, as expounded after the Reformation in a Protestant land, should be taken to bind a nation which persistently repudiated the Reformation as heresy. When as a measure of necessary convenience, we allowed the common law generally to continue in force, we meant to include all the common law in harmony with the national spirit; we never contemplated the maintenance of any construction of the common law affected by the sectarian background.[33]

Regularly returning and warming to this theme throughout his judgment, he later notes 'the judges of the old regime in Ireland were the guardians of the British Constitution in Ireland'[34] leading him to conclude that

> The common law is an integral portion of our jurisprudence; its misconstruction is not. I must be guided by authoritative precedent, where it exists, here there is none . . . Setting pseudodox aside, I must treat the law here at the date of the Constitution as *tabula rasa*.[35]

Gavan Duffy J resolved to

> determine the issue raised in this case on principle and in conformity with the Constitution of Ireland. That Constitution in express terms recognizes the special position among us of the Holy Catholic Apostolic and Roman Church as the guardian of the Faith professed by the great majority of the citizens[36]

Finally, he said

> I hold that the emergence of the national Constitution is a complete and conclusive answer to the objection that I have no judicial precedent in favour of the parish priest. I hold that I am free to give judgment, in the light of the Constitution, on principle, and that I am bound to do so.[37]

---

33 *Cook v Carroll* (n 28) 117.
34 Ibid 119.
35 Ibid.
36 Ibid 116–7. See also *Bunreacht na hÉireann 1937* art 44.1.2 (repealed).
37 *Cook v Carroll* (n 28) 119.

Gavan Duffy J adopts the 'General Principle of Privileged Communications' elucidated by the American jurist, Wigmore,[38] who sees four fundamental conditions to a finding of privilege:

1. The communications must originate in a confidence that they will not be disclosed;

2. This element of confidentiality must be essential to the full and satisfactory maintenance of the relation;

3. The relation must be one which in the opinion of the community ought to be sedulously fostered; and

4. The injury which would enure to the relation by the disclosure of the communications must be greater than the benefit thereby gained for the correct disposal of litigation.[39]

The judge felt these four conditions applied 'so neatly as if they had been made to Father Behan's order'.[40] The judge simply accepts that the first condition applies to the case, that is, that any communications made at the priest's house were made on the understanding of secrecy. It is difficult to see how this can be said with certainty. Cook and Carroll may not have expected the priest to divulge the contents of their interview, but it is difficult to see how an expectation of secrecy can be implied between them. Would the same presumption exist had one or each of the parties brought a supporter? It is difficult to see in what meaningful way there can be an expectation of secrecy when each communication is not solely between priest and parishioner, but is communicated also to a third party. The facts in this case involve a communication made to a priest outside the confessional and ought to be distinguished from an instance of sacramental confession. The latter would only have the priest and penitent present (unless an interpreter was required) and would much more neatly fit the Wigmore test as set out by Gavan Duffy J.

The second element runs into similar problems. The judge thought 'the subject matter of the conference was of a character to make secrecy

---

38 John Henry Wigmore, *Evidence in Trials at Common Law*, rev John T McNaughton (Little, Brown, 3rd ed, 1940) vol VIII [2285].

39 Quoted in *Cook v Carroll* (n 28) 118.

40 *Cook v Carroll* (n 28) 118.

essential to any prospect of a satisfactory outcome'.[41] The element of secrecy may be essential to the priest-parishioner relationship when communication is entered into in confidence, but this situation could arguably be distinguished again on the ground that Cook and Carroll each spoke before a third party. Indeed, both parties waived their privilege and each wanted the priest to divulge what each claimed was an accurate record of the meeting. Again, this part of the test would be satisfied in sacramental confession. The third and fourth categories seem to apply, or at least it did in rural Ireland in 1945.

III The Development of *Cook v Carroll*

A Privilege attaching to the Seal of the Confessional

The scope of the decision in *Cook v Carroll* is difficult to state with certainty. Though the judge goes to great lengths to set aside all former authority on the point, and though he does not expressly state that the privilege applies to the sacrament of penance, it is a fair assumption that the judge did not mean to overturn this Irish concession in the pre-independence common law. Indeed, the privilege is seen as having been strengthened by the case.[42]

In *Johnston v Church of Scientology* the plaintiff sought discovery of notes kept by the Church of Scientology. These notes were taken during spiritual exercises whilst the plaintiff was a member of the church. The defendant sought sacerdotal privilege, claiming that the secrecy of these spiritual practices was akin to the seal of the confessional and ought to be protected under *Cook v Carroll*. The judge recognised the privilege relating to the 'priest penitent relationship in the confessional', but found it to be '*sui generis* and not capable of development'.[43] It is unclear what will satisfy this test. It will normally be clear what constitutes a

---

41 Ibid 118.
42 See, eg, Hogan and Whyte (n 29) 2040; *ER v JR* [1981] ILRM 125; *Johnston v Church of Scientology* [2001] 1 IR 682.
43 *Johnston v Church of Scientology* (n 42) 686.

formal confession in the Roman Catholic Church, but it may be more difficult in other churches. The judge in part based his refusal to apply the privilege on a lack of evidence that 'it was part of the doctrines of the Church of Scientology that any disclosure of what transpired in auditing or training sessions led to some kind of eternal punishment'.[44] How other denominations would show a requirement of confidentiality sufficient to trigger this protection was not considered.

In relation to the Church of Ireland, there is no formal document that refers to the seal of the confessional.[45] Indeed, in 1891 the General Synod passed a motion 'to prevent the introduction of the practice of auricular confession and priestly absolution in the Church of Ireland'.[46] However, the motion recognised 'the duty of the clergy to convey, both in public and in private, to penitent sinners who trust in Christ, the assurance of God's pardon'.[47] It would appear that the aim was not to remove the practice of confessing sins in private to a priest and being assured of God's forgiveness, rather, an attempt was made to distinguish this from the Roman Catholic sacrament of penance. Indeed, the *Book of Common Prayer* recognises that those with 'a troubled conscience who may require spiritual guidance and counsel should consult the minister and seek the benefit of absolution'.[48] It remains unclear whether there is a clear doctrine of the seal of the confessional as inviolable. In *Principles of Canon*

---

44 Ibid 686. For a consideration of the treatment of the usages of the Church of Scientology in the USA, see Eric Lieberman, 'The Underlying Constitutional Basis for the Minister/Parishioner Privilege in the United States and its Application to the Practices of Scientology' at chapter ten of this volume.

45 At best s 53 of pt IV of ch VIII of the Constitution of the Church of Ireland provides: '[e]very act which would have been a breach or violation of the ecclesiastical law of the United Church of England and Ireland, and an offence punishable by such law in Ireland, at the time of the passing of the Irish Church Act, 1869 . . . shall be offences against the ecclesiastical law of the Church of Ireland'.

46 1891 Journal lvii.

47 Ibid lvii.

48 Church of Ireland, *The Book of Common Prayer* (Columba Press, 2004). Ministry to those who are sick, and to others requiring particular pastoral care: at 440. The first Exhortation at Holy Communion also recognises that a penitent may 'open his grief' to a priest and seek absolution: at 198.

Law Common to the Churches of the Anglican Communion,[49] principle 77.1, under seal of the confessional, holds the inviolability of the seal to be a common principle amongst Anglicans. However, as the principle is teased out it is noted at point 4 that the priest may divulge the communication to the extent allowed by the penitent and by church law. Further, in the Church of Ireland, ch XVI of the *Constitution*[50] states that all bishops, clergy, parishes and diocesan bodies shall adhere to *Safeguarding Trust.*[51] SGT seems to place a duty on clergy to report to the civil authorities any disclosure of child abuse, however communicated.[52] Thus it would seem that for Anglicans the principle is not necessarily as strong as it is for the Roman Catholic Church and it is uncertain whether the privilege associated with the seal of the confessional could be relied upon.

B Priest and Parishioner

The term used throughout the judgement by Gavan Duffy J was not 'seal of the confessional', but 'sacerdotal privilege'. He defines the term as describing 'a legal right for a priest to refuse in a court of law to divulge any confidential communication whatsoever made to him as a priest'[53] but he confines his decision to the facts before him noting,

> it cannot be taken as a matter of course that Wigmore's conditions ... will apply to every confidential communication made by anyone to any priest or any clergyman as such, but I must not travel outside the relation constituted by the consultation in strict confidence of a parish priest as such by a parishioner.[54]

The precise meaning of this passage is difficult to define. Gavan Duffy J

---

49 See Anglican Consultative Council, *The Principles of Canon Law Common to the Churches of the Anglican Communion* (Anglican Communion Office, 2008).
50 Ministry with Children 16.1
51 Standing Committee of the Church of Ireland, *Safeguarding Trust: The Church of Ireland Code of Good Practice for Ministry with Children* (2008) ‹ http://www.urney. derry.anglican.org/Safeguarding%20Trust.pdf›.
52 Safeguarding Trust Part 5, An Introduction to Child Protection. "There is one thing that you must not do, that is nothing" at 5.8. "It is a legal require-ment to report any child protection concerns" at 5.9
53 *Cook v Carroll* (n 28) 116.
54 Ibid 118.

began his judgment by asserting that 'no canon law was cited to me and I shall determine the issue without reference to the law of the Church'.[55] The wording seems to suggest that it would be harder to satisfy the Wigmore test were the priest not the parishioner's parish priest, but a stranger to them, or if the parties were not of the same denomination, though it ought to be noted that it does not preclude the possibility. References throughout the judgment to the parish priests' importance in the community create something of an uncertainty that has lured subsequent judges into muddy waters.[56]

In *Forristal v Forristal*,[57] a libel case, it was held that the privilege did not apply in respect of a letter written to a priest on the grounds that the author was not a parishioner of the addressee.[58] The most recent case to consider the matter is *Johnston v Church of Scientology*.[59] Geoghegan J follows Carroll J in *ER v JR*[60] in distinguishing the supposed view of Gavan Duffy J that the extension of the privilege outside the confessional extended only to parish priests and parishioners.

> I am not prepared to follow the views expressed by Gavan Duffy J
> in relation to counseling by a parish priest of a parishioner. Indeed
> it is difficult to see why a relationship between a parish priest and a
> parishioner is any different than a relationship between a priest or
> clergyman of any kind and a person coming from anywhere being

---

55 Ibid 116.
56 *Cook v Carroll* (n 28). '[H]e is regarded as being truly the spiritual father of his people and his traditional devotion to the people throughout the generations has won for him in Ireland the prerogative of extraordinary moral authority . . . Wherever intimate confidence exists between parish priest and people, it wears a sacred character of immense potential benefit to the community': at 118. 'If in a crisis his extraordinary prestige as a parish priest is utilized': at 120.
57 (1966) 100 ILTR 182.
58 The facts would have failed to satisfy the Wigmore test as, not only was he not writing to the priest as his parish priest, but there is little evidence that he was writing to him in his capacity as a priest at all. A letter could also struggle to satisfy the first part of the Wigmore test.
59 [2001] 1 IR 682.
60 [1981] ILRM 125.

counseled by him.[61]

In *ER v JR* Carroll J held that communications between a priest and lay people involved in marriage counseling could be privileged, even where the lay people were not the priest's parishioners. In *Johnston* Geoghegan J expands the concept further in taking the view that the privilege may also apply in certain circumstances to secular counselors, in particular in relation to marriage counseling.[62] Thus, it would seem that subsequent cases have made clear that in Irish common law the privilege exists in relation to the sacramental confession, but exists outside this where Wigmore's test is satisfied, and that it will apply in this form to other clergy outside the Roman Catholic Church and may also apply to secular counseling. These extensions were perhaps to be expected in modern Ireland, but the constant changes to the scope of the privilege afford little certainty that it will rest long in its present form.

C To whom does the privilege belong?

In the *Code of Canon Law* '[t]he sacramental seal is inviolable'.[63] Any knowledge obtained by a priest during confessional cannot be used to the detriment of the penitent. Canon 1548 requires witnesses to tell the truth to a judge who is lawfully questioning them, with certain exemptions, including clerics and matters revealed to them by reason of their sacred ministry.[64] The code does not deal with the question of in whom the privilege vests, or to whom it can be said to belong, framing the issue instead as a binding requirement on the priest based on divine law.

The common law in Ireland has sought to vest the privilege in one or other or sometimes both of the parties to the communication. In *Cook v Carroll* the learned judge states that the privilege belongs to the priest, so that even though the parishioners have waived the privilege, the priest

---

61 *Johnston v Church of Scientology* (n 42) 686.
62 Ibid 686.
63 *The Code of Canon Law* (n 10) canon 983 § 1.
64 Ibid canon 1548 §§ 1–2.

can not be forced to do so also.[65] More interestingly, though obiter, the judge concludes his judgment with a thought he says he wishes had occurred to him at hearing. That is, where three persons are concerned, the privilege must be tripartite.[66] That is to say, 'in a case of this kind I think no publication whatever of the secret conversation is allowable, without the express permission of the parish priest'.[67] The justification given for this is that

> protecting the priest from having to testify is only a half-measure of justice, if others may blurt out the conversation; the essential foundation of the relation established is the acceptance from the outset by all concerned of the inviolable secrecy of the meeting under the aegis of the parish priest.[68]

This corollary has not been followed in later decisions. The court in *Johnston v Church of Scientology* followed the decision in *ER v JR* and the English case of *Pais v Pais*[69] in holding that the privilege belonged not to the priest but to the lay person and was capable of unilateral waiver in the case of an individual, or by mutual consent of spouses. This is an advance both in recognising that the waiver of the lay people could override that of the priest, but moreover, it 'seems to repudiate the idea that the priest counselor himself could have a privilege which he would have to waive'.[70] Arguably this only applies to situations outside sacramental confession and it could be said that the present law still recognises the privilege based on the seal of the confessional as belonging to the priest, possibly to the priest alone, and incapable of being waived by the penitent. This view receives some academic support from Kelly in his respected tome on the *Bunreacht na hÉireann 1937 (Irish Constitution)*,[71] though it remains a view untested in the courts.

---

65 *Cook v Carroll* (n 28) 117.
66 Ibid 120.
67 Ibid 120.
68 Ibid 120.
69 [1970] 3 WLR 830.
70 *Johnston v Church of Scientology* (n 42) 685 (Geoghegan J).
71 Hogan and Whyte (n 29) 2041.

IV Dismantling the Privilege

A Repeal of Art 44.1.2 of the *Bunreacht na hÉireann 1937* (*Irish Constitution*).
Much of the judgment in *Cook v Carroll* relies on the need to develop the
common law in conformity with the newly enacted *Bunreacht na hÉireann
1937* (*Irish Constitution*) and 'the right of the Irish People to develop its
life in accordance with its own genius and traditions',[72] as expressed in
art 44.1.2, which recognised the special position of the Roman Catholic
Church. This section was deleted by referendum in 1972.[73] This raises the
question whether the force of *Cook v Carroll* is lost. In *Johnston v Church of
Scientology*, Geoghegan J said

> I think the waters were muddied in *Cook v Carroll*, with all respect
> to Gavan Duffy J, by the references to ... the then existing article
> in the Constitution referring to the special position of the Roman
> Catholic Church. Gavan Duffy J. appears to have been of the view
> that there were constitutional and legal effects arising out of the so-
> called special position of the Roman Catholic Church. However, in
> other decided cases the view was expressed that it had no such legal
> effect and that it was really nothing more than a statement of fact.[74]

In *ER v JR* Carroll J explicitly stated that the deleted provisions were
neither relevant nor essential[75] to her decision that communications
between a married couple and a clergyman acting as a marriage counselor
were privileged, a view echoed by Geoghegan J in *Goodman International
Ltd. v Hamilton (No 3)*.[76] The most persuasive analysis of *Cook v Carroll* is
that whilst art 44.1.2 provided the scope and the licence required by
the learned judge, the case is actually based and decided upon the four
elements of Wigmore's test. The repeal of the constitutional special
position does not negate the Wigmore test as the authoritative test in
determining whether sacerdotal privilege exists.

---

72 *Cook v Carroll* (n 28) 117.
73 The Fifth Amendment of the Constitution Bill (containing this change) was
    approved by the people by 721,003 votes to 133,430.
74 *Johnston v Church of Scientology* (n 42) 685.
75 *ER v JR* (n 42) 1108.
76 [1993] 3 IR 320, 324.

B A Changing Legislative Landscape

The *Children First Act 2015* (Ireland)[77] and the *Criminal Justice (Withholding of Information on offences Against Children and Vulnerable Persons) Act 2012* (Ireland) ('*Withholding Act*') have both incorporated an element of mandatory reporting of knowledge of abuse. Section 2(1) of the *Withholding Act* provides:

> a person shall be guilty of an offence if ... (a) he or she knows that an offence has been committed by another person against a child ... and fails without reasonable excuse to disclose that information as soon as it is practicable to do so to a member of the Garda Síochána.

However s 2(4) provides:

> This section is without prejudice to any right or privilege that may arise in any criminal proceedings by virtue of any rule of law or other enactment entitling a person to refuse to disclose information.

This section would seem to cover sacerdotal privilege, a fact acknowledged by the Office of the Ombudsman for Children which, in its submission to government on the text of the Bill called on sub-s 4 to be removed, or at least limited so as not to cover sacerdotal privilege.[78] However, the then Minister for Justice, Alan Shatter TD, in introducing the Bill to Seanad Eireann (the Irish Senate) addressed the issue of s 2(4):

> In that regard I would like to state that this provision is simply to allow the courts to use their normal discretion in considering issues of privilege. There has been a lot of media comment suggesting that this Bill has an effect on the 'seal of confession' or sacerdotal privilege. There are no defences in this legislation which would specially apply to information received in the confessional nor is there any specific provision with regard to the confessional. It will continue to be a matter for any court before which a person is prosecuted to determine whether any particular privilege exists

---

77 The *Children First Act 2015* (Ireland) requires mandated persons to report knowledge of harm or potential harm to a child to the relevant authority: at s 14(1).
78 It is therefore recommended that the Withholding Bill be amended so that sacerdotal and counselor privilege are overridden by s 2 of the Bill, given the serious nature of arrestable offences against children.

or applies in the circumstances of any particular case.[79]

The *Children First Act 2015* (Ireland) makes no mention of privilege unlike the much criticised *Withholding Act* and the intention has been not to recognise the privilege. Indeed, the minister noted that the issue of sacerdotal privilege has never been considered by the courts in relation to information pertaining to child abuse.[80] Therefore it would seem that s 11(3) could override the sacerdotal privilege found at common law, though it is uncertain to what extent the courts would find the minister's parliamentary speeches persuasive. The Association of Catholic Priests has already vowed not to comply with the legislation.[81] The Irish Catholic Bishops' 2016 publication *Safeguarding Children: Policy and Standards for the Catholic Church in Ireland*, states that

> All suspicions, concerns, knowledge or allegations that reach the threshold for reporting to the statutory authorities (apart from those received in the Sacrament of Reconciliation) will be reported via the designated liaison person to the appropriate statutory authorities.[82]

The policy quotes the canon: 'the sacrament seal is inviolable, therefore it is absolutely forbidden for a confessor to betray in any way a penitent in words or in any manner and for any reason'.[83]

Whilst the Catholic Church obviously cannot allow for the violation of the seal of the confessional in the face of mandatory reporting requirements in the 2012 and 2015 child protection legislation, it places no restriction on reporting information obtained other than obtained under the seal of sacramental confession. In this, the Church advances a view of privilege narrower than the breadth of the privilege recognised in Irish common law.

---

79 Alan Shatter, 'Second reading speech, Withholding of information on offences against children and vulnerable persons Bill 2012, *An Ronin Dli Agis Cirt (Department of Justice)* 10 May 2012.

80 Ibid.

81 See Michael Brennan, 'Priests: We won't Break Seal of Confession to Report Sex Abuse', *Independent.ie* (Web Page, 26 April 2012).

82 National Board for Safeguarding Children in the Catholic Church in Ireland, *Safeguarding Children: Policy and Standards for the Catholic Church in Ireland* (2016).

83 *The Code of Canon Law* (n 10) canon 983 § 1.

The *Children First Act 2015* (Ireland) imposes an obligation on mandated persons who know, believe or have reasonable grounds to suspect that a child has been harmed, is being harmed, or is at risk of being harmed, to make a report as soon as is practicable.[84] Section 15(g) of sch 2 to the Act list members of the clergy as mandated persons. These mandatory reporting elements came into effect at the end of 2017 and do not introduce a general or universal scheme of mandatory reporting, but only applies to a specified class of persons and to knowledge or belief acquired their professional capacity. Thus, a teacher who acquires the requisite knowledge at a social occasion would not be under any legal obligation. What is unclear from the wording of the Act is whether a mandated person is required to make a report when told by an adult that they were abused as a child. Section 14(2) of the Act refers to the duty to report 'when a child believes . . . and discloses', suggesting that the Act is concerned with disclosures by those who are children at the time of the disclosure. However, s 14(1) could be satisfied in that such a disclosure would relate that a child has been harmed, even it if was a long time in the past. Unusually, the Act carries no penalties for failure to engage with mandatory reporting. Hanly points out that there could be penalties under the *Withholding Act*.[85] However, the *Withholding Act* imposes a narrower obligation than the *Children First Act 2015* (Ireland), the offence in the former only applying in respect of information the individual knew or believed would be of material assistance to the punishment of a person who has harmed a child. Further, the 'reasonable excuse' provision in the *Withholding Act* remains, though no such provision is found under the *Children First Act 2015* (Ireland). Therefore if a priest did not report knowledge of abuse acquired during sacramental confession he will have breached the mandatory reporting requirement under the 2015 Act, but may have a defence under the 2012 Act that he was forbidden by canon law from breaking the seal.

---

84 *Children First Act 2015* (Ireland) s 14(1).
85 Conor Hanly, 'The Reporting of Child Abuse and Neglect in Ireland in an International Context' (2020) 34(2) *International Journal of Law, Policy and the Family* 145.

Mandatory reporting under the *Children First Act 2015* (Ireland) is the first instance of the Irish legislature directly legislating in a way that precludes a priest from relying in any way on the seal of the confession. Neither the Catholic Church in Ireland nor any lay groups have sought to challenge the constitutionality of the *Children First Act 2015* (Ireland) as violating freedom of religion under art 44 of *Bunreacht na hÉireann 1937*. By contrast, there have been several constitutional law challenges to coronavirus lockdown restrictions including restrictions on public worship. The courts have yet to deal with an instance of a priest refusing to report something heard in the course of sacramental confession which the Act would require to be reported. There would seem to be little doubt as to the outcome of such a case should one arise.

V Conclusion

As recently as the Law Reform Commission, looking at contempt of court, considered the law on sacerdotal privilege as 'good law' and concluded 'problems do not appear to have arisen in practice and it has not been suggested to us that the law is in need of any clarification . . . we do not recommend any legislation at the moment'.[86] That said, there is still some uncertainty in the law. The bounds of the privilege relating to the seal of the confession are uncertain, both in terms of how it will be applied and to whom the privilege belongs. Differentiating at all between the seal of the confessional and other forms of sacerdotal privilege lacks neatness and, arguably, justification. The privilege relating to other clergy, communications received outside the confessional and counselor privilege remain unsettled and have been altered every time they have been considered by the courts. The *Children First Act 2015* (Ireland) undoubtedly reduces the scope of the seal of the confessional when considered by the civil courts, though this is a relatively narrow exception to the pre-existing common law principles.

---

86 Ireland Law Reform Commission, *Report on Contempt of Court* (Report No 46, 1994) [4.21].

The fourfold Wigmore test looks less certain in modern Ireland than it did in 1945. Arguably a penitent in Ireland divulging a matter covered by mandatory reporting under the *Children First Act 2015* (Ireland) would struggle to have 'confidence that the communication will not be disclosed', if this was contrary to the civil law, though the canon law provisions remain unchanged. The third element of the Wigmore test looks ripe for reconsideration today, namely, the relation must be one which in the opinion of the community ought to be sedulously fostered. It is unclear whether the community referenced is wider Irish society or the Catholic community who avail of sacramental confession. Whilst the Irish population still overwhelmingly identify as Catholic, 78.3% in the most recent census (2016),[87] they have also shown a willingness to have civil laws which do not reflect Catholic social teaching, as evidenced by the majorities in the recent equal marriage (62%) and abortion (66%) referenda. Given the changing nature of Irish society and the position of the Catholic Church and its part in abuse scandals, it must be in doubt that a court would consider this condition to be met today.

It remains to be seen if the Oireachtas (Irish Parliament) will further legislate to reduce the recognition given to the seal at civil law. The strictness of canon law has now been met with an equal determination on the part of the state to require the seal to be broken in certain cases. In light of these legislative developments the common law position also looks to be in doubt. The fact that the law remains unsettled, coupled with a national mood and attitude to the clergy rather different to that in 1945 would suggest that were a challenge to be brought the privilege may seem as alien to the will of the people as the 'warped'[88] English decisions once seemed to Gavan Duffy J. The ongoing recognition of the seal of the confessional by the Irish civil law is now more precarious that at any point since independence.

---

87 "Census of Population 2016 – Profile 8 Irish Travellers, Ethnicity and Religion, Religion – Roman Catholicism, Demographics", *Central Statistics Office, CSO statistical publication, 12th October 2017.
88 *Cook v Carroll* (n 28) 119.

Part III – Issues of priest / penitent privilege in the USA

8

Gregory Zubacz

A confessor's reflection on some recent trends in America concerning the priest/penitent privilege

Abstract

Revelations about the mishandling of clergy sexual misconduct with minors have prompted political measures to remedy these ecclesiastical shortcomings. There is a growing call for the removal of religious confessional privilege in state evidence legislation. This suggests a general erosion of American religious freedom and one which will create a dilemma for religious confessors.

Keywords:

Seal of confession – religious confession privilege – church-state conflict - evidence legislation – constitutional religious freedoms – freedom of conscience and religion - human rights - mandatory reporting

1 Introduction

As a Catholic priest I watched on with some disquietude at the many events and changes over the past few decades that have unfolded, both within the church and without. Priests were seen by society at large as being beyond reproach, trustworthy heroic men of integrity and goodness who sacrificed the comforts and pleasures of family and worldly life to serve God in their entire person. Their word was to be trusted both on the witness stand and off. Police would avoid investigating them, prosecutors would be reluctant to proceed against them, and most judges preferred that the church handle its own problems internally and not bring embarrassing matters into their courtrooms. Even matters concerning disclosures under the seal of confession were an area of forensic evidence ordinarily to be avoided.[1]

When the Boston scandals broke in 2002 and the residential schools abuse in Canada were exposed, the issue came to the forefront and became impossible to ignore. The breadth of the non-disclosure was as disconcerting as the allegations themselves. This led to an avalanche of further revelations of failures on the part of church administration to both deal with the problem and disclose it. Websites of clergy abuse survivors began to proliferate, as did litigation against the church. Media attention became excoriating and relentless. The politicians began to notice.

Between 1950 and 2002, 4,392 priests out of the 109,694 who served during this period had allegations made against them, representing approximately 4% of the clergy, which appear to have peaked in the late 1970s and then sharply declined by 1985.[2] Most recently, between 2018 and 2019, 2,237 allegations were reported representing a 161% increase over the previous year.[3] This may have been due to archived file reviews

---

1   Lord Donaldson MR, ruling in *X Ltd v Morgan-Grampian (Publishers) Ltd* [1990] 2 WLR 421, makes the poignant statement that 'judges traditionally do not require priests to break the seal of the confessional': at 430–1.
2   John Jay College Research Team, *The Causes and Context of Sexual Abuse of Minors by Catholic Priests in the United States, 1950–2010* (Report, May 2011) 8.
3   Secretariat of Child and Youth Protection, National Review Board and United States Conference of Catholic Bishops, *2019 Annual Report: Recommendations and Findings: Report on the Implementation of the Charter for the Protection of Children and Young People* (Report, June 2020).

and internal audits and not necessarily because of an increase in recent incidents. It is nevertheless critical that statistical trends regarding the incidence of allegations be closely studied on an ongoing basis to determine the effectiveness of the screening and monitoring measures that have been put in place.

At least seven bishops have resigned who were directly or indirectly connected. Between 2014 and 2019, over USD1 billion was paid out for settlements, other payments, support for offenders, attorneys' fees, and other costs.[4] Twenty-four dioceses and religious orders have sought bankruptcy protection.[5] Needless to say, patience is wearing thin both within the church, and without.

Currently, allegations against clergy reflexively result in automatic administrative leave (a euphemism which does not appear in canon law but stands for paid leave) in most dioceses and eparchies until the matter has been investigated and resolved. All dioceses and eparchies now engage heavily in risk management and prevention through thorough criminal records checks of clergy and volunteers, safe environments programs, and an attempt to maintain transparency. In the past two decades, all dioceses and eparchies of the Catholic Church have implemented clergy background checks and put safe environments policies in place. There are now new procedural guidelines added to reduce risk of harm to children and increase responsiveness, transparency, and rapidity of church machinery to allegations, such as the 2002 'Charter for the Protection of Children and Young People'[6] commonly known as the Dallas Charter, and the 2019 motu proprio 'Vos Estis Lux Mundi'.[7]

For the past 200 years, the civil law in America reflected the church discipline out of hard-won respect for religious freedom and the church

---

4   Ibid 43.
5   'Bankruptcy Protection in the abuse Crisis', *BishopAccountability.org* (Web Page).
6   'Charter for the Protection of Children and Young People', in United States Conference of Catholic Bishops, *Promise to Protect: Pledge to Heal* (Report, rev ed, 2018).
7   Apostolic Letter issued Motu Proprio from the Supreme Pontiff Francis, 'Vos Estis Lux Mundi', 7 May 2019.

itself, but the public will to uphold such civil legislative protections is eroding as patience with church authorities is wearing painfully thin. In the past two decades, there have been six grand juries and eight Attorney-General reports in seven different states which have investigated incidents in the Catholic Church.[8] State Attorneys-General from Michigan, Iowa, and Virginia have even publicly intimated[9] the possibility of invoking the provisions of the 1970 federal act commonly known as the *Racketeering Influenced and Corrupt Organizations Act*.[10] This legislation was originally aimed at providing criminal penalties and civil causes of action against organized crime. The successful use of this statute against the Church would certainly be the ultimate disgrace.

With this context having been established, this chapter will examine historically how the canon law of the priest-penitent privilege was accepted into the jurisprudence and legislation of the United States, as well as some recent trends which point towards its future. It will consider early American milestones of jurisprudence in the state courts and survey existing state legislative protections. It will then look at federal jurisprudence concerning the privilege, and the philosophical underpinnings of the privilege using the Wigmore criteria and analysis for the determination of privileges. Some recent litigation touching on the seal of confession, especially with regard to mandated reporting, will be surveyed, as well as some recent legislative initiatives. All this will point towards some policy considerations touching on the potential ramifications of the proposed initiatives to carve out exceptions to the sacerdotal privilege in the case of mandated reporting.

---

8 'Reports of Attorneys General, Grand Juries, Individuals, Commissions, and Organizations', *BishopAccountability.org* (Web Page).
9 Maya Perry, 'AP: States Consider Charging Catholic Church as Crime Ring', *Organized Crime and Corruption Reporting Project* (Web Page, 11 June 2019).
10 *Racketeering Influenced and Corrupt Organizations Act*, 18 USC §§ 1961-8 (1970), enacted by *Organized Crime Control Act of 1970*, Pub L No 91-452, 84 Stat 922 (1970).

II Seal of Confession

A The Seal of Confession in Canon Law

Legal prototypes to the current seal of confession began to appear as early as the fourth century, but it definitively crystallized in its modern form at the Fourth Lateran Council in 1215. It is based in divine law concerning the secrecy of the spiritual elements of confessional communications, as well as the natural law obligation to maintain the confidences of others. The essential provisions of the sacramental seal are stated in canon 983 § 1 of the 1983 *Code of Canon Law*: 'The sacramental seal is inviolable; therefore it is absolutely forbidden for a confessor to betray in any way a penitent in words or in any manner and for any reason'.[11] As such, the seal of confession entails the obligation of secrecy on the part of a confessor, which forbids disclosure of all matters learned in the course of a sacramental confession. Thomas Aquinas stated that generally speaking, the seal of confession covers the actual sins which motivated the confession, and any related information which, if disclosed, would reveal the content of confession and the identity of the penitent.[12] The canon law follows this Thomistic principle. A confessor who reveals such information is to be punished with an automatic excommunication. Canon 1388 § 1 of the 1983 *Code of Canon Law* states:

> A confessor who directly violates the sacramental seal incurs a *latae sententiae* excommunication reserved to the Apostolic See; one who does so only indirectly is to be punished according to the gravity

---

11 *Code of Canon Law: Latin-English Edition: New English Translation* (Canon Law Society of America, 1999) [trans of: *Codex iuris canonici, auctoritate Ioannis Pauli PP II promulgatus, fontium annotatione et indice analytico-alphabetico auctus* (1989)] canon 983 § 1. Canon 733 § 1, the equivalent canon for Eastern Catholics reads: 'The sacramental seal is inviolable; therefore the confessor must diligently refrain either by word, sign or any other manner from betraying the penitent for any cause': *Code of Canons of the Eastern Churches, Latin-English Edition, New English Translation* (Canon Law Society of America, 2001) [trans of: *Codex canonum Ecclesiarum orientalium, auctoritate Ioannis Pauli PP II promulgatus, fontium annotatione auctus* (1995)] canon 733 § 1 ('*Eastern Code*').

12 Thomas Aquinas, *The Summa Theologica*, tr Fathers of the English Dominican Province [*Sent. IV*, d. XXI, q. III, a. I, q. 3, s. 2.]

of the delict.[13]

There have been a number of recent affirmations of the absolute inviolability of the seal of confession in response to challenges to the seal of confession in the civil courts.[14] There are a multitude of complexities and dimensions to the canonical obligations of the seal of confession, but for the purposes of integrating it with the civil jurisprudence, this will suffice for the scope of this writing.[15]

B Early American State Jurisprudence

English law prevailed in America until the American Revolution in 1776. It was not long after the Revolution that the case law began to diverge. The first major state-level case involving the priest-penitent privilege was the famous 1813 New York case of *People v Phillips* ('*Phillips*').[16] In that case, a Catholic priest refused to answer questions concerning the restitution of some items which he had returned on behalf of a penitent. The Court of General Sessions, Mayor Clinton de Witt adjudicating, excused the priest from testifying, not necessarily on the basis of any privilege of the confessional, but on the natural law and the constitutional principle of freedom of religion. The English jurisprudence in the 1790 decision of

---

13 Canon 1456 § 1 of the *Eastern Code* has similar penalties for violations of the seal of confession. It states: 'A confessor who has directly violated the sacramental seal is to be punished with a major excommunication, with due regard for can. 728, §1, n. 1; however, if he broke this seal in another manner, he is to be punished with an appropriate penalty'. However, a canonical trial is required.

14 Apostolic Penitentiary, 'Note of the Apostolic Penitentiary of the Importance of the Internal Forum and the Inviolability of the Sacramental Seal' (29 June 2019); 'Observations of the Holy See to the Recommendations of the Royal Commission', in Letter from the Holy See to the Attorney-General (Cth), 26 February 2020 [No 484.110].

15 For a more detailed survey of the canon law regarding the seal of confession, see Gregory J Zubacz, *The Seal of Confession and Canadian Law* (Wilson & Lafleur, 2009) chs 1–2.

16 1 WLJ 109 (NY Ct Gen Sess, 1813). The earlier case of *Baker v Arnold*, 1805 WL 807 (NY Sup Ct, 1805) is cited by some authors as establishing that a confession to a priest was not privileged. However, this case does not seem to point to any express ruling regarding this issue. This case has not been cited in any jurisprudence concerning the priest-penitent privilege.

Buller J in *R v Sparkes*[17] which appeared to rule against the privilege was not followed.[18] Clinton J rejected *R v Sparkes* in no uncertain terms, declaring it, 'to say the least, erroneous' and 'a heresy in our legal code'.[19] Regarding the first argument concerning the natural law, the Court said that to require the priest to violate his oath would go against conscience.[20] With respect to the second argument concerning constitutionality, the Court stated the free exercise of religion would unquestionably be restrained.[21] These two assertions concerning natural law and constitutionality laid a strong foundation for the recognition of the priest-penitent privilege in American state law.

Historical developments during the Reformation influenced the English jurisprudence concerning the priest-penitent privilege, as did the historical circumstances in America. Laws are of course a product of the lived human experience of history, and this decision may well have been a reflection of the desire of the fledgling 35 year old American judicial system to set itself apart from the English common law system. The contemporaneous acrimony between the United States and England

---

17   Cited in *Du Barré v Livette* (1791) 170 ER 96; Peake 108.

18   The case was summarised by Garrow in *Du Barré v Livette* (1791) 170 ER 96; Peake 108 where he said:

     There the prisoner being a papist had made a confession before a protestant clergyman, of the crime for which he was indicted, and that confession was permitted to be given in evidence on the trial, and he was convicted and executed. The reason against admitting that evidence was much stronger than in the present case; there the prisoner came to the priest for ghostly comfort, and to ease his conscience oppressed with guilt. Besides, in this case the confidence, if any was reposed, was at an end. The confidence was merely as it respected the trial then coming on, without any reference to this cause, which was not then thought of, and supposing it could not be given in evidence on that trial, still it is admissible on the present, when the purpose for which it is given is at an end: at 97.

     Although seeming to rule against the privilege, the case in fact does not actually address the question: see WM Best, *The Principles of the Law of Evidence with Elementary Rules for Conducting the Examination and Cross-Examination of Witnesses*, ed Sidney Phipson (Sweet & Maxwell, 12th ed, 1922) 500; Judge Rupert DH Bursell, 'The Seal of the Confessional' (1990) 2(7) *Ecclesiastical Law Journal* 84, 90.

19   Abstracted in 1 WLJ 109 (NY Ct Gen Sess, 1813); 'Privileged Communications to Clergymen' (1955) 1(3) *Catholic Lawyer* 199, 204. See also Sir James Fitzjames Stephen, *A Digest of the Law of Evidence* (MacMillan, 8th ed, 1909) 205.

20   *Catholic Lawyer* 203.

21   Ibid 207.

during the War of 1812 no doubt played a role.[22] The presiding judge may also have been persuaded by the arguments of William Sampson, famed Irish-American lawyer and opponent of English common law, who asserted the newly-founded American nation was under absolutely no obligation to follow the English jurisprudence.[23]

Four years later, however, in the case of *People v Smith*, the Court held that a Protestant minister was not bound by the same strictures and therefore must testify as to confessional communications.[24] In response, the state of New York passed the first legislation in the United States upholding the priest-penitent privilege for all religions in 1828.[25] The legislators who passed this law may well have been driven more by anti-British resentment than principle, and saw this as making a statement about the authority of English law in America.[26] This factor may have motivated the decision more than any sympathy towards Catholicism, since anti-Catholic sentiment and discrimination is evident throughout United States history.[27]

---

22 Still another reason the American law may have departed from the English law on the issue of the sacerdotal privilege is the larger role that the natural law played in American legal thought, in contrast to the Erastian English legal thought which tended more toward the positive law: see Russell Hittinger, 'Introduction', in Heinrich A Rommen, *The Natural Law: A Study in Legal and Social History and Philosophy*, tr Thomas R Hanley (Liberty Fund, 1998) xv–xvi.

23 See Michael James Callahan, 'Historical Inquiry into the Priest-Penitent Privilege' (1976) 36 *Jurist* 328, 334.

24 2 NYC Hall Rec 77 (NY, 1817), reported in 'Privileged Communications to Clergymen' (1955) 1(3) *Catholic Lawyer* 199, 209–13.

25 See Jacob M Yellin, 'The History and Current Status of the Clergy-Penitent Privilege' (1983) 23(1) *Santa Clara Law Review* 95, 106.

26 See Michael James Callahan, 'Historical Inquiry into the Priest-Penitent Privilege' (1976) 36 *Jurist* 328, 335. See also Douglas Laycock, 'Continuity and Change in the Threat to Religious Liberty: The Reformation Era and the Late Twentieth Century' (1986) 80(5) *Minnesota Law Review* 1047; Walter J Walsh, 'The Priest-Penitent Privilege: An Hibernocentric Essay in Postcolonial Jurisprudence' (2005) 80(4) *Indiana Law Journal* 1037; 'Developments in the Law; Privileged Communications' (1984) 98(7) *Harvard Law Review* 1450.

27 See Douglas Laycock, 'Continuity and Change in the Threat to Religious Liberty: The Reformation Era and the Late Twentieth Century' (1986) 80(5) *Minnesota Law Review* 1047, 1068. For more information on some of the issues facing the Catholic Church in early America, see Elwyn A Smith, 'The Fundamental Church-State Tradition of the Catholic Church in the United States' (1969) 38(4) *Church History* 486.

While *Phillips* was cited federally, it was essentially ignored by state jurisprudence, and English common law seemed to prevail.[28] The jurisprudence generally held that, in the absence of statutory protections, confessions to clergymen were not privileged at common law.[29] Most commentators accepted this jurisprudence at face value, notwithstanding the lack of in-depth legal analysis in most of these state-level cases.[30] Unlike the federal cases, state cases simply followed the English common law which, it has been pointed out, may be regarded as inconclusive, and did not of course take into account the *First Amendment*.[31] If either of these factors were taken into consideration, the outcome of these state level cases may very well have upheld the privilege.

---

28 See Richard S Nolan, 'The Law of the Seal of Confession', in Charles G Herberman et al (eds), *The Catholic Encyclopedia: An International Work of Reference on the Constitution, Doctrine, Discipline, and History of the Catholic Church* (Encyclopedia Press, 1912) vol XIII, 661.

29 See, eg, *Bahrey v Poniatishin*, 95 NJL 128, 130 (1920); *Commonwealth v Drake*, 15 Mass 161 (1818); *State v Morehous*, 97 NJL 285 (1922), revd in part *State v Smith*, 32 NJ 501 (1960); *Re Swenson*, 183 Minn 602 (1931); *Barnes v State*, 199 Miss 86 (1945); *Johnson v Commonwealth*, 310 Ky 557 (1949); *Biggers v State*, 358 SW 2d 188 (Tex Civ App, 1962), an application for writ of error was refused upon the ground that no reversible error existed 360 SW 2d 516 (Tex, 1962); *Rancourt v Waterville Urban Renewal Authority*, 223 A 2d 303 (Me, 1966); *Re Soeder's Estate*, 7 Ohio App 2d 271 (Ohio Ct App, 1966); *Killingsworth v Killingsworth*, 283 Ala 345 (1968); *Keenan v Gigante*, 47 NY 2d 160 (1979). As in England, canon law is treated as foreign law: *Serbian Eastern Orthodox Diocese for the United States of America and Canada v Milivojevich*, 426 US 696 (1976).

30 See, eg, John Henry Wigmore, *Evidence in Trials at Common Law*, rev John T McNaughton (Little, Brown, 1961) vol 8 § 2394; Mary Harter Mitchell, 'Must Clergy Tell? Child Abuse Reporting Requirements Versus the Clergy Privilege and Free Exercise of Religion' (1987) 71(3) *Minnesota Law Review* 723; John Frelinghuysen Hageman, *Privileged Communications as a Branch of Legal Evidence* (Rothman & Co, 1983) 122–3, 127.

31 See Vincent C Allred, 'The Confessor in Court' (1953) 13(1) *Jurist* 3, 21–2.

C American State Legislation

Between 1828 and 1991, all American states had enacted some kind of legislative provisions concerning the privilege.[32] There has been a fair amount of case law commentary regarding these statutory provisions.[33] These statutes are generally applied and construed strictly by the courts.[34] These statutes broadly cover who qualifies as a cleric for the purposes of the privilege, who qualifies as the penitent, mistaken belief, various types of communications, which religious bodies and confessional disciplines qualify for the privilege, the presence of third parties, waiver of the privilege, and sanctions. No statutory provisions have been repealed since they were promulgated. This would suggest that the privilege has at least served its proper policy purpose – that is, the protection of confidential religious communications – and has not hitherto been used improperly from an evidentiary point of view.[35] But new trends are emerging. Since the 1960s, each state has passed mandated

---

32 Ala Code § 12-21-166; Ala R Evid r 505; Alaska R Evid § 506; Ariz Rev Stat Ann § 12-2233; Ark R Evid § 505; Cal Evid Code §§ 917, 1030-4; Colo Rev Stat §§ 13-90-107-8; Conn Gen Stat § 52-146b; Del R Evid r 505; DC Code § 14-309; Fla Stat § 90.505; Ga Code Ann § 24-5-502; Haw R Evid r 506; Idaho Code Ann § 9-203(3); Ill Comp Stat ch 735 § 5/8-803; Ind Code § 34-46-3-1; Iowa Code § 622.10; Kan Stat Ann § 60-429; Ky R Evid § 505; La Code Evid Ann art 511; Me R Evid r 505; Md Code Ann Ct & Jud Proc § 9-111; Mass Gen Laws § 20A; Mich Comp Laws § 767.5a; Minn Stat § 595.02(c); Miss Code Ann § 13-1-22; Miss R Evid r 505; Mo Rev Stat § 491.060(4); Mont Code Ann § 26-1-804; Neb Rev Stat § 27-506; Nev Rev Stat § 49.255; NH Rev Stat Ann § 516.35; NJ Stat Ann § 2A:84A-23; NM R Evid r 11-506; NY Civil Prac Laws & Rules § 4505; NC Gen Stat § 8-53.2; ND Cent Code § 50-25.3-01; ND R Evid r 505; Ohio Rev Code Ann § 2317.02; Okla Stat tit 12 § 2505; Or Rev Stat § 40.260; Pa Cons Stat tit 42 § 5943; RI Gen Laws § 9-17-23; SC Code Ann § 19-11-90; SD Codified Laws § 19-19-505; Tenn Code Ann § 24-1-206; Tex R Evid r 505; Utah Code Ann § 78B-1-137(3); Vt Stat Ann tit 12, § 1607; Va Code Ann § 19.2-271.3; Wash Rev Code § 5.60.060(3); W Va Code § 57-3-9; Wis Stat § 905.06; Wyo Stat Ann § 1-12-101.

33 For a survey and analysis of some of the policy and jurisprudence concerning the privilege statutes, see Appendix I to this chapter.

34 See Robert L Stoyles, 'The Dilemma of the Constitutionality of the Priest-Penitent Privilege-The Application of the Religion Clauses' (1967) 29(1) *University of Pittsburgh Law Review* 27, 32.

35 See Seward Reese, 'Confidential Communications to the Clergy' (1963) 24(1) *Ohio State Law Journal* 55, 58.

reporting statutes. Most states still expressly exempt clergy from reporting if the disclosures fall under penitential communications, or simply do not name them as mandated reporters, but this is a patchwork quilt and a number of exceptions have emerged.[36] These

---

36 Most states directly exempt confessional communications in their mandated reporting legislation: Ala Code § 26-14-3(f); Ariz Rev Stat Ann § 13-3620; Ark Code Ann § 12-18-402; Cal Penal Code §§ 11166, 11165.7; Colo Rev Stat § 19-3-304; Del Code Ann tit 16 § 909; Fla Stat § 39.204; GA Code Ann §19-7-5; Idaho Code Ann § 16-1605; Ill Comp Stat ch 325 5/4; Ky Rev Stat Ann § 620.030(1), (4); La Child Code tit VI art 603(17); Me Rev Stat Ann tit 22 § 4011-A(1)(A)(27); (C); Md Code Ann Fam Law § 5-705(a)(1), (a)(3); Mass Gen Laws ch 119 § 51A(j); Mich Comp Laws § 722.631; Minn Stat § 626.556(3)(a); Mo Rev Stat § 210.140; Mont Code Ann § 41-3-201(2)(h), (6)(b); Nev Rev Stat § 432B.220(4)(d); NM Stat § 32A-4-3(A); ND Cent Code § 50-25.1-03; Ohio Rev Code Ann § 2151.421(A)(4)(b)-(d); Or Rev Stat § 419B.010(1); Pa Cons Stat tit 23 § 6311.1; SC Code Ann § 63-7-420; Utah Code Ann § 62A-4a-403; Vt Stat Ann tit 33 § 4913(a), (h)-(i); Va Code Ann § 63.2-1509; Wash Rev Code § 26.44.060; Wis Stat § 48.981(2)(bm); Wyo Ann Stat § 14-3-210. Some states do not specifically name clergy in their lists of mandated reporters, and/or broadly indicate that 'any individual' or 'any person' is required to report, but do not address privilege: Alaska Stat § 47.17.020; DC Code § 4-1321.02; Haw Rev Stat § 350-1.1; Ind Code § 31-33-5-1; Iowa Code § 232.69; Kan Stat Ann § 38-2223; Neb Rev Stat § 28-711; NJ Stat Ann § 9:6-8.10; NY SOS Law §§ 413-4; SD Codified Laws §§ 26-8A-3, 26-8A-15; PR Laws tit 8 § 446(b); VI Code tit 5 § 2533. Some states directly abrogate the confessional privilege in their reporting legislation and only grant attorney-client privilege and/or marital communication privilege: Conn Gen Stat § 17a-101; NH Rev Stat Ann §§ 169-C:29, 169-C:32; NC Gen Stat § 7B-310; RI Gen Laws § 40-11-11; W Va Code §§ 49-2-811, 49-2-803; NMI Code tit 6 § 5317. Some states grant no privilege at all in their mandated reporting legislation, even to attorneys: Miss Code Ann § 43-21-353(1); Okla Stat tit 10A § 1-4-507; Tenn Code Ann § 37-1-403; Tex Fam Code Ann § 261.101; Wyo Stat Ann § 14-3-205; Guam Code tit 19 § 13201(a).

have been the subject of a fair amount of commentary.[37]

The priest-penitent privilege is generally considered constitutionally protected on the basis of freedom of religion, and to date there have been no real formal challenges to its essential existence in the law of evidence on that basis.[38] Given the current make-up of the United States Supreme Court, it is unlikely that a challenge will appear on this basis in the near future either. However, if a constitutional challenge were made to the privilege legislation, it would likely be on the basis of the separation of church and state (the privilege could be seen as favoring religions with established confessional secrecy practices over those which do not), denial of equal protection (some religions would not meet all the criteria of the legislation), and the issue as to whether revocation of the privilege would in fact violate the constitutional right to the free exercise of religion, as opposed to simply being a reasonable

---

37 See especially Mary Harter Mitchell, 'Must Clergy Tell? Child Abuse Reporting Requirements Versus the Clergy Privilege and Free Exercise of Religion' (1987) 71(3) *Minnesota Law Review* 723, 790–825. See also William A Cole, 'Religious Confidentiality and the Reporting of Child Abuse: A Statutory and Constitutional Analysis' (1988) 21(1) *Columbia Journal of Law and Social Problems* 1; Douglas J Besharov, 'The Legal Aspects of Reporting Known and Suspected Child Abuse and Neglect' (1978) 23(3) *Villanova Law Review* 458; Phyllis Coleman, '"Shrinking" the Clergyperson Exemption to Florida's Mandatory Child Abuse Reporting Statute' (1987) 12(1) *Nova Law Review* 115; David Fenton, 'Texas' Clergyman-Penitent Privilege and the Duty to Report Suspected Child Abuse' (1986) 38(1) *Baylor Law Review* 231; Linda E Frischmeyer and Dennis D Ballard, 'Iowa Professionals and the Child Abuse Reporting Statute -- A Case of Success' (1980) 65(5) *Iowa Law Review* 1273; William N Ivers, 'When Must a Priest Report Under a Child Abuse Reporting Statute? - Resolution to the Priest's Conflicting Duties' (1987) 21(2) *Valparaiso University Law Review* 431; Kathryn Keegan, 'The Clergy-Penitent Privilege and the Child Abuse Reporting Statute: Is the Secret Sacred?' (1986) 19(4) *John Marshall Law Review* 1031; Terry Wuester Milne, '"Bless me Father, for I am About to Sin ...": Should Clergy Counselors Have a Duty to Protect Third Parties?' (1986) 22(2) *Tulsa Law Journal* 139; M Fitzgerald, 'The Sacramental Seal of Confession in Relation to Selected Child Abuse Statutes in the Civil Law of the United States' (JUD Dissertation, Gregorian University, 1991) 219–36.
38 See Robert L Stoyles, 'The Dilemma of the Constitutionality of the Priest-Penitent Privilege-The Application of the Religion Clauses' (1967) 29(1) *University of Pittsburgh Law Review* 27.

limitation on only a small part of overall religious practice.[39]

D Early American Federal Jurisprudence

Federal court jurisprudence in the United States recognises the privilege. In the 1876 decision of *Totten v United States*,[40] the United State Supreme Court dismissed the action on the basis that

> public policy forbids the maintenance of any suit in a court of justice, the trial of which would inevitably lead to the disclosure of matters which the law itself regards as confidential, and respecting which it will not allow the confidence to be violated. *On this principle, suits cannot be maintained which would require a disclosure of the confidences of the confessional*, or those between a husband and wife, or of communication by a client to his counsel for professional advice, or of a patient to his physician for a similar purpose.[41]

This case recognised the privilege, albeit in obiter. But what is remarkable is that the Court placed the privilege on the same footing as solicitor-client privilege, departing from English jurisprudence and restoring the pre-Reformation law.

---

39 See, eg, DW Elliott, 'An Evidential Privilege for Priest-Penitent Communications' (1995) 3(16) *Ecclesiastical Law Journal* 272; Mary Harter Mitchell, 'Must Clergy Tell? Child Abuse Reporting Requirements Versus the Clergy Privilege and Free Exercise of Religion' (1987) 71(3) *Minnesota Law Review* 723, 777–85; Seward Reese, 'Confidential Communications to the Clergy' (1963) 24(1) *Ohio State Law Journal* 55, 87–8; Robert L Stoyles, 'The Dilemma of the Constitutionality of the Priest-Penitent Privilege-The Application of the Religion Clauses' (1967) 29(1) *University of Pittsburgh Law Review* 27; Vincent C Allred, 'The Confessor in Court' (1953) 13(1) *Jurist* 3, 10–1; Ronald J Colombo, 'Forgive Us Our Sins: The Inadequacies of the Clergy-Penitent Privilege' (1998) 73(1) *New York University Law Review* 225; Jane E Mayes, 'Striking Down the Clergyman-Communicant Privilege Statutes: Let Free Exercise of Religion Govern' (1987) 62(2) *Indiana Law Journal* 397.
40 92 US 105 (1875). Similar obiter is found in the jurisprudence of Judge Learned Hand in *McMann v Securities and Exchange Commission*, 87 F 2d 377 (2nd Cir, 1937).
41 *Totten v United States*, 92 US 105, 107 (Field J for the Court) (1875) (emphasis added). For further commentary on this case, see Jacob M Yellin, 'The History and Current Status of the Clergy-Penitent Privilege' (1983) 23(1) *Santa Clara Law Review* 95, 106–7.

The privilege again was recognised in 1958 by United States Court of Appeals for the District of Colombia Circuit in *Mullen v United States* ('*Mullen*'). Here, a Lutheran minister was called to testify regarding confessional communications. The Court (by Fahy J, with whom Edgerton J concurred) stated that the priest-penitent privilege in English common law had ceased to exist. That having been said, the federal courts at the time applied the 1948 *Federal Rules of Criminal Procedure* which allowed for the reinterpretation of evidentiary privileges found in common law.[42] Fahy J stated in his famous dictum, that '[w]hen reason and experience call for recognition of a privilege which has the effect of restricting evidence the dead hand of the common law will not restrain such recognition'.[43] He then went on to say:

> It thus appears that non-recognition of the privilege at certain periods in the development of the common law was inconsistent with the basic principles of the common law itself. It would be no service to the common law to perpetuate in its name a rule of evidence which is inconsistent with the foregoing fundamental guides furnished by that law.[44]

After referring to Wigmore and citing *Phillips*, Fahy J concluded on the basis of the Wigmore criteria that

> Sound policy—reason and experience—concedes to religious liberty a rule of evidence that a clergyman shall not disclose on a trial the secrets of a penitent's confidential confession to him, at least absent the penitent's consent. Knowledge so acquired in the performance of a spiritual function as indicated in this case is not to be transformed into evidence to be given to the whole world. As Wigmore points out, such a confidential communication

---

42 Fed R Crim P r 28. Some of the early challenges in applying this rule to the priest-penitent privilege as well as other privileges are described in David W Louisell, 'Confidentiality, Conformity, and Confusion: Privileges in the Federal Courts Today' (1956) 31(1) *Tulane Law Review* 101. The *Federal Rules of Criminal Procedure* do not directly state the privilege, but they do recognise the state laws on privilege. Note that the American military rules of evidence recognise the priest-penitent privilege: Mil R Evid r 503.

43 *Mullen v United States*, 263 F 2d 275, 279 (DC Cir, 1958).

44 Ibid 280.

meets all the requirements that have rendered communications between husband and wife and attorney and client privileged and incompetent. The benefit of preserving these confidences inviolate overbalances the possible benefit of permitting litigation to prosper at the expense of the tranquility of the home, the integrity of the professional relationship, and the spiritual rehabilitation of the penitent. The rules of evidence have always been concerned not only with truth but with the manner of its ascertainment.[45]

Federal case law since *Mullen* has affirmed the priest-penitent privilege at common law.[46]

E The Wigmore Criteria and Confessional Communications

The American law concerning the privilege, unlike the English law, is based on the axiom that it is 'more desirable to risk concealment of the truth than to disrupt the values that the privilege supports'.[47] In order to determine when this axiom should be applied, John Henry Wigmore (1863-1943), in his locus classicus on the law of evidence, *Evidence in Trials at Common Law*, sets out four criteria: namely (a) that the communications in question need to be made on the understanding that they will be kept secret; (b) that the confidentiality is critical to relationship between these parties; (c) that the relationship is one which the community would consider important enough to be 'sedulously fostered'; and (d) that the injury caused by disclosing the communications would outweigh its evidentiary value in litigation.[48]

---

45 Ibid.
46 See, eg, *Cimijotti v Paulsen*, 219 F Supp 621 (ND Iowa, 1963); *Re Verplank*, 329 F Supp 433, 435 (Gray DJ) (CD Cal, 1971); *United States v Luther*, 481 F 2d 429, 433 (Carter J for the Court) (9th Cir, 1973); *United States v Nixon*, 418 US 683, 709 (Burger CJ for the Court) (1974); *Re Wood*, 430 F Supp 41 (SD NY, 1977); the oft-quoted locus classicus of the law in this area namely *Trammel v United States*, 445 US 40, 45 (1980) where Burger CJ speaking for himself, Brennan, White, Marshall, Blackmun, Powell and Rehnquist JJ stated that '[t]he priest-penitent privilege recognizes the human need to disclose to a spiritual counsellor, in total and absolute confidence, what are believed to be flawed acts or thoughts and to receive and to receive priestly consolation and guidance in return'; *Re Grand Jury Investigation*, 918 F 2d 374 (3rd Cir, 1990).
47 *People ex rel Noren v Dempsey*, 10 Ill 2d 288, 293 (Schaefer J for the Court) (1957).
48 John Henry Wigmore, *Evidence in Trials at Common Law* $ 2285.

Wigmore actually used the priest-penitent privilege as an example of the application of these four criteria. With regard to the first criterion, he concluded that secrecy which is permanent in nature is critical to the proper functioning of a confessional system.[49] Regarding the second criterion, he observed that if disclosure would hinder confession, the relationship between confessor and penitent would be compromised and the practice of confession diminished or altogether lost.[50] In relation to the third criterion, Wigmore indicated that in any society that upholds freedom of religion and tolerance, if some significant amount of the members of the community practise a religion that includes confession, that relation then is one which ought to be sedulously fostered.[51] Finally, relying on Jeremy Bentham, Wigmore states that it would be unfair and imprudent to allow religious confessions in evidence, since they are easy targets in litigation, and that there are other ways that the same evidence could be adduced. For this reason, he determines that the injury incurred by the revelation of confessional communications would be greater than the benefit, and therefore the priest-penitent privilege satisfies the criteria.[52]

The United States federal courts have followed Wigmore's conclusion that the priest-penitent privilege satisfies the criteria.[53] The Wigmore criteria might be useful in interpreting and constructing legislation concerning the seal of confession.[54] It should also be noted that, importantly, Wigmore sought a definitive resolution of this priest-

---

49 Ibid § 2396.

50 Ibid. Mitchell suggests that empirical evidence is not essential but may help to support this criterion: see Mary Harter Mitchell, 'Must Clergy Tell? Child Abuse Reporting Requirements Versus the Clergy Privilege and Free Exercise of Religion' (1987) 71(3) *Minnesota Law Review* 723, 762–5. See also 'Testimonial Privilege and Competency in Indiana' (1952) 27(2) *Indiana Law Journal* 256, 267.

51 John Henry Wigmore, *Evidence in Trials at Common Law* § 2396. There Wigmore points out that the jurisprudence against the privilege in England was based on the refusal to concede that the penitential relationship deserved any recognition due to the historical intolerance toward the Catholic Church: see also G D Nokes, 'Professional Privilege' (1950) 66(1) *Law Quarterly Review* 88, 99.

52 John Henry Wigmore, *Evidence in Trials at Common Law* § 2396.

53 See, eg, *Re Verplank*, 329 F Supp 433, 435 (Gray DJ) (CD Cal, 1971).

54 See, eg, DW Elliott, 'An Evidential Privilege for Priest-Penitent Communications' (1995) 3(16) *Ecclesiastical Law Journal* 272.

penitent privilege, and not a case by case determination of whatever confessional communications were being considered.[55] Certainty of the law is critical in a stable society, and is fundamental to maintaining respect for the rule of law with respect to significant relationships. It is important that penitents know that their confessional revelations and disclosures will always be kept secret, so that they have the confidence to confess without anxiety causing them to hold back that which they need to confess. Mitchell adds that, from a public policy point of view, the priest-penitent privilege may also be grounded in the right to privacy.[56] Certainly, the trend in recent years has been towards increasingly strict privacy laws and respect for confidentiality in spheres well beyond traditional confidential relationships.

F Recent Litigation concerning the Sacerdotal Privilege

In the past decade, there have been a number of cases which have interpreted and applied the legislation.[57] Of these, four cases are noteworthy in that they have grappled directly with the interface between the legislation protecting the privilege and the legal requirement to report risk of harm to children. In the case of *Parents of Minor Child v Charlet*,[58] the Supreme Court of Louisiana ruled a Roman Catholic priest was not a mandated reporter for the purposes of allegations disclosed in confessional communications in Louisiana legislation. In *Ronchi v State*,[59] a Roman Catholic priest to whom allegations were ostensibly disclosed filed a motion for a protective order after being served with a subpoena to testify at the criminal trial. The District Court of Appeal held that the trial court's order contravened the *Florida Religious Freedom Restoration Act*

---

55 See, eg, Mary Harter Mitchell, 'Must Clergy Tell? Child Abuse Reporting Re-quirements Versus the Clergy Privilege and Free Exercise of Religion' (1987) 71(3) *Minnesota Law Review* 723, 767–8.

56 Ibid 768–77, 793–821.

57 For a summary of US cases in the last decade which interpret and apply the sacerdotal privilege, see Appendix II to this chapter.

58 135 So 3d 1177, 1178 (Clark, Johnson and Knoll JJ) (La, 2014).

59 248 So 3d 1265, 1268 (Torpy and Evander JJ, Orfinger J agreeing at 1270) (Fla Dist Ct App, 2018).

of 2005.[60]

However, an equal amount of cases have gone the other way, with trends along religious lines. In *State v Workman*,[61] the defendant admitted allegations of child abuse to two Baptist pastors. Applying the Tennessee legislation, the Court of Criminal Appeals held that privilege does not apply to protect confessional communications in any situation involving known or suspected child sexual abuse. In *State v Willis*,[62] the Supreme Court of New Hampshire came to the same result, also with communications to a Baptist pastor.

While these cases are few, they do suggest a nascent recent trend in litigation towards attempts to break the forensic taboo and challenge what was once the 'off-limits' sacerdotal privilege, at least in cases involving mandated reporting concerning child protection. A study of how different religions have fared under the same legislation based on their confessional theology and practice would also be worthwhile but is beyond the scope of this writing.

G Recent Legislation concerning the Sacerdotal Privilege

Federally, there have been several recent initiatives. On 2 May 2019, Representative Kim Schrier (Democratic Party) introduced the Stronger Child Abuse Prevention and Treatment Bill.[63] Section 108 of that Bill would exempt communications that fall under the clergy-penitent privilege. The Bill has passed the House, been received in the Senate, read twice and referred to the Committee on Health, Education, Labor, and Pensions. On 7 May 2019, two bills, both entitled Speak Up to Protect Every Abused Kid Act,[64] were introduced by Senator Robert Casey (Democratic Party) and Representative Susan Wild (Democratic

---

60 Fla Stat §§ 761.01–061.
61 (Tenn Crim App, No E2010-02278-CCA-R3CD, 13 December 2011) slip op 11–2.
62 165 NH 206 (2013).
63 HR 2480, 116th Congress (2019).
64 S 1353, 116th Congress (2019); HR 2567, 116th Congress (2019).

Party) to amend the provisions of the *Child Abuse Prevention and Treatment Act*.[65] The section concerning mandatory reporting of incidents of child abuse or neglect would also exempt communications under the clergy-penitent privilege.

Following the traditional historical trend between federal and state lines, state legislatures have been somewhat less inclined to protect the privilege. Recently, there was a legislative proposal in California by Senator Jerry Hill (Democratic Party) who introduced a Bill to amend the *Penal Code of California*.[66] The proposed change would have specifically required the disclosure of any penitential communications made between a clergy member and another person employed at the same facility or location as that clergy member, or between a clergy member as confessor and another clergy member. It was set down for first hearing 9 July 2019, but the hearing was canceled at the request of the author.

Some recently passed bills maintain the privilege,[67] while others abrogate it.[68] As of 2020, a number of bills were brought forward that would limit the exemption granted by the privilege with regard to the reporting of child abuse and other some other matters.[69] The legislative trend is leaning towards removing the exemption for the clergy-penitent privilege in cases where children are at risk of harm. This trend is reflected in

---

65 Pub L No 93-247, 88 Stat 4 (1974).
66 Mandated Reporters: Clergy, SB 360, 2019–20 reg sess (Cal, 2019).
67 2019 Mont Laws ch 367 (HB 640); 2020 Wash Legis Serv ch 42 (HB 2762); 2020 Wash Legis Serv ch 302 (SSSSB 5720).
68 NH Rev Stat Ann $ 169-C:29; 2020 Ky Laws ch 74 (SB 72).
69 HB 159, 2020 reg sess (Ky, 2020); HB 265, 2020 reg sess (Ky, 2020); HB 47, 2020 reg sess (Ky, 2020) which would also roll back the limitations periods for sexual abuse; SB 196, 133rd GA, 2019–20 sess (Ohio, 2019); HB 337, 133rd GA, 2019–20 sess (Ohio, 2019); LB 95, 23rd council period (DC, 2019); AB 418, 2019–20 reg sess (Cal, 2019) which provides that the privilege is generally deemed to be waived where a significant part of the communication has been disclosed; SB 1235, 54th legislature, 2nd reg sess (Ariz, 2020); HB 24, 133rd GA, 2019–20 sess (Ohio, 2019); SB 433, 2020 reg sess (La, 2020); Child Abuse Reporting and Investigation, 2020 La Sess Law Serv Act 122 (SB 433) (signed into force 11 June 2020); Dependent or Neglected Children—Reporters, 2019 Ill Legis Serv PA 101-564 (SB 1778); Child Abuse—Sex Offenses, 2019 NC Laws SL 2019-245 (SB 199); 2020 Wash Legis Serv ch 71 (SB 6423); SB 2001; 13th legislature, 2020 reg sess (Haw, 2019); HB 1692, 13th legislature, 2020 reg sess (Haw, 2019).

the increasing focus of legal scholarship concerning the priest-penitent privilege on this tension in the law.[70]

H Public Policy and Legislative Protections of the Privilege

The recent trends concerning the increasing encroachment on the priest-penitent privilege have caused much reflection on these developments and their core ramifications. Fundamentally, becoming a mandated reporter of communications in the confessional theoretically makes the priest an agent of the state. The penitent comes to confession to sort out his or her spiritual shortcomings, but the reporting legislation essentially creates a legal trap for a penitent, with salvation as the bait. The sacrament then potentially becomes the lure, the confessor the fisherman, and the reporting legislation the hook. It also makes the priest the instrument by which the state may work around the penitent's constitutional right to silence.

The church has a vested interest in the spiritual health of all members of society. The state has an unquestionable interest in the protection of vulnerable members of society. This is the essence of the legislative policy conflict between church and state which is being played out in its attempts to make confessional communications another piece of forensic evidence. Certainly, the law of evidence has been trending over the past many decades towards bringing more evidence before the court and letting the judiciary sort it out, rather than blocking it in its entirety under the umbrella of privileged communications. The sacerdotal privilege is one of those areas that it is in the sights of this trend.

The rage concerning the scandals is justified. Justice needs to be done, and needs to be seen to be done. But it should also be observed that anger can reduce personal judgment to that of an infant. When legislative initiatives are taken solely on the basis of conjecture that they will make some real difference, they become a symbolic way of simply corporately

---

70 For a selection of recent US scholarship concerning concerning the priest-penitent privilege, see Appendix III to this chapter.

punishing those who are named in the legislation. The trade-off is that, while an additional piece of potentially probative and corroborative evidence will be available to the prosecution, the one last hope of the malefactor is extinguished. Throughout legal history, the jurisprudence acknowledges that spiritual health and personal reformation has been the linchpin of upholding the civil protections of the privilege. However, the scandals have caused the weight on the scales to begin to tip to the other side. Perhaps the earlier English jurists like Bentham who wrote on the seal of confession being protected as privileged communications had never envisioned the types of things that emerged in the 21st century, and had in mind lesser crimes. We can never know.

But to take the seal of confession away from those who need it most could be like denying a life-saving drug to a person who needs it. It may very well be taking away their very last faint hope of the possibility of amending their lives, seeking treatment, turning themselves in to law enforcement, and ceasing horrific behaviour. The *Louisiana Code* actually recognises this good in art 610. Like a patient who is denied life-saving medical treatment, those who are denied confession will only become worse, sicker, and more diseased as they collapse into themselves and the darkness of the psychological self-imposed imprisonment they have created. The act of confessing to sinful and deeply embarrassing behaviour may be the thing that serves as a last check, a lifegiving nudge to a conscience deadened by habitual sin, a forced reflection on one's failings that is a person's last hope of changing their ways and ceasing their destructive conduct. It would be the substitution of a physical prison and hope, for the spiritual prison and hopelessness they have locked themselves into.

Confession is a much-needed spiritual therapy conducted by a doctor of the soul, the Ἰατρός τῶν ψυχῶν, which by its nature requires privacy. Being unable to approach a physician of the soul is akin to being unable to approach a physician of the body. There being no one left in the material world to confide in, the perpetrator would only sink more deeply into his isolation, and indeed his behaviour may grow worse. Many serial killers reported being emboldened by not having been caught. Their thinking may shift from the possibility of self-amendment and healing, to asking the desperate question that drives the continuation of the most depraved criminal behaviour: what is there to lose at this point? The words of Fyodor Dostoevsky come to mind, as he reflected that '[w]hen losing his hope and purpose, a person slowly becomes a monster'.

Perhaps in the mind of legislators, the real issue is less about the penitents, and more about confessors who might instead offer the penitent an easy way out by covering up their sins. The possibility of cheap forgiveness may only be enabling them to persist in their behaviour with a settled conscience and reassurance of God's love and clemency. The concern of the legislatures may be that the penitent is thinking that some day he may in fact conquer his urges and accept responsibility for his crimes –– but not yet, resulting in further victims. That is the gap the legislation seems to be seeking to bridge. So, the state as parens patriae needs to step in before more are victimised. Prevention is a legitimate concern. But depriving any human being who sincerely wants to change of their last line of hope could never possibly be a good thing either. It may be true that some priests who engage in conduct which is the subject of mandatory reporting might either not confess to the sin, or alternatively might do so in an oblique way, and then possibly to a confessor who is not personally known to them.[71] These sacramental workarounds, however, suggest a situation wherein the priest is being disingenuous and in a state of spiritual self-deception, and is not ready to accept full responsibility. The reporting legislation does not seem to be contemplating a situation like this, in which the confessor receives no probative evidence due to a

---

71 See the discussion in Keith Thompson, 'Should Religious Confession Privilege be Abolished in Child Abuse Cases? Do Child Abusers Confess their Sins?' (2017) 8 *Western Australian Jurist* 95; A Keith Thompson, 'Religious Freedom under the Australian Constitution and Recommendations that Religious Confession Privilege be Abolished', Michael Quinlan, 'An Unholy Patchwork Quilt: The Inadequacy of Protections of Freedom of Religion in Australia', in Iain T Benson, Michael Quinlan and A Keith Thompson (eds), *Religious Freedom in Australia — A New Terra Nullius?* (Shepherd Street Press, 2019).

lack of confessional candour. The legislation rather is contemplating a full and frank disclosure and admission of guilt to a mandated reporter, the likes of which would only realistically happen in the case of a sincere confession, which is exactly what the seal of confession attempts to protect through absolute secrecy. This is the trap.

The reality that frustrates this entire argumentation is that there is no way to study the phenomenon of what people confess and how they do it, because confessional knowledge cannot be used in any way whatsoever, even for the purposes of statistics, study, or bolstering the very assertions made in this paper. In this way, the seal of confession is its own worst enemy in the civil arena, as it can never speak in its own defense in anything other than a theoretical way.

Will these mandated reporting legislative initiatives survive a *First Amendment* challenge to the Supreme Court? It is difficult to predict, but litigation is inevitable. There is a good chance more legislative initiatives will pass which continue eroding the privilege. While acknowledging the good intentions of the legislatures to protect the most vulnerable members of our society by making exceptions to the privilege, the cure may wind up being be worse than the disease. As the Court stated in *Phillips*,

> Secrecy is of the essence of penance. The sinner will not confess, nor will the priest receive his confession, if the veil of secrecy is removed: To decide that the minister shall promulgate what he receives in confession, is to declare that there shall be no penance; and this important branch of the Roman catholic religion would be thus annihilated.[72]

This hearkens back to the early 19th century writings of English jurist Jeremy Bentham, who concludes on the basis of public policy arguments that the priest-penitent privilege should in fact be upheld, notwithstanding the English jurisprudence to the contrary up to that point. He bases his assertion on two grounds. The first ground is that

---

72 *People v Phillips*, 1 WLJ 109, (NY Ct Gen Sess, 1813) reprinted at (1955) 1 *Catholic Lawyer* 199,, 207.

the 'mass of evidence' in litigation would not be lessened. The second ground is that of 'vexation'.

With respect to the first ground, he states that if secrecy is not provided for confession:

> What would be the consequence?—That, of that quantity of confessorial evidence which is now delivered in secret for a purpose purely religious, a certain proportion (it is impossible to say what, but probably a considerable one) would not be so delivered: would be kept back, under the apprehension of its being made use of for a judicial purpose.[73]

Thus, if the privilege is allowed, there will be no evidence of confessional communications brought forward as evidence in court. But, if the privilege is not allowed, no evidence will be generated. Upholding the privilege therefore will not lessen the mass of evidence. Either the admission does not come to court, or it is not made.

With respect to the second ground, he makes the following observation with regard to penitents:

> In the character of penitents, the people would be pressed with the whole weight of the penal branch of the law: inhibited from the exercise of this essential and indispensable article of their religion: prohibited, on pain of death, from the confession of all such misdeeds as, if judicially disclosed, would have the effect of drawing down upon them that punishment; and so, in the case of inferior misdeeds, combated by inferior punishments ... Such would be the consequences to penitents.[74]

In other words, to deny penitents the right to confessional secrecy would amount to 'vexation'. Bentham uses this term in the widest sense of the state targeting penitents as witnesses made vulnerably by the penitential practices of the Catholic religion. The vexation argument also necessarily

---

73 Jeremy Bentham, *Rationale of Judicial Evidence Specially Applied to English Practice* (Hunt and Clark, 1827) vol IV, 587. The reasoning parallels other jurisprudence regarding solicitor-client privilege.

74 Ibid 588.

applies to confessors. With regard to coercing confessors to testify as to the contents of the confessional, Bentham says:

> To confessors, the consequences would be at least equally oppressive. To them, it would be a downright persecution: if any hardship, inflicted on a man on a religious account, be susceptible of that, now happily odious, name. To all individuals of that profession, it would be an order to violate what by them is numbered amongst the most sacred of religious duties. In this case, as in the case of all conflicts of this kind, some would stand firm under the persecution, others would sink under it. To the former, supposing arrangements on this head efficient and consistent, it would have the effect of imprisonment: a most severe imprisonment for life. As to those who sunk under it; what proportion of the number would on this occasion be visited by the torments of a wounded conscience, and to what degree of intensity those torments would amount in the instance of each individual, are questions, the answer to which must on this occasion be referred by a non-catholic to the most competent judges amongst catholics: but a species of suffering, the estimation of which does not require any such appropriate and precise information, is the infamy that could not but attach itself to the violation of so important a religious duty.[75]

Bentham concludes:

> The advantage gained by the coercion, gained in the shape of assistance to justice, would be casual, and even rare: the mischief produced by it, constant and all-extensive. Without reckoning the instances in which it happened to the apprehension to be realized; the alarm itself, intense and all comprehensive as it would be, would be a most extensive as well as afflictive grievance.[76]

He argues that the interests of justice may indeed still be served, while at the same time upholding the privilege:

> Who the misdoer is, the confessor knows better than to disclose; as little will he give any such information as may lead to the

---

75 Ibid 558–9.
76 Ibid 589.

arrestation of the delinquent, under circumstances likely to end in his being crushed by the afflictive hand of the law. But, without any such disclosure, he may disclose what shall be sufficient to prevent the consummation of impending mischief. 'At such or such hour, go not, unless accompanied, to such or such a place: strengthen such or such a door: be careful to keep well fastened such or such a window'.[77]

These conclusions are remarkable in view of the fact that Bentham was both an opponent of privileges as well a champion of Protestantism.

Catholic priests will not disclose confessional communications in violation of their sacred obligation of secrecy and realistically there is no utility in imprisoning priests under such circumstances. By forcing the confessor to make the invidious choice between excommunication and prison for contempt, it would likely be seen as bringing the administration of justice into disrepute.[78]

III Concluding Reflection

Taanit 29 of the Talmud tells the story of how, during the destruction of the First Temple, the young priests climbed to the burning roof, and confessed their failure as stewards. They threw the keys to the Temple up into air, and a hand was seen that reached down through the clouds and took them back. The young priests then flung themselves into the conflagration in disgrace. The good priests now holding the keys of Saint Peter, standing in the double bind of this precarious flaming perch not of their own making, may well be ready to throw themselves into the fire, but will most certainly not release the keys. The cleansing fire going through the church right now has brought about much-needed change and has enabled the church to take the steps necessary to begin healing

---

77 Ibid 591.

78 See the discussion in A Keith Thompson, *Religious Confession Privilege and the Common Law* (Brill, 2011); A Keith Thompson, 'The Persistence of Religious Confession Privilege', in Rex Ahdar (ed), *Research Handbook on Law and Religion* (Edward Elgar Publishing, 2018).

itself of a cancer which was eating away at is core. Time will tell how effective the measures will be. Unfortunately, it appears this fire may inadvertently also consume part of a secular privilege it once enjoyed, which now places the positive law of the state squarely on a collision course with the divine and natural law on which the seal of confession is based, the keys to which confessors will never relinquish. Either the penitent loses the opportunity to confess, or the confessor goes to jail. Everyone knows which one will happen, legislation to the contrary notwithstanding. For this reason, in the hagiography of the church there is a gallery of saints dedicated to those who have done exactly that, such as John Nepomucene, Matteo Correa Magallanes, and the martyrs Felipe Císcar Puig, Fernando Olmedo Reguera, and Jan Kobylowicz. At this point, it is a question of when, not if, the Barque of Peter collides with the dreadnought of the policy of the secular state in the darkness of the night. The Supreme Court will ultimately decide which one will sink.

Appendix I

Survey and analysis of some of the policy and jurisprudence concerning the privilege statutes

Charles David Creech, 'The Clergy-Communicant Privilege: Blessed Are the Meek, For They Shall Remain Silent' (1987) 65(6) North Carolina Law Review 1390; Charles W Quick, 'Privileges Under the Uniform Rules of Evidence' (1957) 26(4) University Cincinnati Law Review 543; LR Adams and ME Polk, 'Privileged Communications—Some Recent Developments' (1952) 5 Vanderbilt Law Review 590; M Fitzgerald, 'The Sacramental Seal of Confession in Relation to Selected Child Abuse Statutes in the Civil Law of the United States' (JUD Dissertation, Gregorian University, 1991) 100–236; J Michael Medina, '"Is There a Time to Keep Silence?"—The Priest-Penitent Privilege in Oklahoma' (1974) 27 Oklahoma Law Review 258; Herbert L Moody, 'The Priest-Penitent Privilege in South Carolina—Background and Development' (1960) 12(3) South Carolina Law Review 440; Edmund M Morgan and John MacArthur Maguire, 'Looking Backward and Forward at Evidence' (1937) 50(6) Harvard Law Review 909; Thomas W Taylor, 'Evidence—Privileged Communications—The New North Carolina Priest-

Penitent Statute' (1968) 46(2) *North Carolina Law Review* 427; Simone Campbell, 'Catholic Sisters, Irregularly Ordained Women and the Clergy-Penitent Privilege' (1976) 9 *University of California Davis Law Review* 527; John J Montone III, 'In Search of Forgiveness: *State v Szemple* and the Priest-Penitent Privilege in New Jersey' (1995) 48(1) *Rutgers Law Review* 263; William E Hurley, 'Privileged Communications in Oregon' (1957) 36(2) *Oregon Law Review* 132; 'Testimonial Privilege and Competency in Indiana' (1952) 27(2) *Indiana Law Journal* 256; Mary Harter Mitchell, 'Must Clergy Tell? Child Abuse Reporting Requirements Versus the Clergy Privilege and Free Exercise of Religion' (1987) 71(3) *Minnesota Law Review* 723; Chad Horner, 'Beyond the Confines of the Confessional: The Priest-Penitent Privilege in a Diverse Society' (1997) 45(3) *Drake Law Review* 697; Julie Ann Sippel, 'Priest-Penitent Privilege Statutes: Dual Protection in the Confessional' (1994) 43(4) *Catholic University Law Review* 1127; Seward Reese, 'Confidential Communications to the Clergy' (1963) 24(1) *Ohio State Law Journal* 55; Michael G Plantamura, 'The Clergyman-Penitent Privilege', in Scott N Stone and Ronald S Liebman (eds), *Testimonial Privileges* (McGraw-Hill, 1983); Jacob M Yellin, 'The History and Current Status of the Clergy-Penitent Privilege' (1983) 23(1) *Santa Clara Law Review* 95; Michael Mazza, 'Should Clergy Hold the Priest-Penitent Privilege?' (1998) 82(1) *Marquette Law Review* 171; 'Developments in the Law; Privileged Communications' (1984) 98(7) *Harvard Law Review* 1450; Fred Kuhlmann, 'Communications to Clergymen—When are They Privileged?' (1968) 2(2) *Valparaiso University Law Review* 265; Robert John Araujo, 'International Tribunals and Rules of Evidence: The Case for Respecting and Preserving the 'Priest-Penitent' Privilege' (2000) 15(3) *American University International Law Review* 639; Donna Krier Ioppolo et al, *Confidentiality in the United States: A Legal-Canonical Study* (Canon Law Society of America, 1988); Vincent C Allred, 'The Confessor in Court' (1953) 13(1) *Jurist* 3; David P Leonard and Victor J Gold, *Evidence: A Structured Approach* (Aspen Publishers, 2004) 583–90; Charles E Torcia (ed), *Wharton's Criminal Evidence* (Lawyers Co-Operative Publishing Company, 13th ed, 1973) vol 3, 85–6; Roy D Weinberg, *Confidential and Other Communication* (Oceana Publications, 1967) 31–5; William H Tiemann and John C Bush, *The Right to Silence: Privileged Clergy Communication and the Law* (Abingdon Press, 2nd ed, 1983) 127–232; Archdiocese of Newark, 'Cleric-Penitent Privilege (USA) With Correspondence' (1995) 102 *Canon Law Society of Great Britain and Ireland Newsletter* 22; Michael Clay Smith, 'The Pastor on the Witness Stand: Toward a Religious Privilege in the Courts' (1984) 29(1) *Catholic Lawyer* 1; 'Slanderous Communication to Clergyman Held Absolutely Privileged' (1965) 11 *Catholic Lawyer* 66; Azizah Al-Hibri, 'The Muslim Perspective on the Clergy-Penitent

Privilege' (1996) 29(4) *Loyola of Los Angeles Law Review* 1723; Anthony Cardinal Bevilacqua, 'Confidentiality Obligation of Clergy from the Perspective of Roman Catholic Priests' (1996) 29(4) *Loyola of Los Angeles Law Review* 1733, 1734; Teresa Stanton Collett, 'Sacred Secrets or Sanctimonious Silence' (1996) 29(4) *Loyola of Los Angeles Law Review* 1747; Barbara Cotton, 'Is there a Qualified Privilege at Common Law for Non-Traditional Classes of Confidential Communications? Maybe' (1990) 12(2) *Advocates Quarterly* 195; Charles Dounahue, 'Roman Canon Law in the Medieval English Church: *Stubbs vs. Maitland* Re-examined After 75 Years in the Light of Some Records from the Church Courts' (1974) 72(4) *Michigan Law Review* 647; Edward A Hogan, 'A Modern Problem on the Privilege of the Confessional' (1951) 6(1) *Loyola of Los Angeles Law Review* 1; Russell G Pearce, 'To Save A Life: Why A Rabbi and A Jewish Lawyer Must Disclose A Client Confidence' (1996) 29(4) *Loyola of Los Angeles Law Review* 1771; Arthur Gross Schaefer and Peter S Levi, 'Resolving the Conflict Between the Ethical Values of Confidentiality and Saving A Life: A Jewish View' (1996) 29(4) *Loyola of Los Angeles Law Review* 1761; Oliver S Thomas, 'Between Scylla and Charybdis: When None of the Choices Are Good' (1996) 29(4) *Loyola of Los Angeles Law Review* 1781; Ari J Diaconis, 'The Religion of Alcoholics Anonymous (AA): Applying the Clergy Privilege to Certain AA Communications' (2014) 99(5) *Cornell Law Review* 1185, 1187; Curt A Benson, 'Keeping Secrets: Privileges and the Examination Under Oath in Property Insurance Policies' (2010) 13(1) *Thomas M Cooley Journal of Practical and Clinical Law* 149; Chad G Marzen, 'Protecting Statements in Catholic Tribunal Proceedings Under the Priest-Penitent Privilege: *Cimijotti v. Paulsen* Considered' (2010) 88(2) *University of Detroit Mercy Law Review* 291, 291–2; A Michael Froomkin and Zak Colangelo, 'Privacy as Safety' (2020) 95(1) *Washington Law Review* 141, 142–3; Jana R Mccreary, 'Tell Me No Secrets: Sharing, Discipline, and the Clash of Ecclesiastical Abstention and Psychotherapeutic Confidentiality' (2011) 29(1) *Quinnipiac Law Review* 77, 78; Victor E Schwartz and Christopher E Appel, 'The Church Autonomy Doctrine: Where Tort Law Should Step Aside' (2011) 80(2) *University of Cincinnati Law Review* 431, 432.

Appendix II

Summary of US cases in the last decade which interpret and apply the sacerdotal privilege

See, eg, *State v Archibeque*, 223 Ariz 231 (Ct App, 2009); *People v Bragg*, 296 Mich App 433 (2012); *McFarland v West Congregation of Jehovah's Witnesses, Lorain Ohio Inc*, 60 NE 3d 39, 47 (Whitmore J) (Ohio Ct App, 2016); *People v Thodos*, 49 NE 3d 62 (Ill App Ct, 2015); *State v Patterson*, 294 P 3d 662 (Utah Ct App, 2013); *United States v Dillard*, 989 F Supp 2d 1155 (D Kan, 2013); *State v Mark R*, 300 Conn 590 (2011); *Lopez v Watchtower Bible & Tract Society of New York Inc*, 246 Cal App 4th 566 (2016); *People v Simental* (Cal Ct App, No E046303, 10 August 2009) slip op 3; *People v Harris*, 34 Misc 3d 281, 283 (Tomei J) (NY, 2011); *Doe ex rel Doe v Catholic Diocese of Rockford*, 38 NE 3d 1239, 1244 (Birkett J for the Court) (Ill App Ct, 2015); *People v Rodriguez* (Cal Ct App, No G046114, 29 November 2012) slip op 3; *Mirlis v Greer*, 249 F Supp 3d 611, 616 (Martinez MJ) (D Conn, 2017); *State v JG*, 201 NJ 369, 375 (Rabner CJ for Rabner CJ, Long, LaVecchia, Albin, Wallace and Hoens JJ) (2010); *State v Gil* (Ariz Ct App, No 2 CA-CR 2013-0508, 23 September 2014) slip op 2; *People v Thomas*, 18 NE 3d 577, 583 (Burke PJ) (Ill App Ct, 2014); *United States v Heller* (D Colo, No 19-CR-00224-PAB, 24 October 2019) slip op 1; *Sampson v Sisters of Mercy of Williard, Ohio* (ND Ohio, No 3:12CV824, 29 January 2016) slip op 2; *Krystal G v Roman Catholic Diocese of Brooklyn*, 34 Misc 3d 531, 544 (Rothenberg J) (NY, 2011); *People v Richard* (Mich Ct App, No 315267, 24 June 2014) slip op 3; *Conti v Watchtower Bible & Tract Society of New York Inc*, 235 Cal App 4th 1214, 1229 (Siggins J for the Court) (2015); *Commonwealth v Vital*, 83 Mass App Ct 669, 673 (Katzmann J for the Court) (2013); *East End Eruv Association Inc v Town of Southampton* (ED NY, No CV 13-4810 (AKT), 13 March 2014) slip op 1; *Commonwealth v Nutter*, 87 Mass App Ct 260, 263 (Berry J for the Court) (2015); *Stevens v Brigham Young University – Idaho* (D Idaho, No 4:16-CV-00530-DCN, 11 June 2018) slip op 2; *United States v Warrick* (ED Va, No 2:12CR189, 21 January 2014) slip op 1; *United States v Burgess* (ED Wash, No 1:14-CR-2022-TOR, 4 March 2015) slip op 2; *Lindhorst v Sullivan* (CD Cal, No LACV17951FMOLAL, 7 June 2018) slip op 4, report and recommendation adopted (CD Cal, No LACV17951FMOLAL, 31 August 2018); *People v Hoffman* (Cal Ct App, No F061127, 5 July 2012) slip op 7, as modified on denial of rehearing on 30 July 2012; *State v Smith*, 197 Wash App 1027 (2017); *Commonwealth v Kebreau*, 454 Mass 287, 301 (Cowin J for the Court) (2009); *Cline v Commonwealth* (Ky Ct App, No 2012-CA-001870-MR, 23 May 2014) slip op 2; *State v McCurdy*, 823 NW 2d 418 (Iowa Ct App, 2012); *Allen v*

Lizarraga (ND Cal, No C 10-4516 CW (PR), 26 September 2014) slip op 7; *Cooke v Town of Colorado City, Arizona* (D Ariz, No CV 10-08105-PCT-JAT, 20 June 2013) slip op 2; *Commonwealth v Garcia*, 86 Mass App Ct 1126 (2015); *Brown v Wimberly* (ED Cal, No 1:14-CV-01812-JLT, 30 June 2016) slip op 2; *State v Hancock* (Tenn Crim App, No M2012-02307-CCAR3CD, 12 December 2014) slip op 4; *Bandstra v Covenant Reformed Church*, 913 NW 2d 19, 39 (Cady CJ for the Court) (Iowa, 2018); *State v Mablin*, 772 NW 2d 269 (Iowa Ct App, 2009); *Williams v State*, 53 So 3d 761, 773 (Irving J for Lee and Myers PJJ, Irving, Barnes, Ishee and Carlton JJ) (Miss Ct App, 2009), revd 53 So 3d 734 (Miss, 2010); *State v Hesse*, 767 NW 2d 420 (Iowa Ct App, 2009); *State v Latham* (Tenn Crim App, No E2006-02262-CCA-R3CD, 20 March 2008) slip op 20; *Amber H v Parfums de Coeur Corp* (Cal Ct App, No A153958, 18 November 2019) slip op 2; *NK v Corporation of Presiding Bishop of Church of Jesus Christ of Latter-day Saints*, 175 Wash App 517, 540 (Becker J for the Court) (2013); *Smith v Hollembaek* (ED NC, No 5:15-CT-3120-BO, 15 December 2015) slip op 1, report and recommendation adopted (ED NC, No 5:15-CT-3120-BO, 14 January 2016); *People v Augustus* (Cal Ct App, No D060939, 3 July 2013) slip op 2; *Cason v Federated Life Insurance Co* (ND Cal, No C-10-0792 EMC, 20 May 2011) slip op 7; *State v Laurel Delaware Congregation of Jehovah's Witnesses* (Del Super Ct, No CV N14C-05-122 MMJ, 26 January 2016) slip op 2; *Roe v Doe* (Cal Ct App, No G057684, 29 June 2020); *JW v Watchtower Bible & Tract Society of New York Inc*, 29 Cal App 5th 1142 (2018), rehearing denied on 31 December 2018, review denied on 27 March 2019, certiorari denied 140 S Ct 217 (2019); *Wall v Wall*, 383 Mont 546 (2016); *Padron v Watchtower Bible & Tract Society of New York Inc*, 16 Cal App 5th 1246 (2017).

Appendix III

A selection of recent US scholarship concerning concerning the priest-penitent privilege

Christine P Bartholomew, 'Exorcising the Clergy Privilege' (2017) 103(6) *Virginia Law Review* 1015; Caroline Incledon, 'The Constitutionality of Broadening Clergy Penitent Privilege Statutes' (2016) 53(2) *American Criminal Law Review* 515; Paul Winters, 'Whom Must the Clergy Protect? The Interests of at-Risk Children in Conflict with Clergy-Penitent Privilege' (2012) 62(1) *DePaul Law Review* 187; Rachel Goldenberg, 'Unholy Clergy: Amending State Child Abuse Reporting Statutes to Include Clergy Members as Mandatory Reporters in Child Sexual

Abuse Cases' (2013) 51(2) *Family Court Review* 298; Kari Mercer Dalton, 'The Priest-Penitent Privilege v Child Abuse Reporting Statutes: How to Avoid the Conflict and Serve Society' (2012) 18(1) *Widener Law Review* 1; Caroline Donze, 'Breaking the Seal of Confession: Examining the Constitutionality of the Clergy-Penitent Privilege in Mandatory Reporting Law' (2017) 78(1) *Louisiana Law Review* 267; Gabriella DeRitis, 'Forgive Me Father, for I Have Sinned: Explicitly Enumerating Clergy Members as Mandatory Reporters to Combat Child Sexual Abuse in New York' (2020) 26 *Cardozo Journal of Equal Rights and Social Justice* 283; Samuel G Brooks, 'Confession and Mandatory Child Abuse Reporting: A New Take on the Constitutionality of Abrogating the Priest-Penitent Privilege' (2009) 24(1) *Brigham Young University Journal of Public Law* 117; Jude O Ezeanokwasa, 'The Priest-Penitent Privilege Revisited: A Reply to the Statutes of Abrogation' (2014) 9 *Intercultural Human Rights Law Review* 41; Megan Clemency, 'Criminal and Civil Liability for Failure to Report Suspected Child Abuse in South Carolina' (2017) 68(5) *South Carolina Law Review* 893; Jordan Paul, 'Deliver Us from Evil: Domestic and International Solutions to Clerical Sex Abuse' (2019) 36(3) *Arizona Journal of International and Comparative Law* 501; Brigid Benincasa, 'Protecting Our Children: A Reformation of South Carolina's Homicide by Child Abuse Laws' (2014) 65(4) *South Carolina Law Review* 735; William A Galston, 'Why the Ministerial Exception Is Consistent with Smith – And Why It Makes Sense' (2016) 53(1) *San Diego Law Review* 147, 147–8; Matthew Johnson, 'Mandatory Child Abuse Reporting Laws in Georgia: Strengthening Protection for Georgia's Children' (2015) 31(3) *Georgia State University Law Review* 643; Stephen M Bainbridge, 'Enhanced Accountability: The Catholic Church's Unfinished Business' (2019) 53(2) *University of San Francisco Law Review* 165; Nina A Kohn, 'Outliving Civil Rights' (2009) 86(5) *Washington University Law Review* 1053; Marci A Hamilton, 'Child Sex Abuse in Institutional Settings: What Is Next' (2012) 89(4) *University of Detroit Mercy Law Review* 421; Craig P Cassagne, 'What is a "Confession per Se?": *Parents of Minor Child v Charlet* Priest-Penitent Privilege and the Right of the Church to Interpret Its Own Doctrine' (2015) 42(2) *Southern University Law Review* 255; Kelly Clark, 'Institutional Child Sexual Abuse—Not Just a Catholic Thing' (2009) 36(1) *William Mitchell Law Review* 220, 222.

9

Giorgio Morelli

The church as a hospital and the seal of confession

Abstract

In this chapter, Father Morelli places religious confession and other confidential religious communications in the context of the Orthodox doctrines of healing and reconciliation to God. Human beings need healing because of their fallen condition. The healing of the soul is more important in God's eternal plan than the healing of the body. But because the healing of the soul cannot take place until efforts to repair wrong have begun, it is entirely appropriate that healing penance require the penitent to report to civil authorities before the prayer of absolution takes place. But that does not mean a priest can disclose related religious communications involved in that practice. The priest acts as an icon for God in the sacrament of penance. What he witnesses is a private communication between the penitent and God and should be distinguished from the reportable conduct of secular counsellors.

Keywords:

Separation from God, healing, the Holy Mystery of confession, the Father Confessor as an icon of God

I Introduction

It is prevalent in the Orthodox Church to view the church as a hospital. To understand healing we must first understand sin, illness, death and love, a task that brings us back to Genesis. Mankind is meant for paradise, and paradise is understood as life in and with God that lasts for all eternity. But our ancestral parents wanted to become as God themselves. The nature of their sin was that they looked to the creation rather than the Creator for the life (which includes knowledge and wisdom) that can only come from God.

But God did not leave our ancestral parents desolate. He began the restoration of all mankind only moments after their expulsion. It started with the clothing of Adam and Eve in animal skins and continued through the covenant with Noah. It follows with a covenant that God made with Abraham that through him God would send a saviour to heal the catastrophic rupture. It is completed in the death and resurrection of Jesus Christ. St Basil expressed it beautifully: 'Thou didst send forth the Prophets; Thou didst perform mighty works by the saints ... who foretold unto us the salvation which was to come'.[1]

The Orthodox Church does not teach that we inherit the *guilt* of Adam. Rather, we share in the sin of Adam in that we are born into a world where the consequences of sin prevail. These consequences are not only the outward brokenness like disease and death, but interior disorder as well. Our nature is corrupted. We are subject to temptation, prone to sin, and share in death.

The rupturing of the relationship our ancestral parents had with God that affected all subsequent generations is the source of sickness and death. Christ, as the One who overcame death, restores the relationship by destroying sin and death. He becomes the *mediator* between mankind and the Father, the bridge over the unbridgeable chasm, the conqueror of death, the *Saviour* of soul and body. His obedience unto righteousness (Christ was the only man not to break the Law of Moses) annuls the

---

1   Divine Liturgy of St Basil the Great, The Anaphora, 24.

penalty of death that fell on disobedient Adam, thereby making His death completely voluntary – a sacrifice – and thus making His resurrection from death possible.[2]

II Healing in the Orthodox Church

In the Orthodox Church, healing of the soul ranks higher than the healing of the body. In fact, the healing of the body is offered as a sign of His mercy and blessing to the person experiencing God's healing and to inspire others to do His will. Healing is to be sought both through prayer and the application of physical sciences, but no complete healing is possible apart from the final resurrection of an individual because the sentence of death still reigns in the mortal body. Further, not all people are healed, despite fervent pleas to God and the applications of the best medicines. Sometime illness needs to be endured.[3]

The subordination of physical to spiritual healing is derived from the Epistle of James. St James said:

> Is there any one among you suffering? Let him pray ... Is any among you sick? Let him call for the presbyters of the Church, and let them pray over him, anointing him with oil in the name of the Lord; and the prayer of faith will save the sick man, and the Lord will raise him up; and if he has committed sins, he will be forgiven.[4]

The church fathers understood this well. St Gregory of Nyssa said: 'Medicine is an example of what God allows men to do when they work in harmony with Him and with one another'. Basil of Caesarea said: 'God's grace is as evident in the healing power of medicine and its practitioners as it is in miraculous cures'.[5]

---

2   George Morelli, 'The Ethos of Orthodox Christian Healing', *Orthodoxy Today* (Web Page, 21 December 2006).
3   Ibid.
4   James 4:13–5 (English Standard Version, 'ESV').
5   John G Demakis, 'Historical Precedents for Synergia: Combining Medicine, Diakonia and Sacrament in Byzantine Times' in Stephen Muse (ed), *Raising Lazarus: Integral Healing in Orthodox Christianity* (Holy Cross Orthodox Press, 2004) 16.

A A Brief Summary of Healing in the Church

It is not overstating the case to say that the emphasis on the healing of persons is one of the great gifts that Christianity has given the world. It started with Christ. The Gospels record numerous instances where Christ healed all manner of diseases, both spiritual and physical. St Luke, himself a physician, recorded the most in his Gospel, and then later showed in his book *The Acts of the Apostles* how this power of healing was granted to the Apostles. It should be no surprise that at the end of the persecutions of the early centuries, healing arts were developed and flourished even to this day.

Orthodox Christianity has a rich history of healers revered as saints. Twin brothers Sts Cosmas and Damian were physicians practicing during the reign of Diocletian and Maximianos in the era before the persecutions ended. Born in Arabia, they became known as 'Anargyroi' (penniless) because they refused to accept any money for their service. They are venerated in both the Eastern and Western churches, but in the East they also carry the title 'Wonderworker' because in addition to healing the body, they also cast out demons and removed other darkness from the souls of men just as Christ had done. They attributed their healing gifts to Christ, whom they called the 'Great Physician', and regarded themselves simply as Christ's instruments of healing, comfort, witness, and sanctification.

Orthodoxy had other great healer saints as well. Hronas detailed the life of St Luke as well as twenty physicians of which eighteen were missionaries and two were priests. One of the priests was St Sampson, the 'Innkeeper and Physician of Constantinople' whose feast day is celebrated on 17 June.[6] St Sampson was originally from Rome at the time when Saint Justinian the Great reigned, but settled in Constantinople. He became so respected for his healing power, prayer, virtue, and love of the sick and poor that Patriarch Menas of Constantinople ordained

---

6   Georgia Hronas, *The Holy Unmercenary Doctors: The Saints Anargyroi, Physicians and Healers of the Orthodox Church* (Light and Life, 1999) 57-63.

him a priest. In humility he often hid his prayerful healing by dispensing medication. He healed the Emperor Justinian who in gratitude donated a grand healing centre to St Sampson that came to be known as 'The Hospice of Sampson'.

B Healing in Byzantium

In the fourth century various healing centres were opened and administered by the Orthodox Church, including homes for the poor, orphans, aged and hospitals.[7] Many of these centres were associated with monasteries. The health care workers, the physicians, nurses, and psychologists of the day were often the monks themselves. St Basil of Caesarea (370-379 CE) was trained in medicine and was reported to have worked with the monks in ministering to the ill and infirm.

St John Chrysostom as Patriarch of Constantinople (390 CE) used the wealth of the church to open hospitals and other philanthropic institutions, which earned him great love from the people. Within two centuries, the rapid growth of these centres necessitated state funding although the church retained the active administration and care-giving in the arrangement. The Emperor Justinian moved the most important physicians into the hospitals, which enhanced the reputation of these centres.[8]

The Pantocrator Monastery was a large healing centre. Its *Typikon* (the book that explains how the monastery should be ordered) reveals that their benevolent work was complex and extensive. A few sections include:

1 External Relations

The remarkable hospital (*xenon*) associated with this foundation capped a long tradition of institutional philanthropy observed in these

---

7   Demakis, (n 5), 17.
8   Ibid 18.

documents since Mount Tmolos in the late tenth century. Chapters throughout provide regulations for the hospital, the old age home, and lepers sanatorium.

(a) The Hospital

The hospital was presided over by an overseer (*nosokomos*) and had sixty beds divided into five wards, one of which was to be reserved for women. Two non-resident doctors (serving in alternate months) and a complement of assistants and orderlies staffed each ward. The doctors were not to undertake any outside work even for unpaid service by imperial command. The women's ward had an extra female doctor. Four extra doctors, including two surgeons, staffed an outpatient department. Two of the outpatient doctors took turns providing services to the monks of the monastery in alternate months.

There were also various service personnel, including a chief pharmacist and three druggists as well as two priests stationed in the hospital chapel. A teacher of medicine was to 'teach the principles of medical knowledge' to student doctors, who were apparently chosen from among the hospital's auxiliaries. Salaries for the various hospital personnel were detailed as well as the supplies needed by the infirmarian and the superintendent, who served as a cellarer. The emperor provided regulations for liturgical services, burials, and commemorations of the deceased.

(b) The Old Age Home

The director (*gerokomos*) of the old age home was chosen from among the monks of the monastery. With the assistance of six orderlies, he would care for twenty-four aged and infirm men in the home; the healthy were specifically excluded, regardless of social class. As in the hospital, a chapel staffed by a priest and reader was available to residents. The emperor provided cash and in-kind allowances for both the staff and the residents.

(c) The Sanatorium

A lepers' sanatorium was established at a site away from the monastery. The emperor sought a 'special remembrance' from its residents, but unlike patients in the hospital, he did not ask them to come to a church to pray for his soul.

(d) Routine Charitable Donations

Less institutionalized forms of philanthropy were practiced at the foundation as well. A bakery (*mankipeion*) provided bread to nourish the residents of both the hospital and the old age home. For non-residents, there were to be charitable distributions at the gate in honor of the foundation's benefactors. Leftovers were to be collected for this purpose after both the midday and evening meals.[9]

Demakis notes five characteristic traits shared by the physician-saints:

1 They were committed to Christ and were holy men before they became healers.

2 They lived as deeply committed Christians in personal prayer, meditation, fasting, and actively prayed for their patients.

3 They were outstanding physicians often 'first in their medical school class'; Medical science was regarded as a serious academic discipline.

4 They had a 'deep and abiding love' for mankind and strove to see 'the image of Christ' in every patient. This was shown in their actions including long working hours, refusal of any payment, turning their homes into hospitals, and the personal care they showed toward their patients ('fed and cared for their patients personally').

5 They attributed their healing skills and medical successes to God.[10]

---

9   Ibid 19-22.
10 Ibid 23.

2 The Church as Hospital - the spiritual dimension of healing

St John Chrysostom presented us with the idea that the entire church of Christ is a hospital, thereby expressing in clearer theological terms the relationship between the healing of body and soul practiced by the early healers. The Parable of the Good Samaritan is the model St Luke used where the good Samaritan exemplifies Christ who, as the great physician, comes to broken mankind (the man beaten by robbers lying on the road) in order to bring healing.[11] The inn in which the good Samaritan delivered the suffering man is the church.[12]

The interrelationship between body and soul is noted in almost every liturgical prayer. Most corporate prayer begins with the Trisagion (Thrice-Holy) prayer that makes the relationship clear: 'All-holy Trinity, have mercy on us, Lord, cleanse us from our sins. Master, pardon our iniquities. Holy God, visit and heal our infirmities for thy name's sake'.[13]

3 Baptism

In fact, the spiritual dimension underlying any healing is most clearly revealed in the foundational sacrament of the Christian life. Baptism, as St Paul taught in Romans 6, is the new birth, the starting point of life in Christ through an entry into Christ's death and a raising into the 'likeness' of His resurrection. The baptismal service begins with several prayers of exorcism that are meant to heal the person of illness and infirmity brought about by the rebellion of the Evil One as indicated above. Originally deacons read the exorcism prayers, but in modern times the priest who performs the baptism reads the prayers. The prayers prepare the baptismal candidate to enter life in Christ and thereby receive the power (through the Holy Spirit received in baptism) to detach from the power of evil that might rule in his soul. These prayers and the baptism

---

11 Cf Luke 10:33 et seq (Douay-Rheims Bible, 'DRB').

12 Hierotheos Vlachos, *Orthodox Psychotherapy: The Science of the Fathers*, tr Esther Williams (Birth of the Theotokos Monastery, 1994) 27.

13 O Heavenly King and Psalm 51 (Psalm of Repentance),' *Orthodox Church in America* (Web page).

that follows are actually a profound healing of the soul's attachment to untoward things, thereby enabling it to attain freedom.

4 Exorcism

Sometimes the healing of the soul calls for drastic measures. A guide for clergy of the Orthodox Church is the *Book of Needs*[14] which includes prayers for expulsion of demons from the soul and for protection from such evil. Clergy entering this dimension of spiritual reality must exercise great discernment since many illnesses have natural causes and a misdiagnosis is easily made. Further, the mental status of anyone requesting such prayers also has to be considered. Pastorally, the best practice is to say a simple prayer for those requesting it, such as those found in the exorcism ritual in Holy Baptism. St Basil, St John Chrysostom, and several other noted saints wrote these prayers.

A prayer by St John Chrysostom that is included in *The Book of Needs* concisely states the goal of our earthly life:

> O Lord Jesus Christ ... We beseech You, look mercifully upon him (or her), and in your great love grant him (or her) relief from his (or her) pain ... that restored to the vigor of health, he (or she) may ... serve you faithfully and gratefully all his (or her) life, and become heir of Your Kingdom, For You are the Physician of our souls and bodies, O Christ.[15]

Another exorcism prayer written by St John Chrysostom reads:

> Everlasting God ... command these evil and impure spirits to withdraw from soul and body ... so he (she) may live a holy, righteous and devout life deserving of the sacred Mysteries of Your only-begotten Son our God.[16]

---

14 A Monk of St Tikhon's Monastery, *Book of Needs* (St Tikhon's Seminary Press, 1987).

15 Ibid 25.

16 Archimandrite, Leonidas Contos, *Sacraments and Services, Book Two* (Narthex Press, 1993), 150.

5 Holy Eucharist

The Holy Eucharist (Holy Communion) continues the healing that began in Holy Baptism. The Eucharist conjoins us to the Great Physician, a point expressed in the liturgical prayer that is read immediately before the elevation of the bread and wine:

> We give thanks unto thee, O King invisible, who by thy measureless power hast made all things ... look down from heaven upon those who have bowed their heads unto thee ... distribute these Gifts here spread forth, unto all of us for good ... heal the sick, thou who art the physician of souls and bodies.[17]

6 Holy Unction

The distinction between spiritual and physical healing is revealed liturgically as well. Orthodox Christians perform the Mystery of Holy Unction for the healing of soul and body and for forgiveness of sins. It is usually celebrated during Wednesday of Holy Week, but can be performed any time. During the service epistle and gospel readings are read, prayers are said, oil is blessed, and each worshipper is anointed with the holy oil as the priest says: 'The blessing of Our Lord God and Savior Jesus Christ: for the healing of soul and body'.

The prayer of the blessing of the oil illustrates the goal of physical healing: that those anointed can glorify God and thus be spiritually healed. The prayer in part reads:

> O Lord, who through thy mercies and bounties heals the disorders of our souls and bodies: Do thou Thyself, O Master, also sanctify this oil, that it may be effectual for those who are anointed therewith, unto healing and unto relief from every passion, of every defilement of flesh and spirit, and every ill; that thereby may be glorified Thine all holy Name, of the Father, and of the Son, and of the Holy Spirit: now and ever, and unto ages of ages. Amen.[18]

---

17 'The Ektenia before the Lord's Prayer,' *Online Novgorod* (Web page).
18 A Monk of St Tikhon's Monastery, *Book of Needs: Abridged* (St Tikhon's Seminary Press, 2002), 64.

Ideally, seven priests perform this Holy Mystery, but fewer, or even a single priest, can celebrate it. It is offered to the healthy as well as the sick for all are diseased in some way.

The Holy Unction service goes back to the earliest days of Christianity. Orthodox Liturgical scholar Fr Alkiviadis Calivas stated:

> In ancient Christian literature one may find indirect testimonies of the Mystery of Unction in Saint Irenaeus of Lyons and in Origen. Later there are clear testimonies of it in Saints Basil the Great and John Chrysostom, who have left prayers for the healing of the infirm which entered later into the rite of Unction; and likewise in Saint Cyril of Alexandria.[19]

Sometimes the emphasis on spiritual healing is taken to mean that attempts at physical healing should be minimized. This is a grave misconception. In the Orthodox moral tradition both spiritual and physical healing should be brought to God. The foundation of this misconception rests in ideas that faith somehow stands in opposition to science. It does not. God is the source of both faith and science and in the end no final conflict exists between the two. Orthodox theologian and ethicist Fr Stanley S Harakas wrote:

> Medical treatment is also seen as a human cooperation with God's healing purposes and goals. In fact, all of Orthodox teaching recognizes a place for human effort, striving and cooperating with God's will. Technically known as 'synergy', this belief requires the exercise of human talents and abilities for salvation, for spiritual growth, for moral behavior, for achievement of human potential … So, in principle, the use of healing, medicines … even surgical operations have generally been understood throughout history in the Church to be appropriate, fitting and desirable ways of cooperating with God in the healing of human illnesses.[20]

---

19 'Holy Unction,' *Greek Orthodox Archdiocese of America* (Web page).
20 'For the Health of Body and Soul: An Eastern Orthodox Introduction to Bioethics,' *Greek Orthodox Archdiocese of America* (Web page).

7 Holy Repentance-Confession

Christ became man and took on our human nature to call mankind to repentance, to conversion, to a 'change of mind' (*metanoia*). Even though our sins are forgiven in baptism, because of our fallen nature and inclination to sin (*amartia* – missing the mark), we continue to fall short during our lifetime either voluntarily or involuntarily. After the fall we are predisposed to self- centred choices directed by the passions (lusts) rather than choices based on agape. St Isaac of Syria tells us: 'pandering to the flesh, produce[s] in us shameful urges and unseemly fantasies'.[21] The passions spring from the heart of the person. Jesus told us: 'For from within, out of the heart of man, come evil thoughts, fornication, theft, murder, adultery, coveting, wickedness, deceit, licentiousness, envy, slander, pride, foolishness. All these evil things come from within, and they defile a man'.[22]

The Parable of the Prodigal Son who left his father's house after wallowing in sin, came to a radical rejection and transformation of his entire perverse way of life and thought, is a model of the Holy Mystery of Confession.[23] That is to say acknowledging (confessing) and asking forgiveness for our sins and thus achieving restoration of the mind and senses to their original purpose in Paradise, which is conformity to the will of God. We can consider the Holy Mystery of Confession to be a continual baptism – a washing away of sin from our souls.

Because of man's inclination to sin throughout lifetime, 're-baptism' is needed. The church fathers have called true repentance, especially a repentance accompanied by 'the gift of tears' to be a second baptism. St Evagrios the Solitary tells us: 'First pray for the gift of tears, so that through sorrowing you may tame what is savage in your soul. And having confessed transgressions to the Lord, you will obtain forgiveness from Him'. St Peter of Damaskos wrote, 'give thanks to Him [God],

---

21 E Kadloubovsky and GEH Palmer (eds), *Early Fathers from the Philokalia: Together with Some Writings of St Abba Dorotheus, St Isaac of Syria and St Gregory Palamas* (Faber & Faber, 1954) 208.
22 Mark 7: 21–3 (ESV).
23 Luke 15:11–24 (DRB).

especially those who have received from Him the power to renew their holy baptism through repentance, because without repentance no one can be saved'.[24]

Sin makes us to be out of communion or what might be called disunion with God and neighbour. St John Chrysostom states: 'Did you commit sin? Enter the Church and repent for your sin; for here is the physician, not the judge; here one is not investigated, one receives remission of sins'.[25] If the church is a 'physician', then this break with God and neighbour needs healing. It is missing the mark of being centred on God and His will. Sin is considered, therefore to be an illness or infirmity. With healing we are restored to a former condition.

The Holy Mystery of Confession was instituted by Christ Himself, in His instruction to the Apostles and their successors, the bishops and priests of His church: 'Amen I say to you, whatsoever you shall bind upon earth, shall be bound also in heaven; and whatsoever you shall loose upon earth, shall be loosed also in heaven'.[26] However, the church always considered confession to be between the penitent and God Himself, with the priest in the position of physician, aiding in healing, guiding the penitent as a spiritual father. Father Deacon John Chryssavgis notes,

> It is the reduction of sin to a punishable legal crime, an act of lawbreaking inviting a penalty that is almost wholly absent in patristic literature. 'Have you committed a sin?', asks Saint John Chrysostom, 'then enter the Church and repent of your sin … For here is the Physician, not the judge; here one is not investigated but receives remission of sins'.[27]

The priest is a witness of the transforming *metanoia* of the penitent to renounce his former life and seek a life in God. Chryssavgis goes on to say

---

24 GEH Palmer, Philip Sherrard and Kallistos Ware (eds), *The Philokalia: The Complete Text Compiled by St Nikodimos of the Holy Mountain and St Makarios of Corinth*, Vol. 3 (Faber & Faber), (1979-1995), 178.

25 John Chryssavgis, *Repentance and Confession in the Orthodox Church* (Holy Cross Orthodox Press, 1990), 13.

26 Matthew 18:18 (DRB).

27 Chryssavgis, 'Repentance and Confession, 13.

[i]n the Orthodox Church, the priest ... [is] not a recipient of secrets, a detective of specific misdeeds. The 'eye', the 'ear' of the priest is dissolved in the sacramental mystery. He is not a dispenser, a power wielding, vindicating agent, an 'authority'. Such a conception exteriorizes the function of the confessor and of confession which is an act of re-integration of the penitent and priest alike into the Body of Christ.[28]

This is especially seen in the prayer of absolution said by priests in both the Greek and Slavonic tradition: 'May Our Lord Jesus Christ [or God] forgive all your sins and transgressions'. Clearly in the Orthodox Church it is Christ in the second person of the Holy Trinity, God, who forgives the sin of the confessor.

8 The Role of the Priest in the Mystery of Holy Confession

The priest is a witness of the repentance and if the repentance is deemed sincere, the priest acts as Christ's instrument dispensing the Holy Mystery of Absolution. The inviolability of the 'seal of confession' is part of the sacred tradition of the church. It is aptly summarized by St Nicodemus the Hagiorite in the *Exomologitarion: A Manual for Confession*.[29] He exhorts:

> Nothing else remains after confession, Spiritual Father, except to keep the sins you hear a secret, and to never reveal them, either by word, or by letter, or by a bodily gesture, or by any other sign, even if you are in danger of death, for that which the wise Sirach says applies to you: 'Have you heard a word? Let it die with you'... meaning, if you heard a secret word, let the word also die along with you, and do not tell it to either a friend of yours or an enemy of yours, for as long as you live ... For if you reveal them, firstly, you will be suspended or daresay deposed completely by the Ecclesiastical Canons.[30]

---

28 Ibid.
29 Nicodemus the Hagiorite, *Exomolgetarion: A Manual of Confession* (Uncut Mountain Press, 2006).
30 Ibid 189–90.

In keeping with the theme of the church as a hospital if a so called 'penance' is given to the penitent by the priest, it is not a juridical act, but an act of healing. It is meant to be a therapeutic intervention healing the disunion of the penitent with God and mankind. For example, if a penitent has confessed being angry with someone, a therapeutic penance might be to attempt to repair. This might require the penitent to approach the person with whom one was angry and to attempt a reconciliation. If the penitent confesses a serious crime, such as sexual abuse, then an appropriate healing penance before absolution would be for the penitent to turn and report to the appropriate civil authorities.

C The Example of Healing Sexual Abuse or Domestic Violence as an Importance Issue of Our Time

The penance given to the penitent is for the purpose of healing. It is entirely appropriate that healing cannot take place until the penitent reports serious sin to the appropriate public authorities as a condition for the prayer of absolution in the Holy Mystery of Confession-Repentance. Serious sin is sin that has been and may continue to be a serious threat to others. Healing of serious sin such as sexual abuse or domestic violence requires psychological and spiritual acceptance of responsibility on the part of the abuser and recognition of the consequences of the abuse. In most cases of severe abuse, healing will not mean reintegration into the usual pattern of life the abuser previously lived. Thus, part of the acceptance of the consequences of serious sin means a radical change in lifestyle must occur. In many cases, individuals who have physically or sexually abused others will have to be removed permanently from their social milieu. Mental health practitioners treating Orthodox Christian patients with evidence based psychological interventions should be informed of their Orthodoxy.[31]

---

31 George Morelli, 'Abuse: Some Pastoral And Clinical Considerations', *Antiochian Orhodoc Christian Archdioces of North America*, n.d. (Web page).

1 Types of Abuse

Four types of abuse have been identified: physical, sexual, emotional and neglect. In cases of severe abuse, victims may experience trauma similar to post traumatic stress disorder ('PTSD') and other psychological disorders such as affective disorders, anxiety, substance abuse, dissociative disorders, compulsive behaviours. It is beyond the scope of this paper to go into all the psychological effects and treatments of abuse. A brief discussion of the trauma reaction will illustrate the severity of the effects of abuse.

Originally trauma was associated with combat (eg combat fatigue). Other incidents became associated with trauma outside the domain of combat. Survivors of horrific railroad accidents and devastating weather events such as hurricanes and tornadoes were shown to have the same physical and psychological reaction as those suffering combat fatigue. Further research extended the understanding of trauma. The American Psychological Association ('APA') defined a traumatic stressor in the diagnosis of PTSD as

> Exposure to actual or threatened death, serious injury, or sexual violence in one (or more) of the following ways:
>
> 1. Directly experiencing the traumatic event(s).
>
> 2. Witnessing, in person, the event(s) as it occurred to others.
>
> 3. Learning that the traumatic event(s) occurred to a close family member or close friend. In cases of the actual or threatened death of a family member or friend, the event(s) must have been violent or accidental.
>
> 4. Experiencing repeated or extreme exposure to aversive details of the traumatic event(s) (eg, first responders collecting human remains; police officers repeatedly exposed to details of child abuse).[32]

Updated trauma research has delineated varied types of traumatic

---

32 American Psychiatric Association, *Diagnostic and Statistical Manual of Mental Disorders* (5th ed, 2013) 271.

stressors such as racial, ethnic or sexual slurs or innuendo as well as describing various symptom clusters such as flashbacks, unwanted intrusive thoughts, dissociation and avoidance.

Individuals who have suffered abuse and trauma are often reluctant to talk about it. It has been shown that an empathic and understanding relationship with the clinician (and or clergy) is important in the treatment process. Ellis et al found that empirically supported therapy relationship variables are common to all specific treatment interventions.[33] Evidence based scientific interventions for abuse and/or domestic violence include cognitive-behaviour therapies, dialectic behaviour therapy, exposure therapies, acceptance and commitment therapy and a couples (dyadic) approach (Gottman relationship therapy).[34]

2 Pastoral Pointer

Orthodox parishes are small. Typically, there is only one divine liturgy on any given day. Many parishioners are like family and know each other. It would not be uncommon for a parish priest to hear about some domestic issues a family may be having. In such cases the priest if approached by a member of such a family, may advise a pastoral counseling session before hearing any confession. Such counseling would not fall under the 'seal of confession.' Of course, any serious infraction that may have occurred outside of the parish community would not be readily known. If in a counseling non-confessional setting, the Orthodox priest becomes aware of an abuse situation, the seal of confession would not apply and the priest would be ethically and morally obligated to conform to local law.

---

33 Amy E Ellis et al, 'The Role of Evidence-Based Therapy Relationships on Treatment Outcomes for Adults with Trauma: A Systemic Review' (2018) 19(2) *Journal of Trauma and Dissociation* 185.

34 John M Gottman, *The Science of Trust: Emotional Attunement for Couples* (Norton, 2014).

3 Other Christian Communities

Few living in today's world can miss the divisions that make up the various Christian communities in the world today. Many would see these as a scandal in direct opposition to Christ's injunction that his followers would all live together as one. He famously prayed 'That they all may be one, as thou, Father, in me, and I in thee; that they also may be one in us'.[35]

There are two major distinctions in the churches of apostolic origin and the reformed communities. The Eastern Orthodox and Oriental churches and the Latin Catholic churches in the West. Both derive their authority in succession from the Apostles. What the Eastern or Oriental churches call the Holy Mysteries of the church are called the sacraments in the Western churches. These apostolic churches conform to the words of St Paul. He commended those 'who remembered [him] in everything and maintain[ed] the traditions even as [he] ha[d] delivered them to [them]'.[36] The Apostles appointed overseers ('*episkopoi*', bishops) to lead these communities. St Luke wrote: 'Take heed to yourselves and to all the flock, in which the Holy Spirit has made you overseers, [the original name for bishops and priests in sacred scripture] to care for the church of God which he obtained with the blood of his own Son'.[37] Christianity is first known through the oral tradition and practice of the church and only then through the written scriptures. The apostolic churches have maintained substantial continuity with this tradition. These churches hold that only a man ordained by a successor-bishop of the apostles can be ordained to the priestly ministry with the function to 'preach, teach and sanctify'. This is the reason why only an ordained priest can provide the blessing of absolution of the penitent's confession of sin to Christ. The confession is sacred and thus under the 'seal of confession' because it is made to God.

In contrast the reformed traditions were mainly started by individuals

---

35 John 17: 21 (DRB).
36 1 Corinthians 11:2 (ESV).
37 Acts 20:28 (ESV).

who departed from the Roman Church. Most of these communities rely only on sacred scripture (the Holy Bible being their authoritative text) for their teaching. Often the Latin term *sola scriptura* is used to denote the reformist view that it is the text itself which provides those who teach in the reformist tradition with their authority. It must be emphasized that, for the Orthodox, sacred scripture can only be understood through the Holy Spirit-inspired church, as is explained in an outstanding book that echoes the mind of the church called *Scripture in Tradition* by the Very Reverend Professor John Breck.[38]

Reformed ministry is one of service and leading worship. One common sacrament may be baptism but the holy mysteries, as known in the Orthodox Church are not acknowledged or performed in reformed churches. Pastors in reformed communities are thus seen by the Orthodox as performing ministry similar to pastoral counseling functions. In some jurisdictions mental health clinicians are considered mandatory reporters. Local laws would have to be consulted to determine if pastoral counselors or ministers performing pastoral ministry are covered by such law. In the Orthodox Church, because a priest does not hear confessions personally as the penitent confesses to God, there is nothing that is reportable under mandatory reporting laws however they are formulated.

4 An Orthodox Response to Abuse

The Orthodox Church has not been unaware of domestic violence, sexual abuse, child prostitution and other critical issues in contemporary society. Such actions are always *amartia* (they miss the mark of righteous human conduct and are sinful). To say these issues have always been there, but have not become widely known, may be true but begs the question of how they should be dealt with by the church. Historically

---

38 John Breck, *Scripture in Tradition: The Bible and Its Interpretation in the Orthodox Church* (Vladimir's Seminary Press, 2001).

these issues have existed in many institutions (in schools, governments and religious organisations) but have been handled differently with responses ranging from cover up, through internal investigation to public disclosure and legal action. The advent of social media has been a factor in focusing the seriousness of the problem and in designating it as a social issue which requires legislative intervention.

The website of the Assembly of Canonical Orthodox Bishops of the United States of America contains a crisis assistance page that highlights domestic violence and abuse and provides access to sexual assault and domestic violence hotlines as well as links to other domestic violence resources.[39] The predecessor, Standing Conference of Canonical Orthodox Bishops in the Americas, in 2005 issued a statement which took a strong stand against abuse. In part it reads:

> Sexual abuse or misconduct will find no safe haven within the Holy Orthodox Church. We, as hierarchs of the Church, commit ourselves and the resources at the Church's disposal to ensure that every child of God, of whatever age, may be safe and secure within the bosom of the Church, and that sexual predators will find no place within her to carry out their crimes. Sin thrives where there is darkness and secrecy, but it cannot stand the light of truth and openness. By pursuing truth and justice, by standing by the victims of crime, by ensuring fair and due process for everyone concerned, and by facilitating repentance unto salvation, the Church will be true to the God she serves and to her faithful people.[40]

This summary of the mind of the Orthodox Church in the Americas on the issue of abuse, confirms that the Orthodox Church will do all it can morally, ethically and legally to stop abuse, short of breaking the seal of confession. In repentance-confession, the penitent confesses to God. The dialogue in confession is primarily between the penitent and God and is about the penitent's sins and includes the penitent's request

---

39 'Seek Support', *Assembly of Canonical Orthodox Bishops of the United States of America* (Web Page).

40 'SCOBA Issues Statement on Sexual Misconduct in the Church', *Assembly of Canonical Orthodox Bishops of the United States of America* (Web Page).

for forgiveness. The priest is a witness to this private dialogue and by God's grace, may offer penance-guidance to aid the penitent toward achieving God's forgiveness and *theosis* (union with Him). In repentance-confession, the priest is not witness to a public act. Outside of the holy mystery, the stand of the church is to promote legal 'fair and due process for [all] concerned'. A distinction should also be made between mandated reporters such as mental health clinicians licensed by the state and the ordained priesthood in the Orthodox Church who are considered commissioned by God, independent of the state. In the United States, the confessional function of the ordained priesthood is protected by the free exercise of religion under the *First Amendment*.

D Repentance-Confession in Healing

Bowby's and Ainsworth's attachment theory is a psychological model that is quite relevant to the healing that takes place in a sincere confession which forms part of the Holy Mystery of Repentance-Confession. As explained by Bretherton, attachment theory states that among humans functional emotional and social behaviour is related to having a secure and consistent attachment with their caretaker. On the other hand dysfunctional attachment patterns such as anxious, avoidant, ambivalent or disorganised attachments are linked to personal distress and social disturbance.[41] Without a relationship characterized by complete trust, confidentiality consistency and empathy, whether in counselling or confession, someone seeking to reform their life is not able to engage in the process completely enough to ensure that the reform sought can begin in earnest.

From an early age the Orthodox Christian knows that God and His love for each of us is always there ready to 'attach' to us. This is expressed clearly in an encounter between St Silouan the Athonite and a hermit:

---

41 Inge Bretherton, 'The Origins of Attachment Theory: John Bowlby and Mary Ainsworth' (1992) 28(5) *Developmental Psychology* 759.

I remember a conversation between [Silouan] and a certain hermit who declared with evident satisfaction, 'God will punish all atheists. They will burn in everlasting fire'. Obviously upset, [Silouan] said, 'Tell me, supposing you went to paradise, and there you looked down and saw someone burning in hell-fire – would you feel happy?' 'It can't be helped. It would be their own fault', said the hermit. [Silouan] answered him in a sorrowful countenance: 'Love could not bear that'.[42]

Every Orthodox Christian comes to know that God is love[43] and that 'His mercy is everlasting'.[44] Therefore, repentance, confession and reconciliation to God are part of the process by which we secure our attachment to Him. Once established, this is a secure attachment. He is always ready to receive us. As previously mentioned, the New Testament scripture 'Parable of the Prodigal Son' serves as a model for all who have sinned and become healed by reconciliation with God and His church. The son left his father's house to live a profligate life. After coming to his senses, he came back to his father and confessed. In the words of St Luke: 'And the son said to him: Father, I have sinned against heaven, and before thee, I am not now worthy to be called thy son'.[45] In St Luke's account, the prodigal's father embraces his penitent son and gives a feast. Neuropsychological researchers have generally confirmed that 'secure attachment, as compared with insecure attachment, [acts] as a physiological reactivity buffer to stress responses'.[46] The prefrontal cortex, an area of the brain that is highly involved in executive functioning skills, is strengthened by secure attachment. In secure attachment the individual feels safe and cared for and the individual's brain can use its energy to develop pathways crucial for higher level thinking. Compassionate and empathic interactions between clinicians and clergy working with people recovering from addiction and lives of crime, are an

---

42 Archimandrite Sophroney, *St Silouan the Athonite* (St Vladimir's Seminary Press, 1999) 48.

43 1 John 4:7 (ESV).

44 Psalms 99:5 (New King James Version).

45 Luke 15:21 (DRB).

46 Anna Buchheim et al, 'Editorial: Neuroscience of Human Attachment' (2017) 11 *Frontiers in Human Neuroscience* 136:1–3, 1.

essential aspect of a healing relationship that enables long term reform. The same principle self-evidently applies to the relationship between Orthodox priests and those who approach them for access to the Holy Mystery of Repentance-Confession.

The key to the reconciliation is confession of misdeeds (*amartia*) and firm commitment to change of heart, repentance and lifestyle (*metanoia*). As St Isaac of Syria tells us: 'Repentance is able to renew within us the grace which we have lost subsequent to baptism through our lax way of life'.[47] God is ever ready to receive us. That is God's mercy. He is a loving father always ready to receive us as emphasized in the writings of the Orthodox 'saint of mercy', St Isaac of Syria. Furthermore, His mercy is far greater than what might be called His justice. This is exemplified in another of St Isaac's counsels:

> As a grain of sand cannot counterbalance a great quantity of gold, so in comparison God's use of justice cannot counterbalance His mercy. As a handful of sand thrown into the great sea, so are the sins of all flesh in comparison with the mind of God. And just as a strongly flowing spring is not obstructed by a handful of dust, so the mercy of the Creator is not stemmed by the vices of His creatures.[48]

One of the major prayers of the Orthodox Church that starts most services emphasizes that God is present everywhere: 'O Heavenly King, Comforter, Spirit of Truth, Who art in all places and fillest all things, Treasury of good things, and Giver of life: come and dwell in us, and cleanse us from every stain, and save our souls, O Gracious Lord!'[49] This fundamental prayer is consistent with God being a 'secure parent'. Orthodox Christians use icons in the temples (church buildings) and in Orthodox Christian homes to enhance prayer and connection with God. Icons, are considered 'windows to heaven' and are aids to cultivate a spiritual perception or appraisal of the relation between God and

---

47   Sebastian Brock, *The Wisdom of Saint Isaac the Syrian* (SLG, 1997) 22.
48   St Isaac the Syrian, *Ascetical Homilies of St Isaac the Syrian* (Holy Transfiguration Monastery, rev 2nd ed, 2011) 244-45.
49   'O Heavenly King and Psalm 51 (Psalm of Repentance),' *Orthodox Church in America* (Web page).

mankind. They are venerated as an aid in understanding God as a Holy Trinity of love. They are not written (painted) realistically but in reverse perspective with the lower field being narrow and the upper field being open. This is just the opposite of a drawing of a railroad track with its parallel lines converging in the distance. In icons, the distance is open to the infinity of God's healing love.

E The Father Confessor as an Icon of God

The emphasis of the Orthodox Church on healing which is the reconciliation between the penitent and God's abiding ever present love, raises the important issue of the relationship between the penitent and the priest who witnesses the penitent's confession and repentance. The priest offers spiritual advice and pronounces the prayer of God's forgiveness. The priest at all times must act in emulation of St Paul's teaching on God's love: 'Love is patient, is kind'.[50] Similar words of admonition are found in the book of Proverbs: 'A mild answer breaketh wrath: but a harsh word stirreth up fury'.[51] This is consistent with studies indicating the importance of compassion and empathy in the therapist-patient relationship.[52] It takes empathic and compassionate discernment and humility before any guidance offered by a priest-confessor as an icon of God, can lead the penitent back to Christ. To quote St Isaac of Syria once again: 'The person who has attained to knowledge of his own weakness has reached the summit of humility'.[53]

III Conclusion

In summary the seal of confession in the Holy Mystery of Repentance-Confession in the Orthodox Church is sacrosanct. It is the pathway to

---

50 1 Corinthians 13:4 (Institute for Scripture Research 1998).
51 Proverbs 15:1 (DRB).
52 Adam Gerace, 'The Power of Empathy' (2018) 40(5) InPsych 16.
53 Brock, The Wisdom of Saint Isaac the Syrian, 6.

God's forgiveness and healing and union with Him. No earthly power or law can take precedence over the inviolability of the seal. The Orthodox Church and Christianity in general are under increasing attack by a secularizing world. However, as Orthodox Christians, we hold fast to our Lord's teaching: 'behold I am with you all days, even to the consummation of the world'.[54]

---

54 Matthew 28:20 (DRB).

10

Eric Lieberman

The underlying constitutional basis for the minister/ parishioner privilege in the United States and its application to the unique practices of Scientology

Abstract

The United States Constitution provides two interrelated protections for religious freedom, the Establishment Clause and the Free Exercise Clause. Yet, due to accidents of history, the privilege protecting secret communications between parishioners and ministers has rarely been analyzed in terms of constitutional protection. Rather, the privilege has been recognized, in various forms, as a matter of common law. This has led to different treatment of the privilege in the states and the federal courts, often with constitutionally suspect results. Analysis of modern doctrinal developments, however, compels the conclusion that the privilege must be accorded constitutional protection, including protection for those religious practices of some churches that provide that privileged communications may be heard by more than one minister and that provide doctrinal protection to a minister hearing a communication as well as to the communicant. The doctrines of the Church of Scientology precisely demonstrate the need for these requirements.

I.   Introduction

The United States' experience with religious freedom is historically unique. The original colonists included adherents of various denominations who left their native lands to escape religious persecution by the dominant churches and their church dominated states. Once in their new homes, however, such settlers often resorted to the same kinds of exclusion and persecution as that from which they had fled. But gradually the original colonies became more accepting of differences and dissenters in their midst, such as Rhode Island under Roger Williams, Pennsylvania under William Penn, and Maryland, where Lord Baltimore established a colony that welcomed Catholics.

By the time of and following the Revolution, the various colonies were populated by numerous formerly persecuted denominations and sects. If the new nation was going to survive as united states, it would need to protect against the imposition of religious persecution by one group over others. As summarized by the Supreme Court of the United States in a seminal opinion on religious liberty:

> The Fathers of the Constitution were not unaware of the varied and extreme views of religious sects, of the violence of disagreement among them, and of the lack of any one religious creed on which all men would agree. They fashioned a charter of government which envisaged the widest possible toleration of conflicting views. Man's relation to his God was made no concern of the state. He was granted the right to worship as he pleased and to answer to no man for the verity of his religious views.[1]

The need to ensure religious liberty to protect the new nation against

---

1   *United States v. Ballard*, 322 U.S. 78, 87 (1944).

sectarian conflict was urgently recognized by Madison, who was charged with drafting the Bill of Rights.[2] The resulting First Amendment thus not only prohibited the establishment of a religion by the government, but also provided a shield against government interference with the free exercise of religion.[3]

> The First Amendment has a dual aspect. It not only 'forestalls compulsion by law of the acceptance of any creed or the practice of any form of worship' but also 'safeguards the free exercise of the chosen form of religion.'... It embraces the right to maintain theories of life and of death and of the hereafter which are rank heresy to followers of the orthodox faiths. Heresy trials are foreign to our Constitution. Men may believe what they cannot prove.... The

---

2   *See The Federalist*, No. 51, p. 326 (H. Lodge ed. 1908).
3   The First Amendment by its terms was addressed only to limitations upon the power of the United States Congress ("Congress shall make no law ..."). Nevertheless, at least one early decision by a New York court, discussed in greater detail below, specifically applied the language of the First Amendment's Free Exercise of Religion clause to protect against disclosure of a confession to a Catholic priest. *People v. Phillips* (N.Y.Ct.Gen.Sess. 1813). As we describe in Part III, the development of the privilege post-*Phillips* proceeded through state courts and legislatures and as a matter of federal "common law." *See, e.g., Totten v. United States*, 92 U.S. 105, 107 (1875); *Mullen v. United States*, 263 F.2d 275, 278 (D.C. Cir. 1959). Indeed, perhaps the seminal Supreme Court case upholding principles of religious autonomy and freedom was decided as a matter of federal common law in 1871, only to be recognized as a core constitutional principle under the Religion Clauses 81 years later. *Watson v. Jones*, 80 U.S. (13 Wall.) 679, 733-34 (1871); *Kedroff v. St. Nicholas Cathedral*, 344 U.S. 94, 115-16 (1952) (*Watson* principle is mandated by the First Amendment, requiring a "spirit of freedom for religious organizations, an independence from secular control or manipulation—in short, power to decide for themselves, free from state interference, matters of church government as well as those of faith and doctrine"). It was not until 1924 that the Supreme Court held that the Fourteenth Amendment's due process clause, ratified in 1868, mandated that the First Amendment speech clause be applied to the states as well as the federal government, *Gitlow v. New York*, 268 U.S. 652, 666 (1925) ("For present purposes we may and do assume that freedom of speech and of the press—which are protected by the First Amendment from abridgment by Congress—are among the fundamental personal rights and 'liberties' protected by the due process clause of the Fourteenth Amendment from impairment by the States") and not until the 1940s that the Court specifically recognized that the Fourteenth Amendment similarly "incorporated" the Religion Clauses. *See Cantwell v. Connecticut*, 310 U.S. 296, 303 (1940) ("The First Amendment declares that Congress shall make no law respecting an establishment of religion or prohibiting the free exercise thereof. The Fourteenth Amendment has rendered the legislatures of the states as incompetent as Congress to enact such laws") and *Everson v. Board of Education of Ewing TP et al.,* 330 U.S.1 (1947).

First Amendment does not select any one group or any one type of religion for preferred treatment. It puts them all in that position.[4]

The Free Exercise Clause was an original American concept and invention unlike anything previously known.[5] The concept of religious liberty embodied in the First Amendment provided a continuing inspiration to oppressed peoples throughout the world and was essential to the expansion of the nation through immigration. It also was fertile ground for new and vital religious communities to arise within the country. Many such religions established varying practices of religious counseling, including but not limited to confessions, and accorded strict confidential protections against disclosure of such communications. State courts and eventually federal courts in the United States, fairly consistently, have honored such confidences despite the different form and structure of the practices in various congregations, as discussed in Part III below.

Before engaging in a fuller exposition of the application of the ministerial privilege by courts in the United States, we first set forth a discussion of the relevant beliefs and practices of the Scientology religion because it presents an opportunity to analyze how the vision of the framers as set out by the Supreme Court in *Ballard* works out in practice. Scientology provides a unique example of a modern expanding religion whose central practices rely upon highly confidential communications between parishioners and clergy. The structure of the confidential communications in Scientology carries out the principles and beliefs of the religion and its community. Indeed, the Scientology Church's ability to practice its beliefs relies on the confidentiality of the communications between its parishioners and ministers. These are described below in Part II of this essay. The communications are protected by the ministerial privilege in the United States as mandated by the Free Exercise Clause of the First Amendment to the Constitution, as addressed in the cases

---

4   *United States v. Ballard*, 322 U.S. 78, 87.
5   See John T. Noonan. *The Lustre of Our Country: The American Experience of Religious Freedom*. Berkeley (University of California Press. 1998).

discussed below.

Indeed, while there are no officially "reported" cases involving the application of the privilege to Scientology ministerial communications with parishioners, several federal and state courts have recognized and applied it and found that ministerial communications come within the ambit of the religious confession privilege.[6]

II.   The Privilege Within the Scientology Church

While Scientology is a relatively new religion with confidentiality practices that do not fit traditional Christian patterns precisely, the purpose of this part is to address whether they are protected by the principles which have been erected under the umbrella of religious freedom established in the *United States Constitution*. As has been true with most new and emerging religions, Scientology churches have been called upon to establish time and again that Scientology is a bona fide religious practice. They have done so in country after country, demonstrating that its central beliefs and practices are categorically consistent with universal standards defining religion.[7]

Scientology religious practices derive from certain fundamental beliefs as set forth in its Scripture, consisting of the writings and recorded spoken words of L. Ron Hubbard, who is the sole source of all the doctrines, tenets, philosophy, practices and rituals of the religion. Prime among these are: that each individual is an immortal spiritual being; that one's experience extends beyond a single lifetime; and that one's capabilities

---

6   *E.g., Funderberg v. United States*, No. C 02-05461 (N.D.Cal. 2004) (finding, *inter alia*, that auditing is "deemed strictly confidential by the Church," it is "conducted by trained auditors," and "the records from such audits are maintained in separate files which are marked 'confidential' and stored in locked cabinets"); *Creel v. Hudson Ins. Co., et al.*, No. 2018-02674 (New Orleans, Louisiana District Court, 2020) (denying motion to compel auditing files), *writ denied*, 297 So.3d 763 (Louisiana Supreme Court, 2020).

7   For a summary of government and judicial decisions around the world that have established the Scientology involves bona fide religious practice, see Appendix I to this chapter.

are unlimited, even if not presently realized. Its Scripture sets forth a precise path leading to certain understanding of one's true spiritual nature and one's relationship to **what Scientology posits as the Eight Dynamics**: self, family, groups, Mankind, all life forms, the material universe, the spiritual universe and the Supreme Being.

Scientology doctrine posits that the individual is basically good; that the individual is seeking to survive; and that one's survival depends upon oneself and one's fellows and one's attainment of brotherhood with the universe. But a Scientologist is not asked to accept anything on faith alone. Rather, one discovers for oneself that the principles of Scientology are true by applying its principles, engaging in the central practices and observing or experiencing the results thereof.

The essential practice of the Scientology religion is a unique form of spiritual counseling called "auditing" from the Latin root *audire*, "to listen." The term aptly describes the central function of a specially trained Scientology minister, called an "auditor," who performs the spiritual counseling.[8] All auditors are Scientology clergy. During an auditing session, the minister uses specific "processes," consisting of exact sets of questions asked or directions given by the auditor to help a parishioner locate areas of spiritual distress, discover things about himself or herself and improve their condition. In Scientology, the State of "Clear" is sought by members. Before achieving that state, the parishioner receiving auditing is often referred to as a "preclear" and his ministerial files of his auditing sessions are referred to as his "Preclear" or "pc" folders. The minister enters notes from the auditing session, which are placed in a folder called a Preclear (pc) folder or auditing folder. As discussed below, these folders are highly confidential. The auditor's notes are not a record of everything said by a parishioner, but are his notes of

---

8 The practices of the Scientology religion consist of "Auditing" (spiritual counseling), and "Training," i.e., learning about the religious beliefs, practices and application of the religion through the study of L. Ron Hubbard's writings and lectures. Scientology churches also host weekly congregational services, ceremonies to honor the major stages of life (naming ceremonies, weddings and funerals) and major events to commemorate the major holidays of the religion.

the ministerial communication, applying Scientology procedures that can only reasonably be understood by trained Scientology ministers.

Many different auditing processes exist and each one, performed in scripturally prescribed gradients, is designed and intended to (1) help individuals rid themselves of spiritual disabilities and (2) increase an individual's abilities. There are hundreds of different auditing processes. Scientology pursues the salvation of man and his spiritual liberation and freedom as the religion's objective for the individual. Personal responsibility is a main road through which Scientologists seek their spiritual freedom; responsibility which requires bettering one's life and that of others. Auditing processes are designed to effectuate all of these goals.

When the specific objective of any one auditing process is attained, the process is ended and another can then be applied to address a different part of the parishioner's life. Questions from the auditor guide the parishioner to inspect a certain part of his life and existence. What is found will naturally vary from person to person, since everyone's experiences are different. However, the individual is assisted in locating not only areas of spiritual upset or difficulty in his or her life, but in locating the source of the upset.

Scientology auditors thus perform the traditional role of ministers, priests and religious functionaries of other faiths – applying the doctrines of the faith through communication with the parishioner to relieve him or her of spiritual travail and to aid in the practical application of the religion to solve the problems of life.

Scientology posits that when a person has committed harmful acts against himself or others, he tends to "withhold" or withdraw himself from activity and from communication about the overt acts or omissions. In Scientology religious doctrine, the deleterious spiritual consequence of a person having attention on the unspoken and unrevealed overt acts (called in Scientology, "withholds") substantially interferes with or prevents one's spiritual progress. Indeed, at the beginning of an auditing session, an auditor determines whether the person may have withholds; if so, confession of the withholds is one of the specific "rudiments" to be resolved at the outset of an auditing session, before proceeding with the next auditing process.

So important is confessional doctrine and procedure in Scientology, Mr. Hubbard held Congresses for thousands of Scientology auditors in Melbourne in November 1959, a "State of Man Congress" in Washington D.C. in January of 1960 and a "Clean Hands Congress" in Washington D.C. in December of 1961, giving lectures regarding the importance of "clean hands" and the auditing procedures to help parishioners to achieve that state. These recorded lectures have been reproduced, distributed and listened to by hundreds of thousands of Scientologists in the 60 years since these early convocations of Scientology ministers.

Thus, while there are hundreds of Scientology auditing processes to increase parishioners' ability in many ways, some Scientology processing actions are primarily directed to providing relief from withholds. Scientology Marriage Counseling, for example, is a precise confessional procedure for alleviating marital difficulties. Based on Scientology Scripture, it addresses the root of all such difficulties: transgressions against the couple's previously agreed-upon moral code that now inhibit their communication to bring about a resurgence of the "affinity and reality" that go with it. Both spouses are present with the minister during the Scientology marriage counseling confessional procedure, taking turns revealing withheld acts to each other and to their minister, secure in the understanding that their communications will remain absolutely secure and will not be disclosed, as set forth in the Scripture of the Church.

There are many other specific confessional auditing procedures in Scientology, including overt acts against oneself, one's family, one's group, Mankind and others. Confessional practice is a ministerial procedure applied within the Scientology doctrine for assisting parishioners in all aspects of their lives.

In Scientology doctrine and practice, the auditor is part of a necessary team of ministers,[9] who facilitate the auditing procedure and the maintenance of confidentiality of ministerial notes of parishioner statements. Each auditor is overseen and supervised by a senior minister denominated a "Case Supervisor." The term "case" is a general term for the summation of an individual's difficulties, past events and acts preventing him from reaching his full spiritual potential and abilities. It is a person's "case" which is addressed in Scientology auditing. The Case Supervisor is highly trained in Scientology auditing "technology" often spending many years studying, auditing and drilling Scientology theory and auditing procedure. The Case Supervisor assures that each auditor is providing 100% standard Scientology practice in accordance with written scriptural materials and lectures.

The Case Supervisor never communicates directly with the parishioner, but operates in what is known as an Ivory Tower, participating through a review of the ministerial notes of the session located in the parishioner's "Preclear Folder." If there are any scriptural deviations in the procedures employed by the auditor, the Case Supervisor is obligated to instruct the auditor in the scriptural materials to correct them, and to program the auditing sessions to assure maximum, standard application of what is known in Scientology as Standard Technology—that is, standard, exactly orthodox application of Scientology Scripture in the auditing. The Case Supervisor's instructions to the auditor are in writing and placed in the Preclear Folder.

Another member of the ministerial team is the Ethics Officer. In Scientology, ethics is defined as "reason and the contemplation of optimum survival." Through the study and application of Scientology

---

9   As emphasized in Part III below, numerous courts in the United States have held that confidential communications made to a "team" of ministers in furtherance of the religious doctrines and practices of a church are and must be protected from coerced disclosure by the Religion Clauses of the First Amendment.

ethics principles, aided by the Ethics Officer, parishioners enhance and ensure their own survival, and their survival through the other "dynamics" through which each person survives: the family, their group, Mankind, the physical universe, all other life, the spiritual universe and the Supreme Being. As ministers of other religions might instruct or guide parishioners in the scriptures of their faith to resolve ethical issues, in Scientology this role is performed by a minister trained in Scientology Ethics–the Ethics Officer.

Accordingly, Scientology auditing must be conducted within a framework of the parishioner's complete trust of the ministers involved. In the course of auditing, the parishioner may disclose information of a highly personal and confidential nature. In other words, a parishioner may tell his minister secrets known to no other. Such information could reveal immoral or unethical acts, or fall within the full gambit of unwanted emotions, events, considerations and histories. Scientology ministers maintain and practice a code of conduct known as the Auditor's Code. It provides exact ethical standards to ensure that all auditing is ministered in an orthodox and ethical manner and that clergy-penitent communications are, and remain, forever, strictly confidential.

The Auditor's Code, by which all auditors and other ministers are bound, requires that a minister may never reveal the secrets and confidences divulged by a parishioner in an auditing session. Such information, given in trust during an auditing session by parishioners to their ministers, is considered sacrosanct by the auditors, the Case Supervisor and by their Churches. Never may that promise of confidentiality be breached. It is strictly forbidden.

It would be an ecclesiastical crime of the highest order for an auditor to reveal parishioner confidences or to permit the disclosure of a parishioner's pc folder, leading to dismissal from church staff and possibly expulsion from the Church for the offender.

Each parishioner is well aware of the relationship between his minister and his Case Supervisor and of the Auditor's Code, and can thereby be assured of strict confidentiality by his own auditor. So there can be no dispute regarding these important issues, parishioners are required to acknowledge the doctrinal issues giving rise to the confidentiality of their communications with their minister and of the pc folders. Each parishioner signs a document recognizing these matters as a condition to receiving auditing in a Church of Scientology, which states in part:

> It is of paramount importance to me that the Church will forever be able to preserve and protect the confidentiality of all folders containing notations of the spiritual progress I attain as a result of participating in Scientology religious services, including, but not limited to, a "Preclear Folder" or "PC Folder" and temporary recordings of sessions and interviews, as well as all other religious files containing notations regarding my spiritual progress (for purposes of convenience, these folders, files and recordings, as defined below, shall be referred to collectively as the "Folders"). The sole purpose of the Folders is to track the progress of my spiritual salvation in Scientology religious terms; they are incomprehensible to anyone who lacks the appropriate religious training for interpreting them and the ecclesiastical authority to review them, as sanctioned by Church of Scientology International ("CSI").

> Maintaining the confidentiality of the Folders is an issue of very great concern to me since, as a matter of fundamental Scientology religious belief, the disclosure of any of the contents of any of the Folders to me or to anyone lacking appropriate Scientology ecclesiastical authority would be spiritually damaging to me, not only in this lifetime, but in future lifetimes as well. In addition, I am aware that I will be guided on my spiritual path by a minister known as a Case Supervisor who reviews records of my sessions and determines which religious services are appropriate for my spiritual growth at that particular time.

Within Scientology practice, the individual parishioner's folders of session notes are accordingly maintained under high security, each folder stamped "clergy/penitent privilege" and maintained under lock and key for the use of the auditor and Case Supervisor. It may be that in months, years or decades, an auditor may need to refer to prior auditing sessions to assist with the current auditing program. Thus, Scientology doctrine holds these past folders to be priceless, and absolutely necessary to assure the spiritual freedom of each parishioner.

Indeed, Scientologists hold that every individual is an immortal spiritual being who has lived before and will live many successive future mortal lives. Upon the death of a parishioner, his or her pc folders are bound and stored for his return in the next lifetime to continue this spiritual journey.

In sum, the Auditor's Code and considerable scriptural doctrine and religious law requires a Scientology minister to maintain as privileged the secrets divulged by a parishioner in an auditing session. The information given in trust during an auditing session by a parishioner to a minister is considered sacrosanct by the Church and Church ministers and is maintained inviolate. All such information is kept *strictly confidential* and privileged by a Scientology minister and the Church now, and forever.

III. The Constitutional Basis for a Ministerial Privilege

In a country in which the role of judicially created constitutional law is so prevalent, it is more than surprising that the Supreme Court of the United States has never addressed the question of whether and to what extent the Constitution requires and protects a privilege of silence with respect to confidential communications between members of a religion and their ecclesiastical leaders or ministers. Instead, the privilege, in various forms, has been enacted by every state and also is recognized by a series of federal "common law" decisions.[10] Nevertheless, as set forth in this essay, it is the Constitution that underlies and compels those statutes and decisions and that ultimately must govern how they are applied.

In fact, the first reported case recognizing the privilege in the United States rested upon the Free Exercise clause. In *People v. Phillips* (N.Y.Ct. Gen.Sess. 1813), the Court addressed whether a Catholic priest could be compelled to testify regarding the contents of a confession. In ringing language, the Court held:

> "Congress shall make no law respecting an establishment of religion, or prohibiting the free exercise thereof." In this country there is no alliance between church and state; no established religion; no tolerated religion—for toleration results from establishment—but religious freedom guaranteed by the constitution, and consecrated by the social compact. It is essential to the free exercise of a religion, that its ordinances should be administered—that its ceremonies as well as its essentials should be protected. The sacraments of a religion are its most important elements. We have but two in the Protestant Church—Baptism and the Lord's Supper—and they are considered the seals of the covenant of grace. Suppose that a decision of this court, or a law of the state should prevent the administration of one or both of these sacraments, would not the constitution be violated, and the freedom of religion be infringed? Every man who hears me will answer in the affirmative. Will not the same result follow, if we deprive the Roman catholic of one of his ordinances? Secrecy is of the essence of penance. The sinner will not confess, nor will the priest receive his confession, if the veil of

---

10 To clarify for those unfamiliar with United States law and government, the nation is governed by a system of federalism, with each of the fifty states maintaining its own laws and judicial system and the national government maintaining a system of regional or specialized federal courts. The federal courts have limited jurisdiction over cases and controversies as established by Article III of the *Constitution* and by federal statute. The state courts have general jurisdiction over all matters except those several areas where federal jurisdiction is exclusive. The United States Supreme Court has ultimate jurisdiction over all cases and controversies in both the state and federal courts that raise a question under the *Constitution* or other federal law, but it is exercised today mostly as a matter of discretionary review, and quite sparingly.

secrecy is removed: To decide that the minister shall promulgate what he receives in confession, is to declare that there shall be no penance; and this important branch of the Roman catholic religion would be thus annihilated.[11]

The *Phillips* Court thus applied the principles embodied in the First Amendment Religion Clauses despite the fact that the Amendment was addressed to the power of the federal Congress. Despite the *Phillips* decision, New York and other states proceeded down different paths in protecting the privilege, chiefly by enacting state statutes of varying scope and breadth. The Supreme Court in dicta recognized the privilege under federal common law as early as 1875:

> It may be stated as a general principle, that public policy forbids the maintenance of any suit in a court of justice, the trial of which would inevitably lead to the disclosure of matters which the law itself regards as confidential, and respecting which it will not allow the confidence to be violated. On this principle, suits cannot be maintained which would require a disclosure of the confidences of the confessional [12]

Nevertheless, the question does not appear to have been the subject of a holding in the federal courts until 1959, when the District of Columbia Circuit upheld the privilege as a matter of common law, even while recognizing that English common law rejected it.[13] The Supreme Court has since acknowledged the centrality of the privilege to the legal system: It is "rooted in the imperative need for confidence and trust," [14] and "recognizes the human need to disclose to a spiritual counselor, in total and absolute confidence, what are believed to be the flawed acts or thoughts and to receive priestly consolation and guidance in

---

11   *People v. Phillips* (N.Y.Ct.Gen.Sess. 1813), quoted in *Mockaitis v. Harcleroad*, 104 F.3d 1522, 1532 (9th Cir. 1997) (Noonan, J.).

12   *Totten v. United States*, 92 U.S. 105, 107 (1875).

13   *Mullen v. United States*, 263 F.2d 275, 278 (D.C. Cir. 1959) ("Sound policy—reason and experience—concedes to religious liberty a rule of evidence that a clergyman shall not disclose on a trial the secrets of a penitent's confidential confession to him, at least absent the penitent's consent").

14   *Trammel v. United States*, 445 U.S. 40, 51 (1980).

return."[15] "In addition to preventing testimony concerning privileged communications, the privilege also [encompasses] the right to exclude documentary evidence of such communications and to quash a summons seeking production of such documents."[16]

Perhaps the leading opinion on the importance and contours of the privilege in the United States was rendered by the United States Court of Appeals for the Third Circuit. After reviewing the history, literature and policy issues relevant, the Court concluded:

> We are satisfied, moreover, that American common law...compels the recognition of a clergy-communicant privilege. Both state and federal decisions have long recognized the privilege. The Supreme Court Rules Committee [i.e., the Judicial Conference of the United

---

15 *Id. See United States v. Nixon*, 418 U.S. 683, 709 (1974) ("[G]enerally, an attorney or priest may not be required to disclose what has been revealed in professional confidence.")

16 26 Charles Alan Wright & Kenneth W. Graham, Jr., *Federal Practice and Procedure* § 5620 (2019). Those state courts that have addressed the issue have held or presumed documents to be within the scope of various statutory formulations of the privilege, including some referring to "testimony" or to the "examination" of a cleric. *See Corsie v. Campanalonga*, 721 A.2d 733, 735-36 (N.J. Super. Ct. App. Div. 1998) (recognizing statute according "privilege" to "[a]ny communication" to protect documents), *rev'd on other grounds*, 734 A.2d 788 (N.J. 1999) (augmenting protection accorded by intermediate court); *Commissioner v. Stewart*, 690 A.2d 195, 197 (Pa. 1997) (treating documents as within scope of privilege against "disclos[ure]" of "information"); *Ryan v. Ryan*, 642 N.E.2d 1028, 1034 (Mass. 1994) (protecting documents under statute forbidding "priest[s]" from "disclos[ing] a confession... [or] testify[ing] as to any communication"); *Doe v. Corporation of the President of the Church of Jesus Christ of Latterday Saints*, 90 P.3d 1147, 1151 (Wash. App. 2004) (protecting against document's disclosure under statute providing that cleric "shall not... be examined as to any confession"); *People v. Campobella*, 810 N.E.2d 307, 321 (Ill. App. 2004) (recognizing protection against disclosure "not only of the admission, confession, or accompanying 'information' as originally articulated... but also of any reiteration or repetition in any form," under statute providing that clergy "shall not be compelled to disclose... a confession or admission... nor be compelled to divulge any information").

States Rules Committee[17]] also recognized the privilege. That is doubtless because the clergy-communicant relationship is so important, indeed so fundamental to the western tradition, that it must be sedulously fostered. Confidence is obviously essential to maintaining the clergy-communicant relationship. Although there are countervailing considerations, we have no doubt that the need for protecting the relationship outweighs them.[18]

While *Mullen* and subsequent federal cases refer to the privilege as a common law rule, the opinion and its consequences inevitably mandate recognition of the privilege as constitutionally based. Not only does *Mullen* concede that it is overruling the common law, but it does so on the basis that the privilege is "so fundamental to the western tradition" and thus a matter necessarily within the due process protections of the Fifth and Fourteenth Amendments. Further, it rests its rationale on religious liberty, a source found in the *Constitution* and not the Rules of Civil Procedure. Moreover, *Mullen,* as well as the various state law provisions, defines the scope and breadth of the privilege in non-uniform ways, typically but by no means exclusively based on the Catholic model. But once the government undertakes to legislate or rule make in the area of religious rights and liberties, *i.e.*, create an exemption from the generally applicable duty to provide evidence, it may not choose to extend the religious privilege only to some denominations and not to others by drawing lines common to some practices but not to others. The *Constitution* imposes guarantees that disallow much of such line drawing.

When a state adopts a statute or rule that specifically addresses a religious practice and relieves a burden on the exercise of the religious practices of

---

17   The *Rules Enabling Act* of 1934 (28 U.S.C. § 2071-2077) authorized the Supreme Court to promulgate rules of procedure, which have the force and effect of law. Over time, the Court delegated the work and oversight of the rule making process to committees of the Judicial Conference, the principal policy-making body of the federal courts. In 1988, amendments to the *Rules Enabling Act* formalized this committee process. Today, the Judicial Conference's Committee on Rules of Practice and Procedure, ("Standing Committee") and its five advisory rules committees "carry on a continuous study of the operation and effect" of the federal rules as directed by the *Rules Enabling Act.*

18   *In re Grand Jury Investigation*, 918 F.2d 374, 384 (3d Cir. 1990).

some religions while not exempting others from that burden, its actions violate the Free Exercise Clause of the First Amendment, unless justified by the most compelling of government interests and achieved by the narrowest means available.[19] In applying its free exercise review, "The Court must survey meticulously the circumstances of governmental categories to eliminate, as it were, religious gerrymanders."[20]

The fact that every state and the federal courts have adopted ministerial privilege rules potentially subjects all such rules to strict scrutiny to the extent that they define the privilege and its application in ways that do not apply to all faiths and practices. And given the universal existence of the privilege in some form, there can be no rational argument that government has a compelling interest in applying that privilege only to certain denominations or practices and not to others, based on their confessional doctrines and practices.[21] Such an interest not only would not be compelling, it would be illegitimate: "To give exemption to some denominations and not to all offends the equality with which all men enter society."[22]

The requirement of governmental denominational neutrality also lies at the core of the Establishment Clause. "The 'establishment of religion' clause of the First Amendment means at least this: Neither a state nor the Federal Government ... can pass laws which aid one religion...or prefer one religion over another."[23] Madison's Memorial and Remonstrance, which formed the basis for the adoption of the religion clauses in the First Amendment, emphasized that denominational neutrality was essential to the concept of religious freedom.

---

19 *Church of Lukumi Babalu Aye v. City of Hialeah*, 508 U.S. 520, 531-32, 546 (1993) ("A law burdening religious practice that is not neutral or not of general application must undergo the most rigorous of scrutiny,... must advance 'interests of the highest order' and must be narrowly tailored in pursuit of those interests.")

20 Ibid 534 (quoting *Walz v. Tax Commissioner of City of New York*, 397 U.S. 664, 696 (1970) (Harlan, J., concurring)).

21 See *Gonzales v. O Centro Espirita Beneficente Uniao Do Vegetal*, 546 U.S. 418, 433.

22 James Madison, *Memorial and Remonstrance*, as quoted in John T. Noonan, Jr., *The Lustre of Our Country* (n 5).

23 *Everson* (n 3),15 (1947).

> Madison's vision – freedom for all religion being
> guaranteed by free competition between religions—
> naturally assumed that every denomination would be
> equally at liberty to exercise and propagate its beliefs.
> But such equality would be impossible in an atmosphere
> of official denominational preference. [24]

"The First Amendment mandates governmental neutrality between religion and religion.... The State may not adopt programs or practices...which 'aid or oppose' any religion.... This prohibition is absolute."[25]"Neither [a State nor the Federal Government] can constitutionally pass laws or impose requirements which aid... those religions based on a belief in the existence of God as against those religions founded on different beliefs."[26]

Application of the Establishment Clause's prohibition of denominational preferences is not limited to cases where the government has explicitly discriminated among denominations. Rather, even where the government action has been expressed in terms that might appear facially neutral, courts have not hesitated to strike down statutes or other government action when the effect upon religious practices is to further such preferences. Thus, in *Larson*, the Court found unconstitutional on its face a solicitation statute that required churches to disclose the use of donated funds, but exempted those churches that received over 50% of their donations from members. The Court rejected the argument that because the 50% rule on its face did not single out any denomination for unfavorable treatment and utilized "secular criteria," it did not create a denominational preference:

> the provision effectively distinguishes between "well-established
> churches" that have "achieved strong but not total financial sup-

---

24 *Larson v. Valente*, 456 U.S. 228, 245 (1981) (quoting *The Federalist* (n 2)); *see also* *Wallace v. Jaffree*, 472 U.S. 38, 69 (1985) (O'Connor J., concurring).
25 *Epperson v. Arkansas*, 393 U.S. 104, 106 (1968).
26 *Torcaso v. Watkins*, 367 U.S. 488, 495 (1960).

port from their members," on the one hand, and "churches which are new and lacking in a constituency, or which, as a matter of policy, may favor public solicitation over general reliance on financial support from members," on the other hand[27]

Similarly, in *Fowler v. Rhode Island*,[28] the Court held unconstitutional a facially neutral statute providing, "No person shall address any political or religious meeting in any public park," which had been applied to arrest a Jehovah's Witnesses minister. The State of Rhode Island conceded that the ordinance did not prohibit religious *services* in the park, but only *speeches* of the kind Fowler gave, which the State maintained was not a religious service. The Court held that the State's attempt to distinguish among denominations as to what was a religious service violated both the Establishment and Free Exercise Clauses.[29] The Court explained, "Appellant's sect has conventions that are different from the practices of other religious groups,"[30] but that "it is no business of courts to say that what is a religious practice or activity for one group is not religion under the protection of the First Amendment. Nor is it in the competence of courts under our constitutional scheme to approve, disapprove, classify, regulate, or in any manner control" religious practices, which would be "merely an indirect way of preferring one religion over another."[31]

As *Larson* teaches, state imposition of a denominational preference is subject to strict scrutiny, and can only be upheld where the preference is in furtherance of a state interest of the highest order and achieves that end by the least restrictive means.[32] There can be no defensible reason, compelling or otherwise, for example, to extend the privilege for communications made to a single clergy person, but to refuse to do so for communications made to two or three clergy or to confidential communications that one clergy person discloses to another according

---

27 *Larson* (n 24), 247.
28 *Fowler v. Rhode Island*, 345 U.S. 67, 69-70 (1943).
29 Ibid 69.
30 Ibid.
31 Ibid 70.
32 *Larson*, (n 24), 247.

to the discipline and doctrine of the faith. The state cannot establish an interest of the highest order to justify denying a religious exemption to one practice where it already has granted a religious exemption to another: "It is established in our strict scrutiny jurisprudence that a law cannot be regarded as protecting an interest of the 'highest order'... when it leaves appreciable damage to that supposedly vital interest unprohibited."[33]

As reported cases demonstrate, numerous denominations (as well as Scientology, as discussed above) provide for confidential communicant-clergy communications where the privileged disclosure either is made to more than one clergy person and/or is disclosed by the clergy person receiving the confidence to senior clergy persons, all in furtherance of the discipline and practice of that particular denomination. In each case, such communication was deemed consistent with and did not destroy the privilege. Indeed, as discussed below, the leading federal decision as well as the highest and intermediate appellate courts of at least several states have held that ministerial privilege statutes must be construed to avoid discrimination among denominations. The rich history of such cases makes clear that it is the *Constitution* that ultimately must govern the application of the privilege.

The United States Court of Appeals for the Third Circuit specifically held as a general matter that "the presence of third parties, if essential to and in furtherance of the communication, should not void the privilege. This statement of the contours of the privilege...tracks the evolving common law."[34] The Court continued that "recognition of the clergy-communicant privilege in this circumstance depends upon whether the third party's presence is essential to *and* in furtherance of a communication to a member of the clergy."[35] We note that this legal standard fully protects clergy-communicant communications in Scientology auditing and eth-

---

33 *Gonzales v. O Centro Espirita Beneficente Uniao Do Vegetal*, 546 U.S. 418, 433 (2006) (quoting *Church of Lukumi Babalu Aye, Inc. v. City of Hialeah*, 508 U.S. 520, 547 (1993)).

34 *In re Grand Jury Investigation*, 918 F. 2d 374, 384.

35 Ibid 386.

ics confessionals, where the limited third parties to whom the communications may be referred are acting in a manner essential to Scientology doctrine and in furtherance of the underlying communication to an auditor or Ethics Officer.

Numerous other cases are in accord, and have been for over a century. In *Reutkemeier v. Nolte*,[36] one of the earliest privilege cases, a member of a Presbyterian congregation made confidential communications, including confession of sin, to her pastor and three ruling elders of the congregation, pursuant to the "Confession of Faith" of the Presbyterian Church, "as well as other standard booklets setting forth the doctrine and policy of that denomination."[37] The Iowa Supreme Court upheld the claim of privilege, holding that the communication was confidential and the elders were "ministers of the gospel."[38]

The Church of Jesus Christ of Latter-day Saints likewise provides for confidential communications to one or more clergy, as well as transmission of such communications to senior clergy in furtherance of the purpose of the communication. In *Scott v. Hammock*,[39] a member of that church made a non-confessional communication to a single Church Bishop to obtain "ecclesiastical guidance," which was considered confidential within the doctrines of the Church. The Bishop thereupon "apparently transmitted the information to a 'Stake' bishop's court [Stake High Council Court]" which had ecclesiastical authority to review the communication.[40] Warning that a construction of the statute to apply only to traditional confessions "would raise a distinct concern about respecting an establishment of religion by advancing one religion and inhibiting another,"[41] the Court not only held that the original communication from the congregant to the bishop was confidential and privileged, but

---

36 *Reutkemeier v. Nolte*, 161 N.W. 290 (Iowa 1917).
37 Ibid 292.
38 Ibid.
39 *Scott v. Hammock*, 133 F.R.D. 610 (D.Utah 1990),
40 Ibid 612.
41 Ibid 618-19.

further held that the bishop's subsequent communication to the High Council Court likewise remained privileged:

> In this case, the communication was passed vertically from one religious authority up to another within the Church hierarchy. Such communication was necessary as a part of the Church sanction process and in carrying out church discipline. *The need for the privilege to follow the communication in such circumstances is obvious and appropriate. Otherwise the privilege would be destroyed and the confidence abridged.* Therefore, the repeating of the defendant's statement and its communication to superior religious authorities must be deemed cloaked with confidentiality and privileged from forced disclosure.[42]

The District Court certified the questions to the Supreme Court of Utah, which likewise concluded that the communications were privileged.[43] A subsequent case provides greater detail in which confidential communications are transmitted from one clergy person to others. In *Doe v. Corporation of the President of the Church of Jesus Christ of Latter-day Saints*,[44] a penitent confessed his sins first to a bishop and then to the Stake High Council Court. The Court explained that under church doctrine, the penitent must repeat his communication to the Stake Court to achieve salvation. The Stake Court included eighteen clergy, including the original bishop, the Stake President, his two counselors, and twelve "high priests," who were essential to the furtherance of the religious purpose of the ecclesiastical procedure. Moreover, if the Stake imposes serious ecclesiastical discipline, it is required to submit a Report of Church Disciplinary Action to the senior officials of the Church. Emphasizing that all such internal communications were confidential and remained secret except to those to whom the communications were made, the Washington Court of Appeals upheld the claim of privilege, finding that the privilege was not "vitiated" by communication of the

---

42 Ibid 619 (emphasis added).
43 *Scott v. Hammock*, 870 P.2d 947 (Utah 1994).
44 *Doe v. Corporation of the President of the Church of Jesus Christ of Latter-day Saints*, 122 Wash. App. 556 (2004),

communication to a third person "when the third person is another member of the clergy."[45]

State v. MacKinnon,[46] involved confidential communications made to clergy of the Missoula Christian Church. A congregant of that church made confidential communications to two members of the clergy in the presence of his ex-wife. The trial court granted MacKinnon's motion to suppress the statements made in those communications, as well as a document relating to the communications.[47]

In addition to the denominations that require or permit communicant-clergy confidential communications to be shared by other members of the clergy, numerous denominations permit such communications to be made in the presence of one or more non-clergy members, usually close family, where such presence is believed necessary to or in furtherance of the religious purpose of the communication. In a ruling involving penitential communications to a Lutheran minister, a federal appeals court held that "the presence of third parties, if essential to and in furtherance of the communication, should not void the privilege" and emphasizing any contrary rule risked "the prospect of restricting the privilege to Roman Catholic penitential communications [which would] raise[] serious First Amendment concerns;"[48] a decision from the state of Louisiana held that communications to a Baptist minister in the presence of the "victim" of alleged aggravated assault was privileged because it was made in expectation of confidence and the minister was acting in "his spiritual capacity as spiritual advisor to two congregants of his church;"[49] a ruling in the State of Georgia found that communications made by a mother and her two daughters, in contemplation of the death of their husband/ father, to a minister of United Methodist Church "to provide pastoral counseling, spiritual guidance," pursuant to church doctrine, were priv-

---

45 Ibid 566, quoting Washington v. Martin, 137 Wash.2d 774, 787 (1999).
46 State v. MacKinnon, 288 Mont. 329 (1988),
47 Ibid 338.
48 In re Grand Jury Investigation, (n 18) 384-85.
49 State v. Ellis, 750 So.2d 418 (La. App. 1999).

ileged and that the privilege was not "waived by the presence of more than one person seeking spiritual comfort or counseling;"[50] in a state court in Michigan, the defendant's statements to a Baptist minister in the presence of his mother were held privileged because they were "made in the course of discipline enjoined by the Baptist Church;"[51] a state court decision in Arizona found that confession to a Mormon bishop in the presence of the penitent's wife was privileged, because the confession was confidential and undertaken in furtherance of the repentance process under church doctrine.[52]

Any denominational preference in favor of the historical one-to-one Catholic model of confession or that of any other denomination and against confidential communications in other religions has thus been disapproved by numerous state and federal courts.

The religion clauses also complement each other in a third essential way that is directly relevant to the question of government power to compel disclosure of confidential communications both between church members and clergy, on the one hand, and among clergy members, on the other. The courts recognize a strong church autonomy right that restricts such interference in ecclesiastical affairs.

It is of significance that the church autonomy doctrine was first enunciated by the Supreme Court as a matter of common law, only later to be recognized as essential to the religious freedoms created by the Religion Clauses. In 1871, the Court, applying federal common law, made clear that matters internal to religious organizations "which concern theological controversy, church discipline, ecclesiastical government, or the conformity of the members of the church to the standard of morals required of them" are beyond the ken of judicial authorities, and that those who participate in such religious bodies do so subject to the

---

50 *Alternative Health Care Systems v. McCown*, 217 Ga. App. 355 (1999)
51 *People v. Bragg*, 824 N.W.2d 170, 187 (Mich. App. 2012)
52 *State v. Archibeque*, 223 Ariz. 231, 236 (Ariz. App. 2009)

internal rules of those bodies.[53] Eighty-one years later, in *Kedroff v. St. Nicholas Cathedral*,[54] the Court held that the *Watson* principle is mandated by the First Amendment, requiring a "spirit of freedom for religious organizations, an independence from secular control or manipulation – in short, power to decide for themselves, free from state interference, matters of church government as well as those of faith and doctrine."

The Supreme Court's recognition in *Kedroff* that federal cases upholding religious freedom that were decided in the nineteenth century under the rubric of the "common law," such as *Watson*, must be accorded constitutional support in the modern era is precisely what has occurred in the lower state and federal courts with respect to the religious confession privilege. It is inevitable that if such a question were to reach the Supreme Court today, it would so rule.

In subsequent cases following *Kedroff*, the Court made clear that the judiciary is constitutionally incompetent to resolve disputes concerning the proper interpretation or application of religious doctrine or practice. In *Presbyterian Church v. Mary Elizabeth Blue Hull Memorial Presbyterian Church*,[55] the Court held that the First Amendment "forbids civil courts from playing such a role" because "in reaching such a decision, the court must of necessity make its own interpretation of the meaning of church doctrines."[56]

In *Lemon v. Kurtzman*,[57] the Court formulated its three-pronged Establishment Clause test. Under that test, government action must have a secular purpose; its primary effect must be one that neither advances nor hinders religion; and it must not create or permit significant entanglement between church and state. While the *Kurtzman* test has

---

53 *Watson v. Jones*, 80 U.S. (13 Wall.) 679, 733-34 (1871).

54 *Kedroff v. St. Nicholas Cathedral*, 344 U.S. 94, 115-16 (1952).

55 *Presbyterian Church v. Mary Elizabeth Blue Hull Memorial Presbyterian Church*, 393 U.S. 440 (1969),

56 Ibid. *See also New York v. Cathedral Academy*, 434 U.S. 125, 133 (1977) ("The prospect of church and state litigating in court about what does or does not have religious meaning touches the very core of the constitutional guarantee against religious establishment").

57 *Lemon v. Kurtzman*, 403 U.S. 602, 612 (1971),

been subject to criticism by those arguing for greater deference to religious free exercise and thus may be subject to modification in the future, the non-entanglement principle remains at the heart of the Supreme Court's jurisprudence on the religion clauses. The non-entanglement principle includes both "substantive and procedural components."[58] With respect to the procedural entanglement component, "It is not only the conclusions that may be reached by [a court] which may impinge on rights guaranteed by the Religion Clauses, but also the very process of inquiry leading to findings and conclusions."[59]

These principles were summarized in *Serbian Eastern Orthodox Diocese v. Milivojevich*,[60] ("*Milivojevich*"), where the Court held that courts may not involve themselves in "matters of discipline, faith, internal organization, or ecclesiastical rule, custom, or law." Of particular note, the *Milivojevich* Court emphasized that matters of internal church discipline were particularly ill-suited to civilian judicial review and are constitutionally forbidden.[61]

Lest there be any doubt about the centrality of the Watson-Kedroff-Milivojevich doctrine of religious autonomy from government interference and control, the cases were central to the Court's more recent decisions specifically recognizing a ministerial exception to such entanglement and articulating such a doctrine of autonomy.[62] In its most recent decision in *Our Lady of Guadalupe School v. Morrissey-Berru*,[63] the Court emphasized that its decision in *Hosanna-Tabor* rested on the church autonomy doctrine and the three prior decisions in *Watson, Kedroff*, and *Milivojevich*:

> The Constitutional foundation for our holding was the general

---

58 *Alcazar v. Corp. of the Catholic Archdiocese of Seattle*, 598 F.3d 668, 672 (9th Cir. 2010), adopted in relevant part as *en banc* decision, 627 F.3d 1288, 1290-91 (9th Cir. 2010).

59 *NLRB v. Catholic Bishop of Chicago*, 440 U.S. 490, 502.

60 *Serbian Eastern Orthodox Diocese v. Milivojevich*, 426 U.S. 696, 713 (1976).

61 Ibid 717 ("questions of church discipline and the composition of the church hierarchy are at the core of ecclesiastical concern").

62 *See, e.g., Hosanna-Tabor Evangelical Lutheran Church v. EEOC*, 565 U.S. 171.

63 *Our Lady of Guadalupe School v. Morrissey-Berru*, ___ U.S. ___, 140 S.Ct. 2049 (2020).

principle of church autonomy to which we have already referred: independence in matters of internal government. The three prior decisions on which we primarily relied [*i.e., Watson, Kedroff, and Milivojevich*] drew on this broad principle, and none was exclusively concerned with the selection or supervision of clergy.[64]

These principles severely limit or prohibit government interference with the ministerial privilege. The privilege lies at the heart of a church's governance, discipline and ecclesiastical doctrine. It is inconceivable under these cases for a United States court to order a minister to disclose a privileged communication contrary to the rules and governance of his church, even in the unlikely event that the parishioner attempts to waive the privilege.

The most important case on point was written by Judge Noonan for the United States Court of Appeals for the Ninth Circuit in *Mockaitis v. Harcleroad*,[65] which was decided under the *United States' Religious Freedom Restoration Act* ("RFRA").[66] RFRA was enacted as a direct response to the Supreme Court's decision in *Employment Division v Smith*[67] which had held that burdens on the religious practices of individuals were subject to ordinary review for reasonableness so long as the burden was one of general applicability and did not address religion per se. RFRA specifically restored strict scrutiny review to any act of government that burdened the free exercise of religion; under RFRA, any burden upon religion must be justified by a compelling governmental interest and be achieved by the means least restrictive of the religious practice. While RFRA later was held to be unconstitutional on federalism grounds as applied to the states in *City of Boerne v. Flores*,[68] its analysis of the application of the strict scrutiny standard to a burden on religion remains applicable not only to federal cases, but also to state cases where strict scrutiny applies under the free exercise clause itself, such as cases where the plaintiff alleges

---

64 Ibid 2061.
65 *Mockaitis* (n 11).
66 See 42 U.S.C. section 2000bb, et seq.
67 *Employment Div., Oregon Dep't of Human Resources v. Smith*, 494 U.S. 872 (1990).
68 *City of Boerne v. Flores*, 521 U.S. 507 (1997).

a burden on a religious belief or practice that creates a denomination-al preference. Thus, the strict scrutiny test (compelling state interest/least restrictive means) applies to any challenge to a restriction on the ministerial privilege that is based on a claim that the state privilege dis-criminates, either intentionally or not, upon the beliefs and practices of a religious body or person.

In *Mockaitis*, the Court held that RFRA was violated when a local pros-ecutor seized an audiotape recording of a murder suspect's confessions to a Roman Catholic priest while the priest was visiting the defendant in the local jail. Although the confession was partially exculpatory and therefore the defendant – i.e., the parishioner – consented to the publi-cation of its contents, the Court held that the religious beliefs and prac-tices of the priest were burdened by the recording and the turning over of the audiotape to the prosecutor. The Court explained:

> No question exists that [the prosecutor] has substantially burdened Father Mockaitis's exercise of religion as understood in the First Amendment. Father Mockaitis was exercising his religion in a priestly function. He was seeking to participate in the Sacrament of Penance understood by the Catholic Church to be a means by which God forgives the sins of a repentant sinner and restores the sinner to life in God's grace. It is a sacrament that from experience the Catholic Church has surrounded with extraordinary safeguards so that the content of the penitent's confession will not be revealed unless the penitent himself chooses to reveal it; and these safeguards have the evident reason that the knowledge, belief, or suspicion that freely-confessed sins would become public would operate as a serious deterrent to participation in the sacrament and an odious detriment accompanying participation. When the prosecutor asserts the right to tape the sacrament he not only intrudes upon the confession taped but threatens the security of any participation in the sacrament by penitents in the jail; he invades their free exercise of religion and doing so makes it impossible for Father Mockaitis to minister the sacrament to those

who seek it in the jail.[69]

The Court further held that the free exercise of the supervising Archbishop was burdened as well. "A substantial burden is imposed [on the Archbishop's] free exercise of religion as the responsible head of the archdioceses of Portland by the intrusion into the Sacrament of Penance by officials of the state.[70]

Mockaitis established as a constitutional principle that any version of the ministerial privilege must recognize that the privilege belongs to the minister as well as the congregant, so long as such secrecy is an essential element of the minister's duty.

Summary

The Scientology central practice of auditing meets all the necessary requirements for full protection in every state and in the federal courts under the constitutional standards set forth above. While the process ultimately employs more than one minister, that characteristic is necessitated by the beliefs and structure of the religion, as in numerous denominations other than Scientology. The cases universally agree that under the First Amendment no disparate treatment may be afforded because of the difference of that practice from more traditional forms of confession. Likewise, while a Scientology auditor is prohibited as a matter of faith and doctrine from revealing what is said or written in an auditing session even if a congregant attempts to "waive" his privilege contrary to his religious covenant never to do so, that provision mirrors the duties of a Catholic priest or ministers of other faiths, and must be respected by judicial and government authorities. At the end of the day, all religions and faiths must be treated equally with recognition of the various forms and practices with which Americans practice their faith.

---

69 *Mockaitis* (n 11),1530
70 Ibid 1531. While the court did not discuss the issue, the case might also have been decided under the church autonomy doctrine discussed above. It is hard to imagine a more egregious violation of church autonomy than for a state official secretly to tape a confession of a prisoner to his priest.

Appendix I

Summary of government and judicial decisions around the world that have established the Scientology involves bona fide religious practice

Governments and judicial decisions of many countries have recognized the religious character of the Scientology Church. In a few countries, the Church has been forced to litigate the issue of its bona fides, either affirmatively or in response to unfounded charges. Inevitably, the Church prevailed in these cases and its religious status has been unequivocally acknowledged. Some of these decisions established the standards in their respective countries regarding what should be deemed a religion. Among these are the following:

- Following the 1963 government seizure of Scientology books and artifacts at the Founding Church of Scientology in Washington, D.C., and six years of litigation, the United States Court of Appeals for the District of Columbia Circuit found the government's acts were unlawful and interfered with religious practice, stating, in part: "On the record as a whole, we find that appellants have made out a prima facie case that the Founding Church of Scientology is a religion. It is incorporated as such in the District of Columbia. It has ministers, who are licensed as such, with legal authority to marry and to bury. Its fundamental writings contain a general account of man and his nature comparable in scope, if not in content, to those of some recognized religions." *Founding Church of Scientology of Washington, D.C. v. United States*, 409 F.2d 1146 (D.C. Cir. 1969).

- In Australia, after false allegations were made to the government in a series of media attacks against Scientology churches, the State of Victoria began an "inquiry" into Scientology in 1965, culminating in banning the practice of Scientology. Western Australia and South Australia followed suit. The inquiry and ban resulted in severe persecution of Scientologists for their beliefs and association. In June 1982, the ban was repealed. Thereafter, the Church sued to appeal the assessment of payroll taxes on the basis of religious exemption. The Church prevailed, during which the High Court established criteria for the definition of religion in Australia and ultimately throughout the Commonwealth, stating: "We would therefore hold that, for purposes of the law, the criteria of religion are twofold: first, belief in a supernatural Being, Thing or Principle; and second, the acceptance of canons of conduct in order to give effect to that belief". It stated, "The applicant has easily discharged the onus of showing that it is religious. The conclusion that it is a religious institution entitled to the tax exemption is irresistible." *Church of the New Faith v. Commissioner of Pay-Roll Tax* (Vic) (1983) 154 CLR 120.

- After the Italian Government had taken official action against Scientologists for holding themselves out as members of a religious organization, in October 1997 the Italian Supreme Court (the Court of Cassation) issued a landmark decision recognizing the religious bona fides of Scientology, and establishing standards regarding the definition of religion throughout the European Community. It stated that "the Church of Scientology... should have been recognized in Italy and thus allowed to practice its worship and to conduct proselytizing activities." The Court concluded that "Scientology is a bona fide religion whose activities, without exception, [are] characteristic of all religious movements." The Court acknowledged that Scientology is a religion whose aim is "the liberation of the human spirit through the knowledge of the divine spirit residing within each human being."

- The European Court of Human Rights issued a unanimous decision in April 2007 upholding the religious freedom of Scientologists throughout the forty-seven nations which ratified the European Convention for the Protection of Human Rights and Fundamental Freedoms (ECHR). By ruling in favor of the Church of Scientology, the Court reaffirmed the right to religious freedom for not only Scientologists, but members of all religions throughout Europe. *Church of Scientology Moscow v. Russia* (application no. 18147/02).

- On October 31, 2007, the National Court in Madrid issued a unanimous decision that the National Church of Scientology of Spain is a religious organization entitled to the full panoply of religious rights that flow from entry in the government's Registry of Religious Entities. This recognition marked the end of an era in which Spanish Scientologists were forced to fight for their rights to religious freedom. The Court recognized the legal status of the National Church of Scientology of Spain as a "religious group" and its fundamental right, in conjunction with its parishioners, to the collective practice and manifestation of religious freedom and its right to the collective practice of the Scientology religion. *Iglesia de Scientology de España v. Ministry of Justice*, Appeal Number 352/2005.

- On December 11, 2013, the Supreme Court of the United Kingdom declared that the London Church of Scientology must be recognized as a place of religious worship under UK law, and thus recognized all other Scientology churches in the UK. *R (on the application of Hodkin and another) v. Registrar General of Births, Deaths and Marriages* [2013] UKSC 77.

Scientology has also been formally recognized as a religious entity in many other countries, including, *inter alia*, Mexico, Argentina, Netherlands, Austria, New Zealand, Brazil, Portugal, Colombia, Sweden, Taiwan, Croatia, Ecuador, Venezuela, India and the Philippines.

INDEX

Made in United States
Orlando, FL
07 February 2022

14549642R10176